KEDLESTON ROAD
Discard

New Thinking in Macroeconom

D1375557

DL 5108547 X

New Thinking in Macroeconomics

Social, Institutional, and Environmental Perspectives

Edited by

Jonathan M. Harris and Neva R. Goodwin

The Global Development and Environment Institute, Tufts University, USA

Edward Elgar
Cheltenham, UK • Northampton, MA, USA

© Jonathan M. Harris and Neva R. Goodwin, 2003

All rights reserved. No part of this publication may be reproduced, stored in a retrieval system or transmitted in any form or by any means, electronic, mechanical or photocopying, recording, or otherwise without the prior permission of the publisher.

Published by
Edward Elgar Publishing Limited
Glensanda House
Montpellier Parade
Cheltenham
Glos GL50 1UA
UK

Edward Elgar Publishing, Inc.
136 West Street
Suite 202
Northampton
Massachusetts 01060
USA

UNIVERSITY OF DERBY
LIBRARY K
ACC. No 5108547
CLASS 339 NEW

A catalogue record for this book
is available from the British Library

Library of Congress Cataloguing in Publication Data

New thinking in macroeconomics: social, institutional, and
    environmental perspectives/edited by Jonathan M. Harris and
        Neva R. Goodwin.
            p. cm.
        Includes bibliographical references and index.
        1. Macroeconomics. 2. Economic policy—Social aspects.
    3. Economic policy—Environmental aspects. I. Harris, Jonathan M.
    II. Goodwin, Neva R.
    HB172.5.N49   2003
    339—dc21

                                                2003054109

ISBN 1 84376 412 1 (cased)

Printed and bound in Great Britain by MPG Books Ltd, Bodmin, Cornwall

Contents

Figures

Tables

Contributors

Nahid Aslanbeigui is Professor of Economics at Monmouth University, West Long Branch, New Jersey.

Peter Dorman teaches economics at The Evergreen State College, Olympia, Washington.

John Eatwell is Lecturer in Economics at the University of Cambridge and President of Queens College, Cambridge, United Kingdom.

David Ellerman is former Economic Advisor to the Chief Economist at the World Bank.

John Kenneth Galbraith is Professor of Economics Emeritus at Harvard University, Cambridge, Massachusetts.

Neva R. Goodwin is Co-director of the Global Development and Environment Institute at Tufts University, Medford, Massachusetts.

Jonathan M. Harris is Director of the Theory and Education Program, Global Development and Environment Institute at Tufts University, Medford, Massachusetts.

David R. Howell is Professor at the Robert J. Milano Graduate School, New School University, New York, New York.

Dorene Isenberg is Professor of Economics at the University of Redlands, Redlands, California.

Anne Mayhew is Vice Provost for Academic Affairs and Dean of Graduate Studies at the University of Tennessee, Knoxville, Tennessee.

Michele I. Naples is Associate Professor in the School of Business at the College of New Jersey, Ewing, New Jersey.

Paul Streeten is Professor Emeritus of Economics at Boston University, Boston, Massachusetts.

Joseph Stiglitz is Professor of Economics and Finance at Columbia University and former Chief Economist at the World Bank.

Lance Taylor is Arnhold Professor of International Cooperation and Development and Director of the Center for Economic Policy Analysis at the New School University, New York, New York.

L. Randall Wray is Professor of Economics and Senior Research Associate with the Center for Full Employment and Price Stability at the University of Missouri – Kansas City, and Senior Scholar at the Levy Economics Institute of Bard College, Annandale-on-Hudson, New York.

Preface: Macroeconomics for the Twenty-First Century

Neva R. Goodwin

Macroeconomic theory has been left behind by some critical facts and trends that are emerging in the 21st century. One large set of discordant facts may be summarized as the limits of the Earth's carrying capacity in relation to both human demands for resources and anthropogenic emissions of destructive pollutants. Other areas in which macro theory, and economic theory in general, have persistently ignored important concerns include the effects of demographic changes; the size, structure and power of multinational corporations; and, most importantly, the harm to social and individual well-being that results from severe and growing economic inequality.

There is nothing new in the equity-related disconnect between the priorities that seem required by reality and the priorities evidenced in economic theorizing. In contrast, a dramatic novelty of the 21st century is the growing consensus regarding the environmental perils associated with continuing economic behavior, and economic theory, as usual. The tectonic shifts that will be required to adjust to this newly realized situation may also have the salutary effect of reopening the social questions that have been for too long the stepchildren of economic theory.

Several characteristics of standard macroeconomic theory have allowed it to continue ignoring the old social problems as well as the growing environmental problems. All of the following characteristics will need to be altered if macro theory is to play a useful role in explaining national and global economic realities, and in supporting policies that lead to increased human well-being.

1. The theory does not address openly several essential questions: Is macroeconomic theory intended to explain and also to guide the macroeconomic system? If so, to what end? What directions of change, or what preferred state of the economy, are implied in the understandings and the guidance afforded by macroeconomic theory?

2. Standard macro theory pays too little attention to problems that cannot or will not be resolved through markets.
3. It assumes that a single macroeconomic theory can apply to all situations, ignoring the increasingly critical differences between understandings, goals and policies appropriate to developed vs developing countries.
4. It ignores issues concerning the total scale of human economic activity, and the speed of change.

This is by no means a complete list. Generalizing further, one could point to how economic systems are presented as though they existed in a vacuum, instead of being embedded in physical contexts of ecology, technology, and the built environment; and in social contexts of history, culture, institutions, politics, ethical and behavioral norms, etc. Or one could note the impediments to change that arise through traditions of describing production in terms of functions whose significant inputs are capital and labor, giving little attention to natural resources in general, and failing to distinguish among resources in terms of their salience for the economy, their relation to technological change, or the ecological side-effects of their use. However, the list above is a sufficient starting point for examining some of the major requirements for fundamental change if macroeconomic theory is to grapple effectively with the most significant national and global economic issues of the 21st century.

THE GOALS OF THE SYSTEM, AND OF THE THEORY

The first item on the list is the most fundamental to the failure of macroeconomic theory to change with a changing world. At the core of economic theory in the West, as it was formally enunciated and taught throughout the second half of the twentieth century, was a claim to be a purely positive science. This claim required that economists overlook a virtually unarguable belief, that an economic system should (normative statement) be designed to work for human well-being in the present and the future. If macroeconomic theory were to be reconceptualized, taking the acceptance of this belief as a starting point, it would then become reasonable to take the next step, and require of economic theory that, at minimum, it assist its users to recognize whether the economic system on which they depend is moving toward, or away from, the goal of contributing to human well-being.

The essential first step, if economic theory is to accept the reasonable normative assumptions just suggested, is to make the distinction between final and intermediate goals. Increased consumption and economic growth as currently measured are both best understood as intermediate goals; that is, they are not simply good in themselves, but are desirable to the extent that they lead to what are recognized as final goals. Efficiency, often cited as another economic goal, is also intermediate: a means to the ends of increased production and consumption. If economic theory is to guide people toward the creation of economic systems that will promote well-being, it must first stop treating efficiency, consumption and economic growth as final goals.

What, then, are the final goals? The term, 'well-being' is increasingly being used as a shorthand expression for whatever we wish to include in our final goals.[1] People will to some extent differ on what these should include, but there is widespread convergence on a number of basic elements such as security, happiness, freedom, fairness, and participation. A critical source of flexibility, that would permit appropriate change in a changing world, is lost to standard models that have not invited assessment of their success against the broad goal of human well-being, but only against the intermediate goals of efficiency in production, increased consumption, and economic growth as currently measured.

It might be argued that these intermediate goals are indeed means to the ends, at least, of security and happiness; but this is not always true. *Security* implies an ability to shape one's own future, and/or reasonable confidence that the aspects of the future that are beyond ones control will nevertheless be as benign as possible. Only the rich, in all countries, have a substantial ability to shape their own futures. For the rest – and even, to some extent, for the rich – a secure future depends on the larger social and physical environment. On the social side, it requires a caring society that will assist individuals who suffer from catastrophic illness or indigent old age. On the physical side, it requires a healthy ecosystem, not one in which there is increasing likelihood of epidemics, pandemics and newly untreatable diseases; of shortages of critical resources, including food and water; of increasingly dangerous and disruptive weather extremes; or of health-threatening environmental pollution. Thus an economic theory that took security seriously as a goal would adapt more quickly to novel stresses and dangers. In the context of the early 21st century, that means that it would be less strongly market-oriented than the theories with which we are familiar: it would give relatively more attention to the social provision of the essentials for security on both an individual and a society-wide basis.

As for the relationship of wealth and consumption to happiness, the first thing to be said is that neither macro nor microeconomics has yet absorbed the impacts that will result from one of the newest social science disciplines, hedonic psychology. Evolving from work begun in the 1950s by Richard Easterlin, and carried forward by Daniel Kaheneman (recently recognized with a Nobel award), Ed Diener, and others, the extensive surveys and scrupulously careful psychological analyses that are the grounding for this area of study have produced several findings with major significance for economics (Kahneman et al., 1999). These include:

(a) The largest bundle of determining factors, accounting for nearly half the difference in average happiness among individuals, are inherited personality traits.

(b) The majority of the rest of the variation among individuals is accounted for by childhood circumstances and ongoing relationships (with friends, family, etc.).

(c) People who cannot be sure of having the basic requirements for survival are likely to be at the relatively unhappy end of the spectrum. (Here we see that security, while often thought of as a final goal, can also serve as intermediate to the goal of happiness.)

(d) However, for people who are accustomed to living above poverty, the influence of wealth or consumption on their happiness is largely a relative matter. To the extent that their comparison group is their neighbors, this is a zero sum game; only some people can derive their happiness from superior wealth, while others must suffer from having, relatively speaking, less. As the globalized world encourages ever-greater proportions of the human population to take wealthy Americans as their comparison group (e.g., on the television show *Dallas*), there is reason for ever-growing dissatisfaction.

(e) The comparison may also be temporal, a matter of whether one is on a rising or a falling trajectory in terms of wealth and income. It is clear that happiness is positively affected as people come up in the world. However, one of the strong findings of hedonic psychology is that people adjust fairly quickly to changed circumstances. A few years after having attained better (or worse) living circumstances, an individual is likely to return to the same base condition of happiness that obtained before the rise (or fall).

What does this mean for macroeconomics? It suggests that economic growth has much to contribute when a population is living below a level of basic needs satisfaction, but less – indeed, it is possible to imagine circumstances where it has nothing – to contribute to the happiness aspect of well-being above that level. Thus, for relatively wealthy populations, economic theory should readjust the balance of its concerns, giving less weight to the issues of efficiency, growth and consumption, at least insofar as these concerns are justified as contributing to the happiness aspect of well-being, and giving more weight to the issue of equity (Veenhoven, 1993; Diener and Oishi, 2000). It should focus somewhat less on the well-being that is expected to result from individual spending, and more on what may be achieved through social investments (Diener and Diener 1995; Diener et. al.,

1995; Frank, 1999). These conclusions are strengthened as we consider (more briefly) the other aspects of well-being that were singled out above.

The freedom of choice which, in certain respects, is often greater in market systems than in other familiar economic systems, is a freedom to choose what the market provides. However the value of this kind of freedom in an individual's life depends greatly on the extent to which the economic system is characterized by fairness and participation.

In the economic context, fairness is often translated as equity. It includes questions about whether individuals get a fair start in life, receiving the kind of nurturing that will enable them to develop their productive capacities as well as their capacity for happiness. The issue of equity also directs us to consider the opportunities that people face when they seek productive employment: are they favored by birth and connections, disadvantaged by skin color, gender, or accent? And how are people compensated for the work they do? Considering, for example, the relative pay of a financier or a chief executive officer on the one hand, versus a teacher or nurse on the other, what do these differences reflect, and are they fair? How much is the value of the freedom to choose in the market mitigated by the inequalities in purchasing power that result from the cascade of life experiences, starting with pre-natal and early childhood care and nutrition, and ending up in highly differentiated earning powers?

When the value of participation is well realized, it may sometimes balance the curtailment of market freedom for those members of society who have less purchasing power. This balance is achieved when the one-person-one-vote system allows people to express their desires for basic needs such as health care and education, which may be provided outside of the market, and not subject to the one-dollar-one-vote restrictions on who can receive these basic needs.

THE THEORETIC VIEW OF MARKETS

The second reason, listed above, for the self-imposed limitations of contemporary macroeconomic theory, was the extent to which the standard models are trapped in the functional logic of the markets whose ideal form they describe. Modern markets are dominated by corporations – increasingly multinational or global in their reach – which are motivated by a constant need to expand their sales. It is probably not an exaggeration to say that this pressure (itself not thoroughly understood or represented within contemporary economic theory), more than any other consideration, drives the global economic system. Among other things, it is a major force behind the consumerist ethos which appears to be in radical conflict with most realistic possibilities for an accommodation between economic systems and the ecological realities and limits they are encountering.

Questions about the kinds of learning that are required in order to derive well-being from the choices and the temptations offered in a market economy (Scitovsky, 1976) were heard less and less often in economics as the last century went on. More obviously economic questions – about who is in charge of corporations and what are the motives of those in charge – have been explored by such critics of the system and the theory as John Kenneth Galbraith (Galbraith, forthcoming, 2004), but they are generally swamped by mainstream assumptions. In most standard models it is simply assumed that the shareholders, as owners, have the moral and effective right to direct the corporation to set maximization of return as the highest, perhaps the only, priority (Friedman, 1962).

The contemporary reality is far otherwise. The ownership of publicly traded shares is divided among individuals and institutional owners. 'Those who hold shares directly (50 per cent of all shares in America, 20 per cent in Britain) are individually so insignificant as to be virtually powerless.' The institutions that hold the remaining half of US stocks and 80 per cent of UK stocks have traditionally acted as though they, also, are powerless. (Monks and Sykes, 2002, p. 10) However pension funds, which represent roughly one-quarter of all share-ownership in the US (including a sizeable proportion of shares in foreign-based companies) have begun to recognize that their ownership decisions may affect not only their immediate portfolio returns but also the long-term health of the economy and society.

This topic is one entry point into the larger question of the purpose of corporations. '[U]ntil 15 years ago it … was accepted that corporations existed to serve the interests of society, and they derived their legitimacy from that object (ibid., p. 22). Given that the economic size and the political and economic power of many corporations is equal to or greater than many national governments, the role of corporations in serving or dis-serving social goals has become an issue of high importance. However, since macroeconomic theory laid aside the question of what are the interests of society it has paid little attention to how modern corporations might serve these goals. Instead it has implicitly and explicitly accepted the corporations' own goal of growth, allowing this to trump all others.

The foregoing suggests that, despite its 20th century positivist ambitions, the currently dominant theory does contain normative elements. However they have not been admitted openly, and therefore their consequences have not been thought through. We inherit a dominant macroeconomic theory that in effect accepts the goals set by corporations (the actors and the theory both aim to maximize consumption), and gives too little attention to questions concerning the social and environmental impacts of corporations.

DIFFERENT MACRO THEORY FOR DIFFERENT CIRCUMSTANCES

Hedonic psychology suggests that neither gross national product growth nor increased consumption can always be regarded as contributing to the achievement of the final goals of well-being. Most generally, consumption that fulfills basic needs or that promotes health, education, and social welfare, should be treated differently from consumption of luxury goods.

In the industrialized world goals to maintain or improve current living standards will need to accommodate significant changes in the content of output and consumption. (The shift from goods to services, called 'dematerialization' or 'ephemeralization' is already underway.) Macro-economic theory has not even broached the essential question of whether it is possible, in the absence of continual growth, for an economy to promote human well-being in the present and the future. A theory that could address this question would need to re-examine many assumptions, including, to start with, assumptions about relationships among the following variables: work, jobs, leisure, income, well-being.

There are different requirements for theory for the developing world, where increased material consumption continues to be an essential intermediate goal, but one to be pursued with a deeper understanding, and better prioritization, regarding the different ways in which an increase in wealth can contribute to well-being. It is becoming evident that a very poor population gains more from broad achievement of elementary and middle school literacy than from the creation of advanced degree programs for a few; or from widely available public health services than from a few hospitals offering the most modern technology to a tiny segment of the population.

One of the most striking – to some, terrifying – aspects of the macroeconomic and macro-social differences between First and Third World countries lies in the area of demographics. In most industrialized countries population growth rates are now below the replacement rate. The decline in births to citizens of countries such as Italy, the Netherlands, or Japan is accompanied by increased longevity. The combined trends mean that the shape of the age profile of these countries has changed dramatically, from the pyramid of a growing population, in which the youngest age cohorts are the largest, to a more rectangular shape, in which the number of retirees is now, and in the foreseeable future, growing relative to the active workforce. By contrast, many Third World countries maintain the demographic pyramid associated with the first industrial revolution, in which the bulge is at the youngest ages.

Each of these situations has serious macroeconomic implications; and they are inextricably interrelated. The industrialized countries face the likelihood of all or most of the following: growing costs for health and other kinds of elderly care, higher tax burdens on the economically active group, lower savings rates, lower investment rates, and a decline in asset prices (Pryor, 2002). The developing countries are already in need of more investment than they can attract; this may be exacerbated by lower savings rates in the industrialized countries. They suffer a shortage of skilled workers who can support the large youth generation (this is especially true in countries where AIDS is decimating the cohort of young adults; China, with its low birth rate, is the great exception, even with the growing threat of an AIDS epidemic). However, given low domestic wages and the growing pull-factor of the need for more workers in the First World, the drain on Third World talent and energy, already significant, will likely continue to grow.

The 'guest workers' in the more developed countries encounter, and by their numbers help to create, social stresses, including confusion of national identity and ethnic hostilities. At the same time, they themselves suffer mistreatment, depression, and the disruption of families and communities. The market solution – let the workers follow the wages, around the world if necessary – is debated, and often resisted, on a variety of well-being grounds which require more attention in economic theory.

For the reasons just listed, and many others, diverging demographics heighten the differences in First and Third World countries, requiring significant differences in the emphasis, the policy results, and even in some of the important assumptions about facts and goals, in the macroeconomics that are taught and applied in the 21st century.

THE SCALE OF THE ECONOMY AND THE PACE OF CHANGE

Like growth and consumption, overall scale is a relative matter: more may well be better up to the point where the balance between the local and/or global scale of human activities goes beyond the carrying capacity of the relevant ecosystem. Past that point, more can be worse. The final item on the initial list of general critiques of standard theory was that the totality of the scale of human economic activity appears nowhere in the theory: not as either an intermediate or a final goal, nor even as a policy variable – except as it is implied in a pervasive assumption that more is always better.

This assumption, with an associated goal of always increasing consumption, dovetails with the imperative that appears (without theoretical justification) to drive major corporations: 'grow or die'. As suggested earlier, with its normative base hidden and unthought-through, standard theory has fallen into the trap of allowing its goals to follow the goals of corporations. While corporations are, in many ways, the most powerful actors in modern economies, a decision to let them set the goals of either economic theory or the general economic system is a decision that should not be made by default.

In contemporary economics it is rare to find attention to the distinction between consumption of essentials vs. luxuries, or to the distribution of consumption expenditures. A recognition of environmental limits implies that the overall economic activities of the human species must be understood in the context of present and future effects on resources and environmental services. At the same time, the importance of local realities must be recognized – the scale, as well as the nature, of local economic activities in relation to the carrying capacity of the appropriately defined local ecosystem.

It is also essential to take into account the pace at which economic impacts are now creating environmental and social changes. Macroeconomic theory could benefit from comparing the rate of economic growth to the rate at which ecosystems can adapt – for example forest and ocean ecosystems, as well as the global climate. Large-scale changes that are likely to arrive in a few decades may not be more important than those that will take hundreds of years to play out, but issues on such different timescales require different kinds of understanding and response. As with the issues of biodiversity, cultural survival, and potentially massive human conflict that arise in connection with the scale of the economy, the rate of change is most obviously critical in dealing with irreversibilities.

CONCLUSION

Not only must a major theoretical revision of macroeconomic theory begin with a clear understanding of final goals; it will also be aided by a set of concrete, practical intermediate goals that can be viewed as steps for moving toward the final goals. Such intermediate goals might be concerned with systems for providing legal justice, education, health care, nutrition, and other social needs, as fundamental requirements for all of the final goals mentioned earlier. As we tentatively propose ideas for a new theoretic approach, we can test these against how well they explain the realities confronting us, and how well they support the policies that seem most likely to take a given economy in a positive, well-being-enhancing direction.

This is an obviously normative stance – starting with an idea of what needs to be done, and then seeking the theoretical explanation. There is good precedent for such an approach; it can be found in Adam Smith[2] and in most of the great economic theorists since his time. To be sure, this approach can be misused – as can nearly any tool. An overt statement of what the theorist is doing – to what goals s/he is adhering – is the best way to assist others to judge both the validity and the value of the proposed theory.

To embrace these suggestions would constitute a seismic shift in economic theory. If ever such a shift was warranted it is now, when demography, technology and corporate structures and strategies have created a new world, while Western and global economic effects on the environment are heading for severe risk, even likelihood, of catastrophic reductions in well-being for the majority of human beings.

NOTES

1. To give just a few examples, this terminology is used in the writings of Amartya Sen and others who are building on the United Nations' work on 'human development'. It is the essential term in the new field of hedonic psychology, described below. It has been central to the work of the Global Development and Environment Institute (www.gdae.org), from its six-volume series, *Frontier Issues in Economic Thought* (Island Press, 1995–2001) through its introductory textbook, *Microeconomics in Context* (Goodwin et. al., forthcoming). (Final goals are discussed in the first chapter of *Microeconomics in Context*.) Why replace the older economic term, 'utility,' with 'well-being'? The reasons have to do with the history of usage of these words. 'Utility' has been accepted as a black box: a word that points to whatever is wanted by the person doing the wanting. Its usefulness has depended upon its not being defined. As it has become clear to some thinkers that economics needs to be concerned with actual human goals, a different word was required: one that could be taken to include what people want, but that invites investigation into both what it is that people do, actually, want, as well as what they will be glad to have if they have it. 'Well-being' is being employed to fill this need.
2. Smith 'backed into' significant portions of his new theory from convictions about policies relating to taxes on international trade: he saw these as harmful to the wealth of his nation, and provided theoretical explanations for the cause and effect relationship he perceived.

REFERENCES

Diener, Ed, Marissa Diener, and Carol Diener (1995), 'Factors Predicting the Subjective Well-Being of Nations', *Journal of Personality and Social Psychology*, **69**: 851–64.

Diener, Ed and Marissa Diener (1995), 'Cross-Cultural Correlates of Life Satisfaction and Self-Esteem', *Journal of Personality and Social Psychology*, **68**: 653–63.

Diener, Ed and Shigehiro Oishi (2000), 'Money and Happiness: Income and Subjective Well-Being Across Nations', in Diener and E.M. Suh (eds), *Subjective Well-Being Across Cultures*, Cambridge, MA: MIT Press.

Frank, Robert (1999), *Luxury Fever: Money and Happiness in an Era of Excess*, Princeton, NJ: Princeton University Press.

Friedman, Milton (1962), *Capitalism and Freedom*, Chicago: University of Chicago Press.

Galbraith, John Kenneth (forthcoming, 2004), *The Economics of Innocent Fraud*, Boston, MA: Houghton Mifflin.

Goodwin, Neva R., Julie Nelson, Frank Ackerman and Thomas E. Weisskopf (forthcoming), *Microeconomics in Context*, Boston, MA: Houghton Mifflin.

Monks, Robert and Allen Sykes (2002), *Capitalism Without Owners Will Fail: A Policymaker's Guide to Reform*, New York: Center for the Study of Financial Innovation.

Kahneman, Daniel, Ed Diener, and Norbert Schwarz (eds) (1999), *Well-Being: The Foundations of Hedonic Psychology*, New York: Russell Sage Foundation.

Pryor, Frederick L. (2002), *The Future of US Capitalism*, Cambridge: Cambridge University Press.

Scitovsky, Tibor (1976), *The Joyless Economy*, New York: Oxford University Press.

Veenhoven, Ruut (1993), 'Happiness in Nations: Subjective Appreciation of Life in 56 Nations 1946–1992', Rotterdam: Erasmus University, RISBO Press.

Acknowledgments

The preparation of this volume has benefited from the support, assistance, and advice of many colleagues. Draft versions of the papers that make up the volume were presented and discussed at a conference sponsored by the Tufts University Global Development and Environment Institute and held at the Pocantico Conference Center of the Rockefeller Brothers Fund. In addition to the authors, others present at the conference, for whose input and encouragement we are indebted, include Frank Ackerman, Steve Cohn, Bruce Mazlish, Julie Nelson, Brian Roach, Hugh Stretton, and Tom Weisskopf. The papers presented here represent the views of the authors, not necessarily those of other conference participants or of the Rockefeller Brothers Fund.

Susan Feiner, Geoffrey Hodgson, and Alejandro Nadal also participated in an electronic macroeconomics discussion forum which helped to formulate the topics for the conference and book. Colleagues at the Tufts University Global Development and Environment Institute, including Timothy Wise and Kevin Gallagher, contributed ideas and comments on the drafts. Essential work on the preparation of the manuscript was done by Mentor Nimani, Samantha Diamond, Melvin Rader, and Dina Dubson, and administrative support was provided by Lia Morris, Ellen Mays, and Mary Knoble.

In addition to support from the Rockefeller Brothers Fund, we are grateful for support from the Richard Lounsbery Foundation for the conference and book, and from the John M. Olin Foundation, the Surdna Foundation, and the Island Foundation for the editing and preparation of the manuscript.

Introduction: New Perspectives on Macroeconomics

Jonathan M. Harris

This volume addresses a variety of issues in contemporary macroeconomic thought. It brings together contributions by analysts working from different perspectives, but with one thing in common: a dissatisfaction with the current state of macroeconomic theory and practice. In the Preface to this volume, Neva Goodwin has expressed the need for a broader approach to macroeconomics, framed in terms of the contribution of economic systems to human well-being, not merely to increased consumption. Within this general perspective, the authors of the following chapters explore specific issues related to economic institutions, social and distributional questions, and the environmental impacts of economic activity. No single alternative to current mainstream macroeconomics is proposed; rather, in the spirit of what Richard Norgaard has called 'theoretical pluralism' (Norgaard, 1989), different frameworks are presented within which both traditional and new macroeconomic problems can be viewed with fresh insight.

The long-term trend in mainstream economic thought about macroeconomic policy has been towards minimalism. In the optimistic Keynesian phase of the 1960s, it was assumed that both fiscal and monetary policy were effective tools for macroeconomic management. But the success of monetarist and New Classical critiques led to a gradual erosion of theoretical support for activist government policy. First fiscal policy fell by the wayside, perceived as too slow and possibly counterproductive in its impacts. The focus moved to central bank monetary policies as the only practical means of government intervention, with the limited goal of price stability. Then rational expectations and New Classical critiques suggested that even monetary policy was ineffective. Thus the role of government appears to be reduced to a cautious effort not to make things worse – in effect a return to an economics of laissez-faire.[1]

Strangely, this theoretical trend towards a narrow perspective on macroeconomics and a negative view of activist government policy stands in clear contrast to what we observe in the real world. In recent years, as the US economy was beset by recessionary trends, the immediate reaction of all political leaders was to call for government policies to stimulate economic recovery. In addition to an aggressive expansionary monetary policy by the Federal Reserve Bank, the Bush administration implemented extensive tax cuts specifically justified as providing economic stimulus.[2] Critics of the administration argued that the tax cuts were biased towards upper-income taxpayers and corporations, and proposed increased benefits for middle- and lower-income wage earners, or expansion of government spending programs, or Federal relief for hard-pressed state governments. But practically no one argued the position implied by the New Classical macroeconomics – that government should stand aside and let the economy find its own equilibrium.

How can we resolve this paradox? Formal economic theory appears to point in one direction, but as soon as problems appear in the real economy, conservatives and liberals alike head in exactly the opposite direction. One approach to resolving the problem is the school of thought known as 'new Keynesianism', associated with theorists such as 2001 Nobel Prize winners George Akerlof, Michael Spence, and Joseph Stiglitz. In their Nobel addresses, these theorists emphasized ways in which the real economy diverges from the idealized general equilibrium model that underlies mainstream macroeconomic thinking. Akerlof (2002) sets out the basis for 'behavioral macroeconomics', which uses plausible assumptions about the way individuals and firms make decisions to develop an alternative to the perfectly competitive general equilibrium model that underlies the New Classical perspective. Spence (2002) applies game theory to explain market structure and performance under conditions of imperfect information. Stiglitz presents an 'information paradigm' in which the concept of asymmetric information helps to explain instability in the macroeconomy (Stiglitz, 2002a; Stiglitz and Weiss, 1992). Thus some explicit microeconomic foundations have been developed for a 'Keynesian' world in which macroeconomic behavior is not self-equilibrating.

Another perspective on the current relevance of a Keynesian perspective is offered by Paul Krugman in his analysis of recent macroeconomic crises in Asia and Japan. Krugman points out that 'old-fashioned demand-side failures can still be a problem' (Krugman, 2000a, p. xiii), that the long-neglected Keynesian concept of a liquidity trap has reappeared in dramatic fashion in present-day Japan, and that developing countries' economies are threatened by the instability of unregulated world financial markets (Krugman, 2000a; 2000b). All of these problems indicate the importance of active government intervention through both fiscal and monetary policy, as well as the relevance of regulatory institutions in stabilizing economies.

The apparent relevance of 'new Keynesianism' may suggest that we should take another look at 'old Keynesianism'. Have economic theorists been too quick to reject a perspective that may fit the real world better than the elaborately detailed abstract models that fill economics journals? Keynesian economics, which gained dominance in the 1950s and 1960s, was discredited by the end of the 1970s due to the apparent failure of 'fine-tuning' – government policies aimed at getting the level of economic activity just right, avoiding both unemployment and inflation. When governments appeared to have failed on both counts, suffering from simultaneously rising unemployment and inflation, it was not unreasonable to conclude that excessively activist government policy had contributed to worsening both problems. This set the stage for more conservative doctrines of a reduced government role – although even the most avid exponents of these doctrines never attempted to dismantle fundamental welfare state institutions such as Social Security and unemployment compensation.

But another interpretation of this history of government policy failure is possible. The variety of Keynesianism which underlay the government policies of the post-World War II period could be called Hicks/Samuelson Keynesianism: the marriage of Walrasian general equilibrium and Keynesian macroeconomics known as the neoclassical synthesis. This synthesis was never without its critics, and the criticism did not all come from the conservative/monetarist side. Some of Keynes's intellectual associates, such as Joan Robinson, argued strongly that the Hicks/Samuelson synthesis eliminated the critical essence of Keynesian thought. This essence consisted, in the view of Robinson and others, of a *disequilibrium* macroeconomics, stressing the inherent instability of capitalist economies. The disequilibrium perspective, generally neglected in mainstream economic thought, is important to consider as we reassess the state of macroeconomics, and the possibilities for a revival of a less narrowly focused discipline.

THE CURRENT STATE OF MACROECONOMICS

The state of mainstream macroeconomics today can be roughly divided between New Classical and New Keynesian perspectives. The New Classical approach is heavily Walrasian. In this view, the macroeconomy is best seen as a system of interlinked markets, all tending towards equilibrium. Disturbances or shocks may temporarily divert markets from equilibrium, but they will tend to return to equilibrium without government intervention. Equilibrium in the labor market means that all unemployment is voluntary, based on workers offering or withdrawing labor at different wages rates. Absent government or union intervention, wage levels will move towards equilibrium, with a 'natural' rate of unemployment based on voluntary decisions by workers. Government intervention intended to stimulate the economy or reduce unemployment can only have a very short-term effect, to the extent that people are surprised by policy actions or subject to money illusion. Once expectations have adapted to a new policy environment, the only long-term effect of expansionary policy will be a higher price level. Clearly the New Classical perspective is well named, since it has eliminated all the essential components of the Keynesian view, returning macro-economic theory to the analyses and policy prescriptions of the 1920s – though with much greater mathematical sophistication.

The problem with this approach is that is so obviously in conflict with reality. No government in the world follows its minimalist policy prescriptions, and with good reason. In the United States, we see that as soon as a stock market downturn leads to a mild economic slowdown, the Federal Reserve Bank springs into action with a series of interest rate cuts. A conservative administration promotes tax cuts to stimulate the economy. These monetary and fiscal adjustments, of course, are standard Keynesian expansionary policy. In addition, the structure of a modern economy includes numerous Keynesian automatic stabilizers such as graduated income taxes and unemployment insurance. Any government that actually dismantled this Keynesian set of policy functions would soon be confronted with catastrophic recessionary conditions, and would undoubtedly reverse their policies or be rapidly thrown out of office by enraged voters.

New Keynesians are more cognizant of economic reality, and less enamored of elegant Walrasian abstractions. They seek to discover imperfec-tions, asymmetries, and coordination failures that interfere with the smooth workings of markets, and can lead to disequilibrium, instability, and involuntary unemployment. They are accordingly less skeptical of the functions of government, harking back to the original Keynesian view that if markets cannot solve economic problems, government intervention is essential. In a review of modern macroeconomics, Olivier Blanchard suggests that the distance between New Classicals and New Keynesians has recently diminished: 'most macroeconomic research today focuses on the macroeconomic implications of some imperfection or another' (Blanchard 2000, p. 1404).

There is a third, non-mainstream, view of macroeconomics which finds fault with both New Classical and New Keynesian perspectives. David Colander, propounding this view, argues that both are founded in a fundamentally Walrasian approach which 'has not taken the complexity of the aggregate economy seriously either in its assumptions of individuals ability to deal with that complexity, or in the structure of its models' (Colander, 1996, p. 3). In order to make economic relationships tractable in theory, mainstream macro assumes relatively simple, price-mediated relationships between variables. Problems of disequilibrium or unemployment in the macroeconomy then arise from such problems as 'sticky' wages or prices that fail to adapt to changes in supply and demand. But what Colander calls a 'post-Walrasian' approach sees the economy as complex and potentially chaotic, with multiple potential equilibria and internal processes different from those of microeconomic price adjustment.

This view harks back to an earlier critique of mainstream Keynesianism, associated especially with Joan Robinson (1971; 1980) and Axel Leijonhufvut (1968). These writers attacked the Hicksian interpretation of Keynesian theory, including IS-LM analysis and Samuelson's formalization of the neoclassical synthesis (Hicks, 1937; Samuelson, 1947). Their argument was that by assuming smooth, well-behaved macroeconomic relationships between interest rates and investment demand the IS-LM formulation abandons Keynes's basic insights concerning the instability of capitalist systems.

More specifically, Leijonhufvut (1968) argued that the neoclassical focus on such phenomena as 'sticky' wages and liquidity traps accepts a basically classical, Walrasian environment, and implicitly endorses the classical view that recessions result from a failure of wage rates to fall, or other 'imperfections' in self-adjusting markets. Leijonhufvut pointed out that this is quite different from what Keynes actually maintained. Keynes argued that recessions and depressions occur despite, or partially as a result of, falling wage rates, with the fundamental cause being unstable investment leading to negative multiplier effects:

> ... the contention that the unemployment which characterizes a depression is due to a refusal by labour to accept a reduction of money-wages is not clearly supported by the facts. It is not very plausible to assert that unemployment in the United States in 1932 was due either to labour obstinately refusing to accept a reduction of money-wages or to its obstinately demanding a real wage beyond what the productivity of the economic machine was capable of furnishing. Wide variations are experienced in the volume of employment without any apparent change either in the minimum real demands of labor or in its productivity. Labour is not more truculent in the depression than in the boom – far from it. Nor is its physical productivity less. These facts from experience are *prima facie* evidence for questioning the adequacy of a classical analysis (Keynes, 1964 [1936], p. 9).

Robinson comments with regard to IS-LM analysis that:

> If Keynes' own ideas were to be put into this diagram, it would show IS as the volatile element, since it depends upon expectations of profit; the case where full employment cannot be reached by monetary means would be shown by IS falling steeply and cutting the income axis to the left of full employment (Robinson, 1971, p. 84).

The implication of this more radical interpretation of Keynes is that government intervention is essential to stabilize an inherently unstable macroeconomy. In addition, it casts severe doubt on the 'rationality' of market capitalist economies and the social optimality of market outcomes. More recently, Leijonhufvut (1996) has called for a 'not-too-rational' macroeconomics, and has suggested an imperfect information model which whose outcomes are sometimes stable, due to buffer stocks of liquid assets, but can become unstable under certain conditions.

We can see, then that in macroeconomic theory *plus ça change, plus c'est la même chose*. The battles between classical, neoclassical Keynesian, and radical Keynesian views are still being fought out, just with more elaborate mathematics. Of these three schools, however, it is the radical Keynesian that offers the best foundation for a revival of macroeconomics. The bland optimism about market efficiency characteristic of classical and New Classical views severely underrates the kinds of problems that concern social and ecological economists, including income, wealth, and power inequity, resource overuse, environmental damage, and institutional weakness. Proponents of New Keynesianism also have much to offer in updating Keynesian perspectives through modern theories of imperfections, asymmetries, and market failures and their connection to macroeconomic problems.

It is therefore worthwhile to return to the basic goals of macroeconomic policy, as set forth by Keynes, his contemporaries, and his immediate successors, and to ask the question whether some of the essential elements of macroeconomics have been lost in the last half-century of evolution of economic thought. 'New occasions teach new duties': the appropriate macroeconomic goals for the 21st century are very different from those that confronted Keynes and his colleagues in the immediate post-World War II period. Yet there are similarities in the scope of problems on a global scale which suggest that the broader view taken at an earlier stage in economic thought may be relevant as we consider the social and ecological problems of the 21st century.

A BROAD VIEW OF MACROECONOMIC POLICY GOALS

Let us review some of the basic functions of macroeconomic policy, broadly conceived.

- *Economic stabilization*, avoiding excessive inflation or recession – the best known function, which has often but mistakenly been viewed as the only appropriate goal for macro policy.

- *Distributional equity*, which played an important role in early Keynesian analysis and in the work of Sraffa, Kaldor, Joan Robinson, and Kalecki.[3]
- The achievement of *broad social goals*, such as income security, education, and universal health care. These were integral to 'New Deal' Keynesian policies, but have become incidental in economists' purely quantitative analysis of the macroeconomy.
- Providing a *stable basis for economic development*. The dynamics of economic growth were explored by Harrod and Domar and later Solow.[4] These theorists generally assumed that growth was good, considering an ultimate steady-state economy only as a theoretical construct. More recently, ecological economists such as Daly (1991; 1996) have suggested that growth should be limited and that a sustainable economic scale, rather than exponential growth, should be the goal of macroeconomic policy. The development of endogenous growth theories, taking into account the role of human and potentially of natural capital in long-term growth, provides another perspective on the importance of policy determinants of growth.[5]

The recent macroeconomic crises in Asia and Japan suggest that the first function is more important than implied in the modern, laissez-faire-oriented approach to macroeconomics. The tendency of unregulated capitalist economies to excessive cycles of boom and bust, emphasized by Keynes and dismissed by New Classicists, gains new relevance in the light of the Asian crisis and the collapse of the U.S. stock market boom in 2001–02. The importance of the second and third functions has been emphasized by critiques of International Monetary Fund and World Bank structural adjustment policies, including those by Joseph Stiglitz (1998; 1999a; 1999b; 2002b). Contractionary macroeconomic policies have devastating effects on social equity, as well as on income distribution, with the heaviest burden of economic contraction being borne by the poorest. Expansionary, export-led growth is no panacea: growing income inequality and loss of social safety nets threatens the 'success stories' of rapidly developing nations such as China. Issues of fairness in distribution and social investment need to be included in a redefined set of economic policy goals (Sen, 1999; Streeten, 1998 and this volume).

Regarding the fourth function, even the World Bank (1992) acknowledges that the scale of global growth poses enormous environmental problems. Whether or not some version of Daly's approach to growth limits is adopted, it is clear that economic growth needs to be steered in an environmentally sustainable direction, implying some degree of macroeconomic planning (not in the sense of a centrally planned economy, but in the sense of indicative planning for long-run energy and resource use, as implied for example by the Kyoto process). All four functions, not just the first, will be important in the macroeconomics of the 21st century. This will require a rethinking and reorientation of both theory and policy, at the national and international levels.

We can thus identify some of the strands that are appropriate for the development of a new macroeconomics:

- a return to the original Keynesian vision of a non-equilibrium macroeconomic system, prone to instability, cycles of inflation and recession, and imbalances of aggregate demand and supply, personal and corporate savings and investment, and external balance of payments crises;
- a renewed emphasis on distributional issues, linking the inequities of market income distribution to instability in the macroeconomic system;
- a focus on the development of appropriate macroeconomic institutions at both the national and international levels, intended not simply to modulate aggregate demand, but to direct the flows of surplus and promote social investment;
- a new linking of macroeconomic and environmental policy, recognizing the limits of microeconomic and market-based environmental policies.

NEW PERSPECTIVES ON MACROECONOMIC THEORY AND ISSUES

The chapters in this volume address different aspects of this broader macroeconomic perspective. In Part I, dealing with national institutions and policies, John Eatwell and Lance Taylor apply an updated version of the Keynesian perspective to the unique fiscal realities of the United States at the beginning of the 21st century. Starting from a Keynesian demand-side perspective, they follow Godley (1999) in extending Keynesian analysis to take account of financial stocks as well as flows. The results emphasize the interdependence of the US with the global economy, and the need for activist US fiscal policy to prevent a balance of payments crisis and possible economic collapse. Anne Mayhew gives an overview of monetary policy, examining the institutional origins of the Federal Reserve System, and pointing out the limits of the Fed's ability to manage the US economy. David Ellerman and Joseph Stiglitz analyze the problems of formerly socialist economies trying to make the transition to a market system, and suffering the macroeconomic effects of 'shock therapy' based on market ideology, but lacking a sufficient institutional basis for economic stabilization.

The authors in Part II examine macroeconomic issues in an international context. Paul Streeten seeks to deconstruct the ideology of globalization. He focuses on the destructive effects of globalization on national institutions, the introduction of destabilizing financial flows, and problems of income disparity and increasing inequality. The lack of appropriate institutions for the management of 'the blind forces of globalization' means that the potentially positive effects of expanded trade are not effectively used to advance well-being, and the promises of neo-liberal ideology prove hollow. Nahid Aslanbeigui further explores the financial problems of a globalized economy, with its tendency to crises and inadequate institutions for countervailing government policies to stabilize economies and promote more equitable outcomes. Michele Naples reviews the establishment and breakdown of institutional frameworks for macroeconomic stabilization, foreseeing further problems with global economic instability. All three of these authors point to the need for a revised understanding of macroeconomic systems to guide the needed reforms in the global economy.

In Part III, the focus is on the social impacts of macroeconomic policies. David Howell criticizes the orthodox perception of unemployment as caused primarily by technological change and institutional rigidities. He locates the fundamental cause of high unemployment in excessively contractionary fiscal and monetary policies. Randall Wray explores the limits of conventional expansionary policy in reducing unemployment, arguing that a substantial residual level of unemployment among the least skilled is unresponsive to standard macroeconomic policies. He suggests that specific public employment institutions are needed to resolve the problems of people stuck at the bottom of the labor market. Dorene Isenberg looks at similar problems in the housing market, tracing the rise of homelessness to a faltering government commitment to provide affordable housing either directly or through market subsidies. She sees the need for new policies to prevent worsening inequity in housing in the 'global age'.

Part IV deals with the relationship of environmental problems to macroeconomic policy. Peter Dorman focuses on the environmental issue of deforestation, finding a link between external debt and deforestation. Forests, he argues, are not appropriately managed as 'assets' in an international financial system that generates strong pressures for their liquidation to meet financial liabilities. Harris and Goodwin review arguments on growth and its limits, concluding that the nature of economic growth will have to be changed fundamentally to take into account its environmental impacts. Standard assumptions of ever-increasing consumption and technological progress must be revised to promote sustainable economic systems, and policies on tax incidence and public investment reoriented to the same goal.

In the Afterword, John Kenneth Galbraith, who called attention early to the problem of resource and environmental problems in his 1958 article 'How Much Should a Country Consume?' turns his attention to growth and consumption limits in the Japanese economy. He suggests that Japan may lead the way in moving towards an economic system oriented less to material consumption and more to less tangible, but perhaps more significant, elements of human well-being.

The articles presented here thus span a wide area of social and environmental issues, pointing the way to broader and more productive macroeconomic theories and policies. Students of contemporary macroeconomics who are puzzled by its narrow perspective and seeming disengagement from many real-world problems may find in these contributions some elements of an alternative perspective. It is the belief of the editors of this volume that macroeconomics must respond to the diverse challenges raised in these articles, or become ever more irrelevant to the provision of solutions to the problems of human well-being. The scope of macroeconomics must include social equity, environmental sustainability, and global public goods, returning the discipline to its more ambitious goals of an earlier era, but updating those goals to take into account the new issues of the twenty-first century.

NOTES

1. See, for example, the discussion of rational expectations and monetary policy in Lucas (1972) and Sargent and Wallace (1981).
2. Critics such as Paul Krugman (2001) argued that the true motivation for the Bush tax cuts was a redistribution of income in favor of corporations and the wealthy, but the economic stimulus argument was always cited by the Administration in support of their proposals, in an odd historical echo of Richard Nixon's assertion that 'we are all Keynesians now'.
3. See, for example, Robinson (1980) and King (1996).
4. See, for example, Solow (1987).
5. See Barro and Sala-i-Martin (1995).

REFERENCES

Akerlof, George A. (2002), 'Behavioral Macroeconomics and Economic Behavior', *American Economic Review*, **92** (3): 411–33.

Barro, Robert J. and Xavier Sala-i-Martin (eds) (1995), *Economic Growth*. New York: McGraw-Hill.

Blanchard, Olivier (2000), 'What Do We Know about Macroeconomics that Fisher and Wicksell Did Not?', *Quarterly Journal of Economics*, **115** (4): 1375–1409.

Colander, David (ed.) (1996), *Beyond Microfoundations: Post-Walrasian Macroeconomics*, Cambridge: Cambridge University Press.

Daly, Herman E. (1991), 'Elements of Environmental Macroeconomics', in Robert Costanza (ed.), *Ecological Economics: The Science and Management of Sustainability*, New York: Columbia University Press.

Daly, Herman E. (1996), *Beyond Growth: The Economics of Sustainable Development*, Boston, MA: Beacon Press.

Galbraith, John Kenneth (1958), 'How Much Should a Country Consume?', in Henry Jarrett (ed.), *Perspectives on Conservation: Essays on America's Natural Resources*, Baltimore, MD: Johns Hopkins Press.

Godley, Wynne (1999), *Seven Unsustainable Processes: Medium-Term Prospects and Policies for the US and the World*, Annandale-on-Hudson, NY: Jerome Levy Economics Institute, Bard College.

Hicks, John R. (1937), 'Mr. Keynes and the Classics: A Suggested Interpretation', *Econometrica*, April: 147–59.

Keynes, John M. (1964 [1936]), *The General Theory of Employment, Interest, and Money*, New York: Harcourt, Brace. (Original publication London: Macmillan.)

King, John E. (ed.) (1996), *An Alternative Economic Theory: The Kaleckian Model and Post-Keynesian Economics*, London: Kluwer Academic.

Krugman, Paul (2000a), *The Return of Depression Economics*, New York: W.W. Norton.

Krugman, Paul (2000b), 'Thinking About the Liquidity Trap', *Journal of the Japanese and International Economies*, **14** (4), December: 221–37.

Krugman, Paul (2001), *Fuzzy Math: The Essential Guide to the Bush Tax Plan*, New York: W.W. Norton.

Leijonhufvut, Axel (1968), *On Keynesian Economics and the Economics of Keynes*, New York: Oxford University Press.

Leijonhufvut, Axel (1996), 'Towards a Not-Too-Rational Macroeconomics', in David Colander (ed.), *Beyond Microfoundations: Post-Walrasian Macroeconomics*, Cambridge: Cambridge University Press.

Lucas, Robert E. (1972), 'Expectations and the Neutrality of Money', *Journal of Economic Theory*, **4** (April 1972): 103–24.

Norgaard, Richard (1989), 'The Case for Methodological Pluralism', *Ecological Economics*, **1**, February: 37–57.

Robinson, Joan (1971), *Economic Heresies*, New York: Basic Books.

Robinson, Joan (1980), *What Are the Questions? And Other Essays*, New York: M.E. Sharpe.

Samuelson, Paul A. (1947), *Foundations of Economic Analysis*, Cambridge, MA: Harvard University Press.

Sargent, Thomas J. and Neil Wallace (1981), 'Rational Expectations and the Theory of Economic Policy', in Robert E. Lucas and Thomas J. Sargent (eds), *Rational Expectations and Econometric Practice*, Minneapolis: University of Minnesota Press.

Sen, Amartya (1999), *Development as Freedom*, New York: Alfred A. Knopf.

Solow, Robert M. (1987*)*, *Growth Theory: An Exposition*, New York: Oxford University Press.

Spence, Michael (2002), 'Signaling in Retrospect and the Informational Structure of Markets', *American Economic Review*, **92** (3): 434–59.

Stiglitz, Joseph E. (1998), 'More Instruments and Broader Goals: Moving Toward the Post Washington Consensus', WIDER Annual Lectures No. 2, Helsinki.

Stiglitz, Joseph E. (1999a), 'Reforming the Global Economic Architecture: Lessons from the Recent Crises', *Journal of Finance*, **54** (4), August: 1508–21.

Stiglitz, Joseph. E. (1999b), 'Responding to Economic Crises: Policy Alternatives for Equitable Recovery and Development', *Manchester School*, **67** (5): 409–27.

Stiglitz, Joseph E. (2002a), 'Information and the Change in the Paradigm in Economics', *American Economic Review*, **92** (3): 460–501.

Stiglitz, Joseph E. (2002b), *Globalization and Its Discontents*, New York, W.W. Norton.

Stiglitz, Joseph E. and Andrew W. Weiss (1992), 'Asymmetric Information in Credit Markets and its Implications for Macroeconomics', *Oxford Economic Papers*, **44** (4): 694–724.

Streeten, Paul (1998), 'Globalization: Threat or Salvation?' in A.S. Bhalla (ed.), *Globalization, Growth, and Marginalization*, New York: St. Martin's Press.

World Bank (1992), *World Development Report 1992*, New York: Oxford University Press.

PART I

National Institutions and Policies

1. Stock-Flow Traps in the American Economy[1]

John Eatwell and Lance Taylor

The American economy is running into a trap. Its jaws are the growing imbalances between, on the one side, outstanding *stocks* of financial assets and liabilities, and, on the other side, *flows* of interest payments, imports and exports, and consumer spending. It is impossible to predict just how and when the trap will be sprung. But today's developments ensure that it will snap shut, with predictably damaging consequences.

Stock-flow traps are not new. They were at the root of the recent financial crises in Mexico, East Asia, Russia, and Brazil. In Asia, stocks of short-term debt were large relative to the flow of economic activity, provoking a crash when the loans were called. Hikes in interest rates on their governments' foreign debt had similar impacts on Russia and Brazil. What is new is that the richest country in the world is walking into same sort of situation. The similarities between the US and these earlier examples are clear and unnerving.

THE POSITION OF THE UNITED STATES

Paradoxically, the reason why stock-flow imbalances now imperil the US economy is because, in some ways, the external position of the dollar is so strong. The dollar is the world's key currency. In 1995, it accounted for almost 65 per cent of total official holdings of foreign exchange or 'international reserves' (this share was down from 80 per cent in 1975, but was still four times as large as that of the Deutschemark, the then second most important reserve currency). Almost half of international trade payments, foreign holdings of bank deposits, and developing country debt are all denominated in dollars. The dollar also serves as the anchor and reference for many other countries' exchange rates. Both the public and private sectors in the US borrow abroad almost exclusively in terms of dollars, so that as far as their liabilities are concerned they can ignore swings in the exchange rate (the same is not true of their foreign currency assets, of course).

But for how long can the US maintain this freedom from pressures in international markets? The situation today dates from the American policy decision around 1970 to pursue a 'passive' approach to the balance of payments.[2] Since then, the current account has been in large and growing deficit paid for, as shown below, by the routine absorption of around two-thirds of the rest of the world's surplus savings. The US economy today can grow only by increasing its foreign borrowing. Who does that borrowing, whether government or corporations or households, is vital to the maintenance of growth and employment in America. Moreover, the US borrowing strategy has become an important element in maintaining demand around the world. If that strategy were forced to change there would be serious implications for the future stability and growth of the global economy.

The result of high levels of US borrowing has been the accumulation of an enormous stock of external debt. The foreign debt of the US consists of a range of financial liabilities issued by government, business, and households, and held by foreigners. If foreign players decided to sell a significant proportion of their claims on the US, there would be major repercussions in all financial markets inside America and around the world.

Injections and Leakages

From the point of view of economic theory, the situation can be analyzed in terms of injections and leakages from the overall macroeconomic flow. A standard Keynesian analysis indicates that from the side of demand, the level of economic activity is determined as a balance between, on the one hand, 'injections' such as investment, public spending, and exports and, on the other hand, 'leakages' such as saving, taxes, and imports. In terms of the standard national income and product accounts, the supply of goods and services that results is equal to value-added generated within the economy (or gross domestic product), plus 'imports' including all outgoing payments on current account.

Godley (1999) suggests an interesting elaboration of Keynesian analysis to take into account demand originating from different institutional sectors of the economy. It extends naturally to the study of shifts in flows (and ultimately stocks) of financial obligations, which over time can lead to macro instability. Potential stock/flow imbalances are conspicuous by their absence in Keynes's own analysis:

Perhaps the largest theoretical gap in the model of the General Theory was its relative neglect of stock concepts, stock equilibrium and stock-flow relations. It may have been a necessary simplification for Keynes to slice the time so thin that the stock of capital goods, for instance, can be treated as constant even while net investment is systematically positive or negative. But those slices soon add up to a slab, across which stock differences are perceptible... it is important to get the stock-flow relationships right (Solow, 1983, p. 164).

Along lines suggested by Godley, one can ask hypothetically 'what would have been' the level of supply had it been determined exclusively by an injection and leakage from just one of the three main sectors – private, government, and the rest of the world. For example, the government curve illustrates the balance between the injection of government spending, G, and the corresponding leakage into taxation, $T = tX$, where t is the tax rate and X the total value of supply. If injections and leakages came only from the public sector, then since total injections equal total leakages, we would have $G = tX$, or $X = G/t$. This is the sectoral demand. Similar calculations may be made for the household and foreign sectors. For the household sector alone, investment would have to equal savings, $I = sX$ or $X = I/s$, where s is the savings rate. For the foreign sector alone, exports would have to equal imports, $E = mX$ or $X = E/m$, where m is the marginal propensity to import.

In practice, X will be a weighted average of these terms, with the weights depending on the 'leakage' rates s, t, and m. Since a financial deficit in one sector has to be balanced by a surplus elsewhere, macro financial balances have to satisfy the identity

$$(I - sX) + (G - tX) + (E - mX) = 0 \qquad (1.1)$$

Sectoral Multiplier Effects on Output

Without making predictions about whether the American economy will have recovered strongly from its 2001–02 recession (the outcome will be known by the time this book comes out, in any case!), it is interesting to see how its data fit into this theoretical pattern of injections and leakages. The lines in Figure 1.1 show the evolution of supply and private, government, and foreign contributions to effective demand since World War II, in nominal terms in the upper panel and real terms below. Three observations come from the diagram:

First, since 1982, the 'foreign' curve has generally been below the supply line. This means that the external deficit (the excess of payments outgoing on current account over those coming in) has had a contractionary effect on economic activity, with current account leakages (imports) outweighing injections (exports). This drag was briefly lifted in the early 1990s, as a consequence of dollar devaluation of about 30 per cent between 1985 and

1990 (which stimulated exports and cut back the import share of supply), the Bush recession (which also reduced import penetration), and transfers from the rest of the world of about $100 billion in connection with the Gulf War. All these favorable factors receded after 1992, and the gap between supply and foreign effective demand steadily widened.

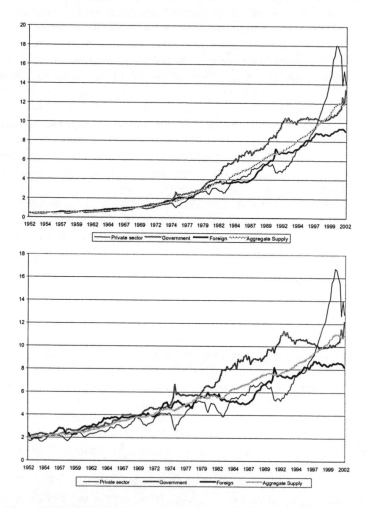

Figure 1.1   Multiplier effects on output from each sector – trillions of nominal dollars (upper) and real 1996 dollars (lower)

Second, governments at all levels – federal, state, and local – combined to stimulate demand through 1997. The federal deficit was responsible for this outcome, because state and local governments suffer from chronic budget balances or surpluses. As the 'government' curve shows, the policy choice to run a federal surplus to 'pay down the debt' along with the fact that fiscal stimulus tends to drop off as the economy expands (tax revenues rise and transfer payments such as unemployment compensation fall) led to a contractionary fiscal stance from 1995 through 2000. Thereafter, government began to support demand again.

Third, with demand from the rest of the world lagging and fiscal demand in retrenchment, in the late 1990s the private sector had to pick up the slack. Its effective demand grew very rapidly after 1992, due to rising investment and a falling saving rate. Private demand peaked at the end of 1999 and with the onset of recession there was a very rapid decline. By the end of 2001, the private and public sectors were both offsetting the net export drag, but with strongly divergent trends. It will be interesting to see if the two sectors go back to (respectively) dampening and supporting aggregate demand as they did from the mid-1970s through the mid-1990s.

These demand shifts had financial consequences. As shown in (1.1), if a sector's effective demand lies above total supply, it has to borrow to finance the excess. Quarterly increases in net claims among the sectors are shown in Figure 1.2 (again, nominal data in the upper diagram and real below). Two private sector curves are included, for household and 'other' flows of investment minus saving (with the latter basically coming from non-financial and financial business).[3] Except for the 1992 blip, US imports consistently exceeded exports, $E - mX < 0$, so the economy was decumulating net foreign assets.

Flow accumulation of government debt ($G - tX > 0$) reached its peak in mid-1992 and then began to decline; government began to build up positive net claims – or reduce its net liabilities – in 1997. There was another reversal in 1999–2000 and by 2001 the government sector once again was running up debt in the range of $100–200 billion per year. With an external deficit on the order of $400 billion in nominal terms, the private sector had to run the offsetting internal deficits.

Both private sectors behaved in unhistorical fashion in the 1990s. In prior decades, the household sector ran a consistently positive financial balance (or negative deficit in the diagram), which tended to vary counter-cyclically between around $300 billion in real terms in recessions and $100 billion in booms. But beginning in 1992, its level of gross saving fell from about $600 billion to $200 billion in 2000. Investment rose from a bit over $200 billion to $400 billion, so households started to run a historically unprecedented deficit in 1997.

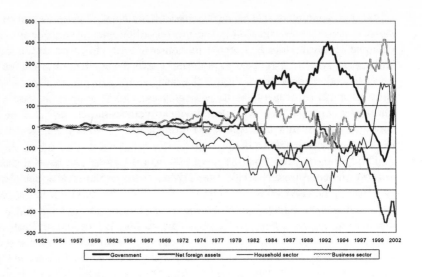

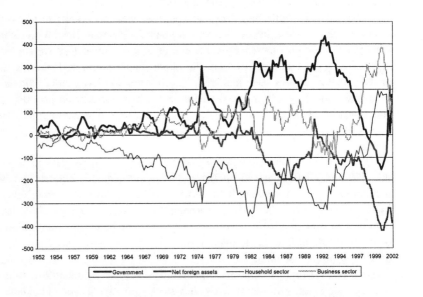

*Figure 1.2   NIPA-based financial needs of the government, foreign sector,
            household and rest of the private sector – billions of nominal
            dollars (upper) and real dollars of 1996 (lower)*

The business sector had tended to run deficits during upswings and then revert to approximate financial balance or a small surplus in recessions as in the early 1980s and 1990s. But as with households, the business deficit took off in the 1990s. In 1991–92, both saving and investment were about $700 billion. They climbed in tandem (with investment rising somewhat faster) to about $1.0 trillion in 1997–98. Thereafter, investment shot up to almost $1.3 trillion in 2000 with saving falling off to $850 million (with investment dropping significantly faster) in 2001. As Figure 1.2 shows, the swing of business into a consistent deficit position occurred in 1994–95; the household shift came a year or two later. Thereafter, both sectors' deficits climbed hand-in-hand, amply collateralized by rising asset prices, into the bubble that began to deflate in the year 2000.

In other words, the Clinton boom was uniquely supported by net increases in private sector liabilities. The fiscal deficit played a negligible role in stimulating demand, in sharp contrast to previous upswings. In the first half of the 1990s, the public sector did issue liabilities to finance the foreign deficit. But in the second half of the decade private debtors took over that function.

As of late 2002, how the rapid reversal of trends in private and public sector deficits in 1999–2000 will play out remains to be seen. What can safely be said is that if the structural foreign deficit remains in the $400 billion range and the household and business sectors continue to move toward the surpluses they used to run in economic downswings, then there will have to be a large fiscal stimulus if effective demand is to be maintained. Otherwise the foreign deficit will have to be sharply reduced by recession and/or devaluation as in the early 1990s. Figures 1.1 and 1.2 illustrate interesting times.

GLOBAL MACROECONOMICS

The patterns shown in Figures 1.1 and 1.2 could not have developed without the massive liberalization of international capital markets that commenced in the 1970s.[4] The US has only been able to run current account deficits for so many years because financial markets were open and increasingly dominant institutional investors in all countries initiated a large and sustained flow of foreign capital toward Wall Street. But the persistent American deficit has produced a peculiarly unbalanced structure of global financial stocks and flows, which may well threaten the future stability of the world economy.

At the world level, there are three main financial actors – the US, the 15 countries of the European Union (EU) functioning as a rather tightly coordinated group, and Japan. At the core of the EU is 'Euroland', with 11 members that now share a single currency, the euro. China and the other historically rapidly growing economies in East Asia play supporting roles, with the rest of the world (ROW) picking up the slack. Table 1.1 summarizes current account performances from 1993 to 2002.

The first point to note is that international payments data do not add up as they should. As shown in the last line the world seems to run a substantial current account deficit with itself – an impossibility because the sum of all nations' current accounts should be zero. After all, one country's exports are another country's imports. The statistical error is comparable in magnitude to the flows of the major players. So the scales, though probably not the directions of the forces about to be discussed are imprecise.

The two surplus players in the late 1990s were the EU-15 and Japan. Europe ran a current account deficit earlier in the decade, but then switched to a surplus partly as a consequence of the contractionary macro policy packages most countries adopted as part of the run-up to the introduction on the euro on 1 January 1999. While Japan has remained in surplus, the EU shifted back into deficit as of 2000. Since 1993 the US has run the major deficit; by 2000 this was over $400 billion. An American current account gap in the $200–300 billion range injects effective demand to the tune of about 1 per cent of world GDP into the global macro system. This is a non-trivial amount. The world economy can be very sensitive to '1 per cent' shocks. That was about the size of the 1973 oil price shock.

There are four key international financial flows:

First, the US has a structural deficit, financed by borrowing from abroad. It has used the resulting capital inflows to support steady if unspectacular GDP growth beginning in the early 1990s, based on stable although not low real interest rates. Calling the decade's results a 'boom' is an exaggeration. Trend output growth was around 50 per cent higher in the 1960s.

Second, Japan has been stagnant since its 'bubble' economy burst around 1990, and runs a secular surplus. As a consequence of the collapse of the bubble, its internal credit supply has been limited, leading to slow growth, a weakening yen through 1997, and a strong current account surplus with corresponding capital outflows.

Third, during the 1990s Europe's growth was slow and its foreign surplus large. During most of the 1990s, the sum of the European and Japanese surpluses exceeded the American deficit, but since 1998. But since 2000 Europe's current account balance has shifted back into deficit, and the US deficit has greatly exceeded the Japanese surplus.

Fourth, as far as the ROW is concerned, the newly industrialized economies (NIEs) of Asia have generally recorded a trade surplus. China and developing Asia had an overall deficit during the first half of the 1990s, then switched to a surplus position after the Asian crisis, as the countries of the region attempted to export their way out of depression. The region's famous

Table 1.1 Summary of payments balances on current account (US$ billions)

	1993	1994	1995	1996	1997	1998	1999	2000	2001	2002
US	-82.7	-118.6	-109.5	-123.3	140.5	-217.1	-331.5	-435.4	-446.0	-445.8
Japan	132.0	130.6	111.4	65.8	94.1	121.0	106.8	117.3	115.4	124.0
EU	11.1	20.1	57.3	91.4	122.1	73.7	22.4	-24.3	-23.3	-20.5
NIE	20.8	16.1	5.9	-0.9	16.8	67.2	65.2	51.7	43.2	43.0
China	-11.9	7.7	1.6	7.2	37.0	31.5	15.7	12.5	7.2	3.1
Developing Asia	-33.0	-18.9	-42.4	-38.9	8.8	47.0	46.7	35.9	22.5	11.6
Africa	-12.3	-12.3	-16.9	-6.3	-8.0	-20.5	-15.5	1.3	-3.7	-5.5
C. & E. Europe	-8.4	-3.4	-2.8	-15.0	-16.9	-20.3	-23.2	-20.4	-21.8	-22.7
Russia	2.6	8.2	4.9	3.8	-0.4	-1.6	22.9	45.3	35.6	26.5
Mid. East	-27.3	-3.7	-0.7	9.6	5.5	-28.6	6.0	56.7	47.6	22.6
ROW	-48.3	-76.4	-48.2	-42.5	-107.6	-138.2	-68.7	-14.1	-32.0	-37.4
World	-57.4	-50.6	-39.4	-49.1	10.9	-85.9	-153.2	-173.5	-255.3	-301.1

Source: IMF Economic Outlook (2002).

bilateral current account surplus with the US consistently exceeded its overall surplus. The difference is the deficit that the East Asian economies ran with the EU and with Japan. In effect, they were absorbing some of the excess saving in the EU and Japan and recycling it toward American shores. After all, the US external deficit had to be financed from somewhere.

How do the national economies supporting these flows interact? In terms of its output dynamics, the US current account deficit is pro-cyclical. When world activity is low, the US deficit, and hence US borrowing, rises, pumping demand into the rest of the world. Similarly, when world activity is high the US deficit falls, limiting the injection of demand into the rest of the world. America's net borrowing varies against the cycle, meaning that financial flows into the US have behaved in a globally stabilizing fashion.

For a nation that borrows, however, capital movements are not a matter of its own volition. A better way to describe the current role of the US is to say that its creditors – Japan directly and the EU at one remove – have agreed to lend pro-cyclically to finance the American injection of global effective demand. The inflows illustrated above have built up a huge stock of debt. Just as in East Asia before 1997, there is the potential for huge, rapidly destabilizing capital outflows. The federal government's T-bills, in particular, could be sold off very rapidly.

External Dangers?

The most recent runs on the dollar took place in the 1970s and 1980s. The former helped provoke the Volcker interest rate shock, a significant recession worldwide, the developing country debt crisis, and other major adjustments. Doubts about the dollar in the mid-1980s were instrumental in triggering the 1987 stock market crisis. A decade is a long time in terms of such events. What scenarios may unfold if the US in particular and the world system more generally get into trouble once again?

So far, the US has managed to borrow in globally stabilizing fashion and faces only potential flow-flow and stock-flow disequilibria. There are risks, however, on both fronts. With regard to borrowing, the real decisions will be made in Europe and Japan. The latter has been under international pressure for years to restructure its economy so that aggregate demand can be driven by domestic spending as opposed to exports. To date, very little has been achieved and the Japanese current account surplus continues to be recycled via Wall Street. This situation may very well continue.

Europe, on the other hand, has already shifted from surplus to deficit. Europe may continue to grow more rapidly now that the Maastricht process has ended and the euro has been born. In that event, higher activity levels and interest rates in the EU would draw in imports and capital flows. It is also possible that the introduction of the euro, the only currency with a potential status in international trade and finance similar to that of the dollar, will create a potentially unstable currency duopoly. International arrangements may soon need to be put into place to limit fluctuations among the dollar, euro, and yen. But suppose this does not happen, and speculative pressure mounts against the dollar.

A sell-off of dollar securities would produce sharp falls in US bond prices, and hence a rise in interest rates. Would higher interest rates stop the rot, would they be 'credible'? The potential disequilibria – portfolio shifts away from the US, bigger interest obligations on its debt, and growing financial stress on the household sector – could begin to feed on one another, and on the views of the markets. At that point, with an expectational run on the dollar fuelled and not staunched by higher interest rates, dollar devaluation, austerity, and the other usual policy moves, all hopes for global macro stability could disappear. A massive international rescue campaign would certainly be required, with worldwide implications impossible to foretell.

A medium-term policy mix for the US, then, will require an expansion in government spending to offset the solvency problems that the private sector (especially the household sector) will soon confront. Monetary expansion will not do the trick, since some domestic sector has to borrow to offset the current account deficit. But still more is required. The dollar is perhaps not so 'over-valued' as it was in the mid-1980s, but a real exchange rate correction could help reduce the external deficit and slow the debt accumulation process just described. Talk of depreciation in the 20–30 per cent range is in the air, and as of 2002 this process appears to have begun.[5]

Can American policy-makers convince themselves to expand fiscally after years of arguing that balancing the budget is the only sensible policy course? How can the Fed respond to conflicting pressures for low interest rates to stimulate activity and high rates to deter capital outflows? The exchange rate is essentially determined in speculative markets. Short of imposing capital and exchange controls, can the authorities somehow evade market expectations that the dollar must depreciate, with consequent reductions in American real spending power and wealth?

It may be some time before these stock-flow imbalances clamp down on the US economic system. But as time goes by the size of the trap becomes ever greater. The jaws will surely be sprung.

NOTES

1. This is a revised version of an article that appeared in *Challenge*, vol. 42, no. 2, September/October 1999.

2.   Prior to 1970, adherence to the Bretton Woods international financial system required the US to limit deficits and the outflow of dollars, to avoid a run on the dollar at its fixed gold exchange rate.
3.   Household and business sectors were not disaggregated in Figure 1.1 because the former has low gross savings rates which generate a spectacularly unstable curve for $I_{household}$ / $S_{household}$ where $I_{household}$ is interpreted as investment in residential construction. Per Gunnar Berglund and Codrina Rada did the real work in putting Figures 1.1 and 1.2 together.
4.   The history is recounted in Eatwell and Taylor (2000).
5.   As more than a curiosum, the dollar must depreciate over the medium term if the US hopes to keep its trade deficit stable as a share of GDP. Imports into the US respond more strongly to income growth than do imports of its trading partners to their own higher incomes. If US income is to expand as rapidly as the rest of the world's, therefore, the dollar has to weaken steadily to cut back on American import demand

REFERENCES

Eatwell, John and Lance Taylor (2000), *Global Finance at Risk: The Case for International Regulation*, New York: New Press.

Godley, Wynne (1999), 'Seven Unsustainable Processes: Medium-Term Prospects and Policies for the US and the World', Annandale-on-Hudson, NY: Jerome Levy Economics Institute, Bard College.

Solow, Robert M. (1983), 'Comment on Godley', in G.D.N. Worswick and J.S. Trevithick (eds), *Keynes and the Modern World*, Cambridge: Cambridge University Press.

2. Can the Fed Give Us Macroeconomic Stability? Lessons from History

Anne Mayhew[1]

As the United States has experienced recession and slow recovery in the first years of the 21st century, the general consensus seems to have been that the most powerful, and perhaps the only tool, to ensure a return to full employment and robust economic growth is that wielded by the Federal Reserve System (FRS), and its Open Market Committee. This understanding has developed in a climate in which discussion of fiscal policy, once seen as the more powerful stabilizing alternative to monetary policy has at best been confused, and more often dismissive. Both professional and public disagreements over the causes and consequences of federal budgetary surpluses and deficits and over the desirability of federal spending have made it more difficult than it once was to argue concisely for fiscal stimulus through either tax cuts or increased government expenditures.

The importance of monetary policy been powerfully reinforced in the public mind by that fact that when, during recent years, television or newsprint reporters, or the Congresses of the United States, or various high-level business groups, have wanted to know how well the American economy is performing, and what its performance may be in the future, they have turned to one man. That man is the Chairman of the Federal Reserve System, Alan Greenspan.

Not only does Chairman Greenspan pronounce on these weighty matters; he is also widely regarded as having, by virtue of his position, the power to change the direction of the economy. Is the economy growing too slowly? Are we in recession, with plants idle and workers unemployed? Many congressmen, many economists, and much of the public have come to regard Chairman Greenspan as the man who can correct this unhappy state of affairs. When we had different problems, back in the 1980s and 1990s, and the economy was growing at a rate that many thought was too fast, with the consequence that prices were rising in an inflationary manner, Congress, the Presidents in power, and the public looked to Greenspan to slow the economy down. In the 1950s and 1960s, and even into the 1970s, the public and

Congress might well have looked to the Chair of the Council of Economic Advisors (CEA) for answers about the macroeconomic performance of the economy, and to both the Chair of the CEA and the Chairman of the Federal Reserve System for stabilization policies. Now, however, the Chairman of the FRS has become the only source for both prognostication and action.

Why is the Chairman of this system accorded such respect? Does he have the power that we believe he has? Why have so many people discarded fiscal policy to the junk heap of misguided history, and come to place such faith in monetary policy? While those who studied economics in the 1950s and 1960s, and even earlier, will probably be able to answer these questions, they will not all agree on the answers. Even more to the point, readers whose knowledge of macroeconomics dates only to the 1980s and since, will probably have no idea that we have gotten where we are through a process that has many twists and turns, determined as much by political and military events as by economic rationality. The story to be told in this chapter is one of how political and social change can have a profound impact on economies. It is also a story that can be told in two quite different ways. And it is a story full of irony.

To understand how the Chairman of the Fed has come to be understood as the supreme commander of the American economy requires both an understanding of what the Fed is and how and why it was created. It also requires an understanding of how the role of the Fed in the major macroeconomic upheavals of the 20th century has been interpreted by economists and public officials; this will be the goal of the second part of this chapter. First, however, it is necessary to understand the basic structure of the Fed and its reason for being.

THE EARLY FED

In December of 1913, the Congress of the United States passed the Federal Reserve Act, and in August of 1914 the Federal Reserve Board took office. It had taken years of study and a fierce debate to create the Fed because the United States had had a long history of state chartered and state controlled banking. In the 1820s and 1830s a federally chartered bank, the much-reviled Bank of the United States, had briefly exerted a degree of central control, and in the years during and just following the Civil War, the National Banking Act had served to bring most banks under Federal control. However, from the creation of the earliest banks in 1780s right through to 1913, most US banks were authorized to do business by the states in which they operated, and they were controlled (to the extent that they were) by the states. Banking was, in 1913, still an industry with may small and independent banks. Throughout large parts of the country any effort to centralize control of the banks in a new federal agency was viewed with deep suspicion as a way to give the already large and powerful New York City bankers control over the economic lives of the American population.

Why, then, was the Fed created? During the 1870s, 1880s, and 1890s the United States experienced a series of steep downturns in the economy, a series of panics and depressions, that were accompanied by falling wages, falling prices, and business failures. It was widely and understandably believed that these panics and depressions were largely a result of inelasticity in the money supply. That is to say, it was believed that the inability, or unwillingness, of the banking system to supply reliable money in sufficient quantity constrained economic activity so severely that the entire economy went into a slump.

To understand why that view made sense to most people, consider the options of, let us say, the owner of a local hardware store in a medium or small-sized American town in the 1880s or 1890s. This businessman would finance inventories by borrowing on a short-term basis from his local bank, a small bank that would have held an account with a 'correspondent bank' in a larger city.

The system of correspondent banking that developed up in the US over the 19th century allowed relatively easy payment across a rapidly growing economy. Banks in small towns could earn interest by depositing money in banks in bigger towns, and banks in bigger towns could earn interest by depositing money in New York City, and checks such as the one that would have been written by the hardware merchant to a supplier in a larger city could be cleared through the system of correspondent banks.

The problem was that a financial crisis, even a small one, in one place could spread like an epidemic across the country. Local weather conditions could affect agricultural revenues in the still largely agricultural US so severely as to leave inventories unsold in the hardware store, and a chain reaction could ensue. The hardware merchant, unable to repay the bank loan, would want to refinance. However, the local banker, as sympathetic as he might have been, would have been caught in a bind. To meet its own requirements in the face of non-repayment, the local bank would be likely to withdraw funds from the correspondent bank in a larger city to maintain its reserves.

Here you have the beginning of a panic that could easily spread from Podunk to Pittsburgh to New York City and even to London, if New York banks drew upon their deposits there. In effect, the American banking structure in the late 19th century was a huge pyramidal structure, with funds flowing upward toward commercial banks in New York in good times, but outward through the pyramid when hard times or panics hit.

By the end of the 19th century, the reasonable solution was not to change the pyramid, but rather to insert Federal Reserve Banks into the system so that they could quell local panics when they arose and prevent their spread from bank to bank. The pre-Fed system was one in which all banks were commercial banks. Their goals were to earn enough to cover costs and so survive, and, if possible to earn profits and dividends for their owners. What the Federal Reserve Act of 1913 did was to create Reserve Banks that would operate in their districts to rediscount commercial paper for member banks. All state chartered banks (which were by far the majority) could join the new system, and all nationally chartered banks (which were usually the larger banks) had to join. District lines were drawn (this was a highly political process) and the new Federal Reserve Banks were located in New York, Philadelphia, Cleveland, Richmond, Atlanta, Chicago, St. Louis, Minneapolis, Kansas City, Dallas, and San Francisco. A Federal Reserve Board was created, but the real power was to be in the regional banks.

This new system would solve the old problems, it was believed, because banks, faced with non-repayment of loans for reasons of local weather or other conditions exogenous to the smooth functioning of the economy, could acquire needed liquidity through the regional Federal Reserve Bank without reducing liquidity of other commercial banks. As the Federal Reserve Banks and the Federal Reserve System had been created to serve the public interest rather than its own commercial interests, the expectation was that the FRS bank would indeed set a low discount rate in the face of exogenous problems with liquidity.

How would the Reserve Bank of Philadelphia survive if it lent cheaply? The Federal Reserve System would have a reserve from the proceeds of sale of bank stock to member banks, and, more importantly, they could issue a newly created form of money, Federal Reserve notes (which would, however, have to be secured by deposits of gold in the Federal Reserve Banks, so that the specie flow mechanism, or its late 19th century equivalent, would provide overall constraint). They were also permitted to buy and sell government bonds as needed to secure their financial condition. From these sources they could shore up the holdings of the Reserve Banks if they were required to engage in heavy lending to the commercial banking sector.

The Origins of Open Market Operations

The details of how the Fed might have operated under these rules need not detain us, for here we come to the first great irony of our story. The Fed never operated as intended, and it did not do so because by the time the doors of the Reserve Banks opened in August 1914, another monumental event was unfolding. On 4 August 1914 Britain declared war on Germany and World

War I had begun. Although the creators of the Fed and those who awaited business when the doors of the new banks opened could not have known it, within a matter of months the economic conditions of the Western world changed and the role of the Fed changed as well.

Remember that the Federal Reserve Banks were designed to rediscount commercial paper in order to prevent local conditions from spreading from region to region. The important tool in the arsenal of the newly created Fed was their ability to alter the rediscount rate to accommodate to the needs of trade, and to provide liquidity that the whole, totally commercial, pyramidal system had lacked. This was meant to be a largely automatic system in which the rules of good banking in reverse would be applied: instead of trying to lend more at high rates when demand for funds was high as commercial banks would, the Federal Reserve Banks were to lend at low rates when demand for liquidity was high, and so automatically keep the commercial system operating.

During the first year of operation, the Fed found little reason to do anything. Gold imports to the United States, and a booming economy, left commercial banks with little need to turn to the Fed. However, as the war progressed and as America became more involved, the Treasury (after years of surplus in the late 19th century) needed to borrow, and the Fed was able to perform a useful role by lending to commercial banks that offered government securities as security for their loans. The Fed rediscounted government obligations at less than the rate that the government bonds paid to their holders. This facilitated purchase of government bonds because banks could borrow from the Fed at a low rate, and lend (or use) the proceeds to buy bonds that would pay more than the Fed was charging. This was lucrative for the commercial banks and the public and it made it possible for the federal government to sell more and more bonds. Such practices were made easier by amendments to the Federal Reserve Act.

In the years just before World War I, Federal government debt had been at a relatively low level, and government securities did not play a big role in the nations financial system. However, by the end of World War I government debt had increased substantially, and the holdings of government securities by the Federal Reserve Banks themselves, and by their member banks, had substantially changed the financial system. Before the War, lending against, and purchase of, commercial paper had been the key to Fed control over the monetary system. After the war it became obvious that buying and selling government debt could play an even more important role, and Open Market Operations (buying and selling government securities on the open market) became an important part of the toolkit of the Fed.

However, the tool had to lie there for a while before it was recognized for what it was, and certainly before it was effectively used. The tool itself now looks simple enough and relatively powerful. If the Fed buys government securities from commercial banks at a relatively high price, so that the commercial banks have reason to sell, the reserves of those banks are increased. The Fed pays the banks for the securities by crediting the accounts that the banks have with the Fed banks; the payment can take the form of simple bookkeeping entries, or FRS notes, if the banks want. If the Fed wants to reduce the liquidity of commercial banks it can offer to sell securities at a low price and reduce liquidity in the system.

In the early 1920s, however, the Federal Reserve Banks bought securities not to ease liquidity among commercial banks but to have interest-earning assets in their own portfolios. Even during the short but severe depression that followed World War I, the Fed was content to lower the discount rate and wait for commercial banks to come to them for rediscounting. When they didn't come, the Federal Reserve Banks used their idle assets to buy bonds so as to earn income for themselves, and each of the FRS district banks did this purchasing on its own. It took some time before the Fed began to realize that open market operations had become a tool that they could use.

One reason for the slow recognition of the potential effectiveness of open market operations was the slow evolution of what it was that the Fed was supposed to do. The Federal Reserve Act, as passed in 1913, was 'An act to provide for the establishment of Federal Reserve banks, *to furnish an elastic currency, to afford means of rediscounting commercial paper, to establish a more effective supervision of banking, and for other purposes* '. Congress had not specified that the Fed should combat depressions or recessions, nor had it specified that the Fed should adopt policies to achieve price stability. It is almost certainly true that many people involved in the creation of the Fed had thought that if an elastic currency could be achieved, these other goals would be achieved as well. However, the Fed did not, during the 1920s, explicitly concern itself with the goals of maintaining full-employment and stable prices, goals that were only articulated for the federal government and its agencies after World War II. Nevertheless, during the 1920s the officials of the Fed did begin to recognize that open market operations could affect the position and behavior of banks.

THE FED IN THE 1920s AND 1930s

For most of the 1920s it was also true that public officials and the public did not worry all that much about the business cycle, or about economic conditions. After a short depression at the beginning of the 1920s, the US economy boomed, and the only explicit concerns of the Fed were with the stock market speculation that developed late in the 1920s. Then, as that most cataclysmic downturn, the Great Depression, began in mid-1929, unemployment grew, prices fell, factories closed, bankruptcies were widespread, and banks closed their doors, unable to meet their obligations. In spite of considerable effort, President Herbert Hoover and his administration could not stop the downward slide. Widespread discontent with economic conditions led to the election of a new president, Franklin Delano Roosevelt, in 1932.

In a desperate and often chaotic effort to restore economic health, Roosevelt and his administration created a variety of programs, known collectively as the New Deal. Although most of the New Deal programs had roots in earlier proposals, and in prior American thought about needed economic reforms, the policies and programs taken together marked a departure in that the federal government became much more deeply involved in trying to guide the American economy toward a high level of performance. This can be described as a move away from an era of laissez-faire policies, or as a continuation of the Progressive movement that had been temporarily ended by World War I and its aftermath, or in a variety of other ways. However you describe it, the New Deal marked a landmark, and a controversial one.

However, the controversy over the New Deal paled, for even while the creators of the New Deal were still trying to understand how best to guarantee maximum economic performance, another war washed over the United States, and once again changed the character and direction of domestic institutions. Even before Pearl Harbor and the declaration of war by the US, the growing involvement of the US in providing armaments to those nations that became, after 1941, our official allies, had effectively ended the depression, and by 1941 and 1942 the new problem was how to find enough people to serve in the armed forces and to run the farms and factories as well. There was, for all practical purposes, no unemployment, factories operated 24 hours a day, incomes rose, and instead of overall price declines, we had to worry about increasing overall price levels.

As economists, congressmen, the President's staff, and much of the public looked at what had happened, it seemed obvious that the great increase in government spending associated with the war had ended the depression. This government spending had resulted in employment and income for those directly employed, but it had also had a ripple (or multiplier) effect on the whole economy. That this had happened made a lot of sense to many people because from 1932 and 1933 onward (and from even earlier in fact; see the work of Herbert Hoover when he was Secretary of Commerce in the early 1920s!), the idea that direct government expenditures could 'prime the pump' had been forcefully argued (Barber, 1985). The argument had gained legitimacy among many economists with the publication in 1936 of John

Maynard Keynes's *The General Theory of Employment, Interest and Money* (Keynes, 1936). Keynes offered an explanation of why and how otherwise healthy capitalist economies would periodically fail to achieve full employment, and why government intervention would be necessary to remedy the problem.

Although the programs of the New Deal as created and implemented from 1933 through 1938 or so were little affected by Keynes's arguments, many of those same programs came to be justified during the 1940s and 1950s as 'Keynesian', and were described as insufficient in that government expenditures were not as large as those called for by World War II. The consensus was that the New Dealers had been on the right track, and what World War II showed us was that you only needed to get the magnitudes right in order to solve the problems of recession and depression. To this consensus was added the notion that if you 'fine-tuned' government expenditures just right you could also avoid the excessive demand generated by too much government and private expenditure and so prevent the inflation that had threatened during the 1940s.

THE ERA OF A FISCALLY MANAGED ECONOMY

As a consequence of two wars, one great depression, and a lot of other intervening events, the expectation of the Federal Reserve System in 1946 was very different from what it had been in 1913, or even in 1923. In 1913, when Congress passed the Federal Reserve Act the best thinking was that the Fed would provide macroeconomic stability by providing an elastic currency. By the time the Employment Act of 1946 was passed, the thinking had changed. Although it would remain the responsibility of the Fed to facilitate the actions of the federal government, it would be responsibility of the President of the US, advised by the newly created Council of Economic Advisers, to recommend policies that would adjust federal spending to the levels required to ensure economic stability.

This new consensus was not without controversy because it implied that the federal government would need to run deficits in some years (as it had during the Great Depression and the World Wars) and surpluses in other years. Nevertheless, there was a broad consensus that we had discovered the tools needed to maintain economic stability and economic growth. It was not long, however, before that consensus was shattered by further unexpected events.

During the late 1960s and the 1970s, a new set of problems arose, problems that shattered the consensus and profoundly altered economic thinking. The problem was 'stagflation'. After a decade in which the

American economy appeared to behave in the expected manner, things went awry. During the 1960s, recession was counteracted in the 'Keynesian' manner by a mid-decade tax cut, and the economy then grew at an even more rapid than anticipated pace as an apparent consequence of increases in government expenditure associated with the Vietnam War. We appeared to be replaying the now-familiar scenario: increase expenditure by cutting taxes, but then increase expenditure directly by increased government expenditures, and you get too much total expenditure, so prices rise. Unemployment is gone, but you have inflation.

What happened as the 1970s wore on, however, was that the American economy experienced both relatively high rates of unemployment *and* high overall price increases. There were many explanations for why this combination, which was not supposed to happen, was happening. OPEC-induced increases in oil prices received a lot of blame for inflation, which was held not to be demand-induced. Changes in the labor force were blamed for relatively high unemployment. There was no shortage of explanations. However, the explanation that gained favor among a lot of economists, and particularly among those economists who were to have the greatest influence on public policy during the Reagan and the first Bush administration, and among a lot of influential journalists as well, owed much to another important book. This book, *A Monetary History of the United States*, by Milton Friedman and Anna Schwartz (1963), was a complete revision of the economic history of the Great Depression of the 1930s, as it had been told from the 1930s through the 1950s and 1960s. (*A Monetary History of the United States* was published in 1963 and might have been known only to specialists in the field had it not been for the stagflation of the 1970s, much as Keynes's *General Theory* would have remained a specialists' book if not for the Great Depression.)

A New Monetarist Perspective Emerges

The modern monetarist view, which is what Friedman and Schwartz advanced, was that the Great Depression was not a result of basic flaws in American capitalism that required periodic correction by government intervention, but rather the result of incompetent monetary policy. The monetarist-revisionists argued that, far from showing the need for active counter-cyclical monetary and fiscal policy, the years 1929–33 show how destabilizing a government agency can be. What Friedman and Schwartz did was put the Fed back in the center of stage and blamed the Great Depression on a failure of the Fed. To reach their conclusion the story of the 1920s and 1930s must be retold, and retold quite differently.

In the Friedman and Schwartz version, it was the Fed's failure to engage in sufficient open market operations in 1930 that turned a mild recession into a major depression. Friedman and Schwartz argue that the Fed's inadequate response to the downturn led to substantial and sustained falls in the deposits held by the public (which, in combination with currency, is often called the money supply or M1). This, they argue was a consequence of (a) the public's decision to change the composition of the money supply by holding currency rather than deposits as they did not trust banks, and (b) a consequence of larger reserve holdings by the now cautious and frightened banks.

It is at this point in the story that difficult issues of causality arise. There is absolutely no doubt that the public lost confidence in banks. When Roosevelt took office one of the first things that he did was extend the policy already in place in some states, and declare a bank holiday to prevent the 'runs on banks' that led panicked depositors to show up in mass at bank after bank and remove their deposits, causing many banks to fail and others to close their doors for extended periods. There is also no doubt that the money supply decreased. The question is why? How did it happen? In the story that underlay the Keynesian interpretation of the depression, the banking crises and the decline in the money supply were consequences of decreased demand for bank loans by business firms for new purchase of capital equipment, of an unwillingness of banks to lend to out-of-work consumers, and of the many other problems in the economy.

For Friedman and Schwartz this story has the direction of causality reversed. They argue that had the needed elasticity been provided by the Fed, then the other problems that surfaced in the American economy would have been minor.

For those who doubt the Friedman and Schwartz version, the crucial question is whether the Fed had the power to provide elasticity in a way that would have made a difference. Here, we must go back to the 1920s and even earlier. Friedman and Schwartz assume that the Fed's goal was to insure economic stability. They can assume this without great concern for the historical record which suggests slow evolution of this goal over the 1920s and 1930s, because of a basic model in which both price level and level of total output (GDP) are a product of the money supply and the (relatively) constant velocity with which that money is used. If this model offers a good explanation of how the economy works then, whether they knew it or not, the Fed by providing sufficient elasticity through its combination of discount rates and open-market operations would provide economic stability.

Critics of the Friedman and Schwartz model respond by saying that the Fed did, in fact, act quickly in late 1929, and in 1930 and 1931, to ease the reserve positions of member banks, and many of the largest banks held excess reserves. The Friedman and Schwartz response is that the Fed should have done still more to increase liquidity. What is crucial to the disagreement, however, is not the level of reserves or the degree of liquidity, but the underlying assumptions of both sides about how the economy works.

For Friedman and Schwartz, and for all of those who are 'monetarists', the economy can be envisioned as a complex of actors all of whom respond with a high degree of sensitivity to price changes in the things that they buy and sell. Banks buy promissory notes and sell liquidity. Changes in the prices of promissory notes, interest rates, and in the price of liquidity (the rediscount rate and the buying/selling prices of government bonds) determine bank behavior. Bank customers, both borrowers and depositors, also respond to prices, as do all other agents in the economy. If you want to change the economy, change crucial prices and the rest will follow.

While Friedman and Schwartz do agree that non-price events such as wars, drought, and bad economic policy decisions, may alter behavior, they also argue that if the monetary authority (the Fed in this case) gets the price of money back to the right level to restore stability, and does so quickly, then stability will recur. Friedman and Schwartz assume that over the long-term the economy will grow as capacity (resources, population, knowledge) allows, and departures from that long-term path can be short-lived, if the price of money is kept at the right level. It was a failure, say Friedman and Schwartz, to get money to the right price quickly enough in 1929 and 1930 that led to the Great Depression.

On the other side of the debate, those at the Brookings Institution who studied the Great Depression while it was underway, the creators of the New Deal, and those who advocated 'Keynesian' policies in the 1940s and 1950s, had another vision of the economy. What they saw was a period in the 1920s when new technology (among other things, electrical appliances and the automobile in the 1920s) created a high demand for funds for investment in new plants. This was a period when employment was high and wages generally good, so that consumers had money to spend from their earnings, and were willing to borrow as well. (The 1920s saw a boom in installment purchases, a form of purchase on credit that preceded widespread use of credit cards.) In such an era, banks could and did lend a lot. Then came a period when additional new factories were not needed because new technologically created opportunities had been exhausted, and when households and their creditors started to worry about debt, and both borrowing and spending declined. (The downward trends were greatly exacerbated in this view by international events, but that is another story.) Bank deposits declined as borrowers borrowed less, and as the process snowballed downward, increased liquidity did little to reverse the trend.

In this non-monetarist view of the economy there are a large number of things other than price that affect spending by both business firms and by households, with no simple way to incorporate all into a model, though the original interpretation of Keynes offered a way to express the complexity in relatively simple way. Consumption is described as a function of all of those things such as household income, consumer confidence, availability of consumer credit, and other things that effect household spending; investment spending is a function of all things that affect business investment such as prior levels of investment, expectations about the future, the cost of borrowing, and so on. In this approach, aggregate demand C + I (with foreign demand and government purchases of goods and services added in) becomes the determinant of GDP and the price level, and it is easy to see that changes in goverment spending, or in taxes which affect C and I, become the important levers to use in maintaining stability. In this view of the economy there is no one price that can be controlled by the Fed (or any other agency) to bring GDP to a level that will provide full employment and price stability.

Thus we have two quite different accounts of how the Great Depression occurred, but the disagreement has been much more than a disagreement among economic historians. It has been a disagreement about how to manage the economy of the 1960s, 1970s and beyond. Friedman and Schwartz said that reliance on fiscal policy (taxing and spending), which had characterized the administrations of Roosevelt, Truman, Eisenhower, Kennedy, and Johnson, was misplaced. You did not need to manipulate G to get stability. All that you needed to do was to manage the price of money and the economy would automatically right itself.

In fact, those who accepted the Friedman and Schwartz story went further and said that the use of fiscal policy to stabilize the economy was likely to have destabilizing effects. It is ironic that Friedman and Schwartz, even though they argue that the Fed could have prevented the Great Depression from becoming great, also conclude that the behavior of the Fed reveals the inevitable tendency of government agencies to react inappropriately (too little, too late or too much, too late). This same criticism has been levied as a general proposition against the use of fiscal policy: by the time Congress acts to cut or increase taxes so as to cause households to increase or decrease consumption, or by the time Congress increases or decreases government spending, it was likely to be too late.

Those who criticized the 'Keynesian' views that were dominant in the 1940s, 1950s and 1960s, on the general grounds derived from Friedman and Schwartz's retelling of the story of the Great Depression, were joined during the 1970s and 1980s by an increasing number of economists and other analysts who argued that either the US economy had changed to render Keynesian-style fiscal policy ineffective, or that it had always been foolishly naive to think that such policy could work in the political context of the US There had indeed been a lot of changes in the economy: changes in the labor force and the patterns of employment, increased international involvement, and so on. And it had been difficult to persuade Congress to act quickly or at all in affecting fiscal policy. The classic case occurred during the Vietnam War buildup when, with unemployment very low it would have made fiscal sense to increase taxes to prevent overall price increases. It proved difficult indeed to persuade Congress to raise taxes to support an unpopular war!

The combination of stagflation, a loss of confidence in policies of aggregate demand management, and the availability of an alternative story (the Friedman and Schwartz story) of economic stability, as well as the development in economics of financial asset theories, have caused many economists and journalists to accept the Friedman and Schwartz version of the role of the Fed and of its potential. This is in many ways a curious turn of events. Although there are very good reasons to doubt that that fiscal management of the economy could ever have worked as imagined in the texts of the 1950s and 1960s, there is no good reason to accept that a properly managed Fed can create macroeconomic stability. At best, what Friedman and Schwartz have provided is a story in which a timid FRS did too little, too late. The faith that has been placed by many in the Fed that Alan Greenspan manages in the early 21st century is not well grounded in that story.

A NEW PROBLEM? A NEW CONSENSUS?

Over the years since the Fed was created, problems in the economy, problems that sometimes rose to the level of crises, led to changes in the Fed, and these changes led, in turn, to changed perceptions. It seems likely that we are currently in the middle of yet another change that will produce a new consensus. It is always difficult to see the direction of change at the time when it is taking place. Yet several things seem clear enough.

In spite of the public perception that the Chairman of the Fed has powerful ability to forecast and to control, continued inability of the Fed to positively affect unemployment rates and overall economic performance will seriously erode this confidence. The Federal Funds Rate is currently very low and likely to go lower but it may not be sufficient to bring about rapid economic recovery. It has been well documented that consumer spending was the mainstay of recent economic growth in the US, and low interest rates are unlikely to be sufficient to restore this source of growth. Although the low rates can affect sales of automobiles and new housing, it is not clear that this will be sufficient to offset declines in consumer confidence and the impact of lower earnings on the interest-bearing assets upon which a number of US households now depend for a portion of their income.

Economists have a language developed from the older 'Keynesian consensus' to describe what seems to be happening. The central banking authority 'can't push on a string'; it can 'lead the horse to water but not make it drink'; there is a 'liquidity trap' in which additional funds are simply held because of the low return on alternative asset forms and because of the uncertainty attached to those other assets; a decline in both business and consumer confidence has reduced the 'marginal efficiency of capital' and the 'average propensity to consume' at all relevant levels of GDP.

If history is a guide, however, we are unlikely to restore to popular usage these phrases from earlier texts and unlikely to restore the consensus they described. How international economic and political instability, the possibility of war, the impact of demographic changes on both private and public pension funds, an underfunded public sector, and any number of other realities of the early 21st century will come together to produce a new consensus is unclear. What is clear is that the conditions of economic growth in a decentralized economy that produced the initial Fed, the changed conditions of World War I that produced the interwar Fed, and the era of fiscal management that resulted from World War II did not endure. Neither will the monetarist era of the last quarter century of the 20th century, when US economic growth did seem relatively automatic if you got the prices right.

It is only a matter of time, and perhaps now a matter of a fairly short time, before it becomes clear that the Fed, for all of its ability to make changes in the price of federal funds that then ripple through all asset pricing, cannot control the level of economic activity in the US. It was not created to do that, and the evidence is that it never has been able to do that.

The temptation to predict what will come next is quieted by recognition that few saw that the original Fed would be substantially altered by World War I, or that World War II and then the stagflation of the 1970s would again alter the role of the Fed. All that can be said is that what happens next will be different.

NOTE

1.   Office of the Provost, the University of Tennessee, Knoxville, TN 37996; email: AMAYHEW@UTK.EDU. There are a number of excellent accounts of the creation and evolution of the Federal Reserve System and of the macroeconomic events described in this chapter. For the beginning student and for others as well I would particularly recommend Elmus Wicker (1966), *Federal Reserve Monetary Policy 1917–1933*; Elmus Wicker (1996), *The Banking Panics of the Great Depression*; an early Keynesian interpretation, and Thomas Wilson's *Fluctuations in Income & Employment* (1970). For excellent treatment of the international context, which is vitally important today but almost

entirely ignored in my essay, I suggest Charles P. Kindleberger (1986), *The World in Depression, 1929–1939.* For an insightful overview of the evolution of public policy, including fiscal policy and the remarkable views of Herbert Hoover, I suggest William J. Barber (1985) *From New Era to New Deal: Herbert Hoover, the Economists, and American Economic Policy, 1921–1933.*

REFERENCES

Barber, William J. (1985), *From New Era to New Deal: Herbert Hoover, the Economists, and American Economic Policy, 1921–1933*, Cambridge: Cambridge University Press.

Friedman, Milton and Schwartz, Anna Jacobson (1963), *A Monetary History of the United States, 1867–1960*, Princeton, NJ: Princeton University Press.

Keynes, John Maynard (1936), *The General Theory of Employment, Interest and Money*, London: Macmillan.

Kindleberger, Charles P. (1986), *The World in Depression, 1929–1939*, Berkeley, CA: University of California Press.

Wicker, Elmus R. (1966), *Federal Reserve Monetary Policy 1917–1933*, New York: Random House.

Wicker, Elmus R. (1996), *The Banking Panics of the Great Depression*, Cambridge: Cambridge University Press.

Wilson, Thomas (1970 [1948]), *Fluctuations in Income & Employment*, 3rd edn, New York: Pitman Publishing.

3. New Bridges Across the Chasm: Macro and Institutional Strategies for Transitional Economies

David Ellerman and Joseph Stiglitz[1]

INTRODUCTION

The 20th century was marked by two great economic experiments. The outcome of the first set, the socialist experiment that began, in its more extreme form, in the Soviet Union in 1917, is now clear. The second experiment is the movement back from a socialist economy to a market economy. Ten years after the beginning of the transition in Eastern Europe and the former Soviet Union, how do we assess what has happened? What are the macroeconomic and institutional lessons to be learned? Surely, this is one of the most important experiments in economics ever to have occurred, a massive and relatively sudden change in the rules of the game. As rapidly as the countries announced the abandonment of communism, so too did Western advisers march in with their sure-fire recipes for a quick transition to a market economy.

A decade after the beginning of the transition in Eastern Europe and the former Soviet Union (FSU), and two decades after the beginning of the transition in China, the picture is mixed. Each country started the course of transition with a different history, a different set of human and physical endowments. Some had lived under the yoke of central planning and authoritarianism for most of the century, while in others it was imposed only in the aftermath of World War II. Those countries bordering Western Europe with encouraging prospects of European Union integration were clearly in a different position than the land-locked countries of Mongolia and the former Soviet republics in Central Asia. Counterfactual history – what would have been but for the policies that were pursued – is always problematic, and especially so when there are so many variables with which to contend. Yet, the disparity between the successes and failures is so large that it calls out for interpretation and explanation, and in any case, the public debate is well underway.

Some have formulated the public debate about the transition as a question of fast versus slow. But that seems a poor formulation since one can find successes and failures on both sides of the fast–slow dichotomy. Some countries, such as Russia, tried to 'jump over the chasm in one leap', but their leap did not reach the other side and now they will take much longer to climb back out of the chasm. Other countries progressed more incrementally and found that well-designed incremental reforms, such as the Chinese agricultural reforms, can proceed quite rapidly. Yet other countries tried to just 'go slow' and sat on one side of the chasm erecting many half-bridges that went nowhere – many pseudo-reforms that were dead-ends.

It is time to harvest some of the rich lessons from the first decade of the transition experience. The Western advice to Russia and many of the countries of the FSU has surely been one of the largest policy disasters in recent history – the advice before and after the East Asian crisis being another example (see Stiglitz, 2002). In view of the remarkably different results in the transition between Russia and China, those who promulgated the 'Washington Consensus' advice to Russia and the FSU would like to avoid drawing any damning lessons by terminating the debate with one-liners such as:

- 'Russia is not China';
- 'Of course, mistakes were made, but that doesn't mean the basic policies were wrong'; and
- 'The policies were right but were just not implemented'.

While each one-liner has some truth, it is the job of intelligent analysis of past experience to draw deeper lessons in spite of the ever-present differences between cases and the inevitable differences between the past, present, and future.

Going beyond analysis, the task is also to suggest building new bridges across the chasm, which means to change institutions in a determined but incremental way. We begin by outlining four macro-strategies or bridges, many of them drawn from the experience over the last decade in transitional economies. Then we turn to some of the broad institutional lessons.

FOUR BRIDGES

Russia's transition from communism to a market economy has been far harder than most people anticipated just a decade ago. The rise in prosperity that the market economy had promised has not materialized: far from it, as GDP has fallen by 50 per cent,[2] and the fraction in poverty has soared from 2 per cent to 50 per cent (Milanovic, 1998). We need to recognize these sad facts no matter how we analyze the causes.

At each stage of a country's history, it builds on what it has inherited from the past. The legacy of the Communist era was more than an aging and inefficient capital stock and the absence of the institutional infrastructure required to make a market economy and a social democracy work: it included a disillusioned workforce, a broad sense of cynicism (especially towards the state), and an unhealthy disrespect for the rule of law (see, for instance, Murrell, 1996).

Today, over a decade later, it has a new legacy: there is a growing group of young entrepreneurs, but also a 'Mafia' that has perhaps grown even faster. As the institutions of the state have broken the social contract time and time again, failed to deliver on implicit and explicit promises, and been used as instruments for private gain at public expense – with a few becoming vastly enriched at the same time that the majority has become impoverished – the sense of cynicism towards the state and the rule of law is today perhaps even stronger than it was a decade ago. While a decade ago the country looked forward to the prospect of creating a more egalitarian democratic capitalism – unencumbered by the inequalities inherited from a feudal past – today the country must face the task of creating a market economy with a level of inequality that rivals the worst in the world. And while there have been some strides in creating democratic or at least electoral institutions, they also show the power and dangers of an excessively concentrated media.

There are those who hoped that privatization, no matter how it was done, would create demand for the institutional infrastructure of a market economy and the rule of law, replacing the grabbing hand of the state with the invisible hand of the market.[3] Neither history nor economic theory provided grounds for these hopes – the conventional wisdom is that it is the middle class that gives rise to the demands for these institutions, and the last decade has added another data point in support of that generalization. If anything, the last decade in Russia has seen the evisceration of the Russian middle class and the creation of a new and even more concentrated oligarchy, with little interest in the rule of law, effective competition, or a fair bankruptcy regime. The oligarchs who were 'empowered' by the Russian 'reforms' want to consolidate and strengthen their power in a rather bizarre hybrid system, and have little interest in creating the long-term institutional preconditions[4] for a private property market economy or a genuine political democracy.

What is the macroeconomic agenda that the country should pursue? We argue that what is required are the following broad macro-strategies:

- recognizing that the country needs a growth strategy, and not just fiscal consolidation;
- recognizing that the current state of massive tax arrears (and other liabilities to the state, direct and indirect) provides a unique opportunity to rectify some of the mistakes of the past decade;
- recognizing the importance of rebuilding the economy 'from the bottom up', with a healthy investment climate for the whole private sector, but particularly starting with the promotion of domestic medium-sized and small enterprises both as start-ups and spin-offs from larger enterprises; and
- recognizing that the creation of a vibrant social democracy will entail recreating social capital.

Growth and Inflation

There is a broad consensus among economists that economic growth in Russia would have been impossible if hyperinflation had continued; hence strong action – even shock therapy – to stop the hyperinflation was called for. But too often, policies went beyond simply bringing down inflation to reasonable levels. Cutting inflation to lower and lower levels – no matter what the cost – became a fetish, despite overwhelming evidence that there are little if any gains in productivity or growth from reductions in inflation below 20 per cent.[5] And the costs of pushing inflation to these low levels have not been inconsiderable. Some argue that the excessive tightening of monetary policy has been a contributing (but not the only) factor in the growth of arrears and of the barter economy – to the point where it was estimated that 70 per cent of all transactions were via barter.[6] While inflation may weaken the price system because individuals do not have accurate knowledge of relative prices, barter may be even more effective in undermining the price system. Thus, the attempt to strengthen the price system by curtailing inflation may well have backfired. In addition, there is an argument that if there is some degree of downward wage and price rigidity, then moderate inflation may actually be desirable (see Akerlof et al., 1996); and the critical rate of inflation may increase with the magnitude of the adjustments in the economy that are required. Because the economies in transition require more adjustment, the 'optimal' rate of inflation may accordingly be higher than in other economies, so that results derived from other economies provide an underestimate of the critical rate.

Overall, macroeconomic policy has been so contractionary – given the inflation paranoia – that it has probably played a significant role in the economy's contraction. (To be sure, misguided structural policies, discussed below, may also have played a role.) These contractionary policies have included an overvalued exchange rate, maintained by usurious interest rates that have choked off all new investment and entrepreneurial activities. The recent expansion of the economy (e.g., in import substitutes) can be directly attributable to the 1998 devaluation, bearing testimony that at least some of the economic downturn was due to misguided macroeconomic policies.

It is now widely recognized that aggregate demand and aggregate supply are closely intertwined.[7] Excessively contractionary macroeconomic policies, especially tight monetary policies, undermine the net worth of firms, forcing them into distress; even short of that, supply is reduced.[8] The adverse effect on aggregate supply means, of course, that even if and when aggregate demand is resuscitated, the economy will not immediately recover. It would be wrong to infer from this that the initial, underlying problem was insufficient aggregate demand. It is right, however, to conclude from this that addressing problems of aggregate demand will not suffice as a policy response.

Fiscal Policies and Privatization

A second major mistake of the preceding decade has been the focus on the speed of privatization, without paying due attention to its manner or the presence of institutional infrastructure. The presumption underlining this was a version of Coase's conjecture: all one had to do to ensure eventual efficiency was to turn over the assets to private hands, and the profit motive would subsequently ensure that the assets were owned or managed by those most capable of doing so (Coase, 1937). Subsequent experiences have confirmed that, indeed, incentives matter; but private markets, in the absence of appropriate institutions, can provide stronger incentives for asset stripping and diversion than for wealth creation. The stronger version of this hypothesis, for which there was never any theory or empirical basis – that the creation of private property rights would automatically provide incentives for the creation of an appropriate institutional infrastructure – was equally misguided.

The manner of privatization – with a few oligarchs accumulating huge amounts of wealth – has not only failed to generate the promised benefits in terms of efficiency, but has undermined social capital and led to a lack of confidence in the market economy, and even, to some extent, in democratic processes.

The focus on privatizing existing assets diverted attention away from creating new enterprises.[9] And the manner in which privatization proceeded not only failed to pay due attention to issues of corporate governance,[10] but did not serve to facilitate the creation of new enterprises.[11] Moreover, the strategy did not make the enterprises that were put up for foreign sale attract many foreign bidders; and over time, the absence of the rule of law has further served to discourage foreign investment.

While privatization in a manner inappropriate for the institutional infrastructure (see below) led to asset stripping rather than wealth creation, privatization prior to establishing the mechanisms of tax collection deprived the country of needed fiscal resources for public expenditures, thereby further undermining the social contract, as pensioners saw their benefits decline while the wealth of the oligarchs increased.

It would have been a relatively easy matter to enforce revenue collection from a substantial fraction of the GDP – that part generated by natural resources – had the government had the will, and had the international financial institutions made this a precondition of providing funds. There are well-established methods of monitoring, and international benchmark prices, on the basis of which it would be easy to levy taxes. This can still be done. Moreover, such taxes come as close to being pure rent taxes as any other except those imposed on land, and are accordingly less distortionary than other forms of taxation.

New Enterprise and Job Creation

This brings us to the third major pillar of the proposed new strategy: the investment climate in general, but starting with the climate for domestic enterprise and job creation. Previous policies not only did not focus on this, but seemed almost deliberately designed to suppress new enterprise and job creation – high interest rates made borrowing prohibitively expensive; an overvalued currency put domestic firms at an unfair trade advantage in tradables, whether exports or import substitutes; and the low revenues achieved from privatization, and obtained from the large privatized enterprises, sometimes led to high implicit taxes on the newer, less powerful firms.

Rebuilding Social Capital

The fourth pillar is perhaps the most difficult: re-establishing the social contract and reinvesting in social capital.[12] Rebuilding social capital is not a task that can be done from Moscow. Too many, both inside and outside Russia, think hope can only come in the form of the 'good Czar' finally getting into the Kremlin. We might draw an analogy with the Civil Rights Movement in the US during the 1960s and 1970s. How are people who have been held down and who have been socially passive finally able to mobilize themselves to become socially active and to gain some measure of control over their own affairs? Certainly not by just waiting for the right president in the White House. Local bottom-up organizations of civil society are necessary – the new atoms and molecules of social capital. But local mobilization is rarely sufficient, since local and subnational governments are often part of the problem. Thus there needs to be a pincer movement of pressure from below and pressure from above to break the old molds and allow new forms to evolve.

Thus any strategy for economic rejuvenation designed in Moscow should have as a key component the ways and means for facilitating local empowerment through employee-owned enterprises, rejuvenated unions, new cooperatives, and other people-based 'third sector' associations of civil society.

PUBLIC–PRIVATE PARTNERSHIPS AND CHANGING THE INVESTMENT CLIMATE

Reform Based on Credible and Effective Government

We want to begin by dispelling the idea that one can base a transition strategy on weakening the government (the 'grabbing hand' theory) and then expect a vibrant market economy to rise up automatically in its place.[13] We have seen from the Russian experience alone that there is no automaticity in the development of market institutions in the post-socialist environment. Nor can we wait until there is a full complement of institutions before moving forward. Strategies need to take into account what positive institutions are in place now and might realistically evolve in the near future. Strategies should not presuppose that some ideal set of institutions that has taken many decades to develop in the West (and still has its 'Enrons' and 'S&L' crises) can be quickly 'installed' in the post-socialist environment.

It is as if you are at sea and your ship is in distress. If you just abandon the ship, another ship will not automatically appear to save you (only East Germany had that option). Nor can you just pull into a dry dock and repair the ship before going back to sea. You must learn to repair your ship at sea, starting with the most pressing problems and moving forward increasing your self-confidence in resolving your problems and staying on a true course.

Instead of focusing on abandoning or weakening the state, the focus should be on redirecting government (which may well involve downsizing), which might involve a variety of public–private partnerships and support for 'third sector' non-governmental organizations. Market failures are too extensive for the private parties to develop the institutions automatically. But government failure is the legacy of the socialist past, so we must explore new avenues, partnership between public and private sectors and the intermediate third sector of non-governmental organizations that are neither purely public nor private.

Filling the 'Socialist Blackhole'

The post-socialist economies suffer from the legacy of the 'bigger is better' mania of their socialist past. In the advanced western economies, we see the finished products and the advertisements of the big firms, but it is not as widely known that each large firm is supported by many small and medium-sized enterprises (SMEs). For example, fully one half of the German GDP is produced by the small and medium-sized firms called the 'Mittelstand' companies. They are largely insider or family-owned and do not appear on the stock markets.

In the post-socialist economies, there was a preponderance of huge vertically integrated 'firms' while smaller firms hardly went beyond the kiosk-economy of small traders. The missing SMEs represented a huge hole in the size distribution of firms that was called the 'socialist blackhole' (see Figure 3.1 and Vahcic and Petrin, 1989). One of the larger goals in restructuring large 'production units' (one hesitates to call them 'firms') should be to help fill the socialist blackhole by spinning off smaller 'planets' or 'satellites' as SMEs.

We will point you toward success stories of post-socialist countries (e.g., Hungary, Poland, and Slovenia) as well as to successes from long ago in Western countries at an early stage of development. There are methods of restructuring large companies, such as hiving off of the viable parts in medium-sized firms that are short of liquidation bankruptcy. There are ways to actually implement liquidation bankruptcy laws without creating social chaos by fostering direct redeployment of the assets (e.g., by entrepreneurial middle managers from the old firm) in small business start-ups (see Ellerman and Kreacic, 2002). There are methods of government assistance that countries have found to foster the small and medium-sized enterprise sector. And there are changes in the education system for both the student and adult populations that will help develop the skills and mind-sets that are fruitful in a market economy. Development can be approached as a transformation of society (see Stiglitz, 1998). The transition from communism to a market society is no less a transformation of society, entailing not only changes in institutions but changes in ways of thinking. A crucial question is how best to bring about these changes.

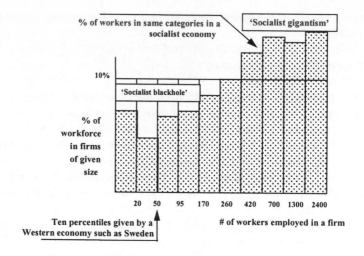

Source: All data 'stylized', from Vahcic and Petrin (1989).

Figure 3.1   Socialist blackhole

Rethinking Restructuring

Much confusion has been caused by the fact that certain words were used under communism with totally different meanings from how those words are used under capitalism. Consider the word 'bank'. Under capitalism, banks garner funds, then allocate them, based on a process of screening among different applicants. They then monitor that the funds are spent in the way intended, and finally they take actions to see that the loans are repaid. Under communism, banks did only one of these: they collected funds. Other than that, they were engaged basically in bookkeeping; the real allocation decisions were made elsewhere (e.g., Gosplan). By the same token, firms under communism had little to do with the concept of firms under capitalism. The concept of the firm in a capitalist system is fundamentally a legal one, a locus of decision-making authority, with certain rights and obligations, including (residual) control of certain assets. The rights of others to intervene in the decision-making of the firm was restricted – though to be sure influence could be exercised by a variety of means. By contrast, under communism, the state, particularly through the ministries, could intervene in any decision, though in practice much was delegated to lower units. And while the lower units may have had certain de facto property rights, they had no de jure rights, and so the central authority could override any allocation decision they made.

In a sense, one could think of the national economy as a single large firm, with the President of the country acting as the CEO or the Chairman of the Board, the heads of ministries being heads of different subsidiaries, and the banking system being the accounting department. 'Debts' were simply intra-firm bookkeeping entries. The transition from communism to the market economy can be thought of as a national bankruptcy, in which the debts of the separate units, being nothing more than intra-firm bookkeeping entries, could simply be ignored. Only the deposits of households into the banks were of importance – they were part of the 'social contract' that had to be preserved. (Ironically, it was these obligations that were in fact wiped out through hyperinflation in the period immediately following the end of the Cold War.)

The principles guiding such a national bankruptcy are similar to those guiding a more conventional bankruptcy: the essential question is how should various assets be best deployed. But the circumstances of the two situations differ sufficiently that one must be careful to rethink how to answer that question. For instance, two guiding principles in corporate restructuring in well functioning economies are the following: first, it makes less difference who is the owner than that there be well-defined owners. That is because, so long as there are well-defined owners, they will have an incentive to redeploy assets in ways that maximize market value. This is the essence of the Coase theorem (or, as it is more aptly called, the Coase conjecture). Even in well-functioning capitalist economies there are strong caveats to the Coase theorem; important corporate governance problems can arise with dispersed ownership, with managers using their discretionary powers to advance their interests at the expense of shareholders, or majority shareholders doing so at the expense of minority shareholders. But good legal structures and a strong banking system typically put important checks on abuses. But in the economies in transition, incentives to maximize value are attenuated, when there are no markets on which to sell shares, or those markets are far from competitive or well functioning. Corporate governance problems are further exacerbated by the inadequacies of the legal structure and the weaknesses in the banking system. Many of the specific proposals noted below are intended to address these concerns.

The second guiding principle is the preservation of social, organizational, and informational capital – when it has positive value. That is why there is a presumption for keeping intact production units within a firm; the value of an enterprise as an ongoing production unit is greater than the value of the underlying capital goods (this is sometimes referred to as the firm's goodwill). On the other hand, there are economies and diseconomies of scale and scope, and there are transactions costs and other costs associated with using markets and non-market mechanisms – all of which affect the boundaries of a firm, in particular, what should go on within a firm. Again, though the principle remains the same, the differing contexts have strong implications: much of the 'goodwill', the informational and organizational capital, relate to a quite different economic system. The differing institutional infrastructures – including the problems of corporate governance referred to earlier – imply differing organizational solutions.

From 'Bigger is Better' to 'Small is Beautiful'

Why do SMEs tend to work well and overcome some of the endemic problems of large firms? When there are many people in a firm, each person might feel they could only have an effect inversely proportional to the number of people in the firm – which would be such a small effect that they are not strongly motivated. The firm is just too huge to feel that you can make a difference. One can imagine how it must feel to be a rank-and-file worker in gigantic post-socialist firm, just a small cog in a gigantic wheel. In a small or medium-sized firm (say, up to 500 workers), an individual might be able to see the difference that he or she, or the team they work in, can make. That alone should call forth more individual effort. The entrepreneur in a small firm is 'big frog in a small pond instead of a small frog in a big pond'.[14] Moreover, people can more easily see what others are doing, so that noncooperative behavior will face more social approbation.

From the viewpoint of decision-making, small firms have less bureaucratic hierarchy and are thus more agile in responding to changing conditions. In America, they are called 'gazelles' because they can change direction so quickly. Information has a shorter distance to travel from top to bottom and from bottom to top. And management will tend to be newer and more entrepreneurial in a small and medium-sized firm. This is especially true in the transitional economies where those in charge of the 'subunits' are likely to be younger than those at the top of the larger organizations. They will be building for the future – rather than, as in some of the larger firms, just trying to hold together the remnants of the past.

Spin-offs have the opportunity and the incentive to add new customers and new suppliers. In all the large firms of the developed, developing, and transitional economies, managers and workers in some small subunits may realize that their skills and capabilities could be used to produce other products and satisfy other needs than those emphasized in the plans of the larger unit. In entrepreneur-friendly environments, they could spin off or breakaway and form a new small firm to pursue those other lines of business.[15] They are no longer a captive part of a vertically integrated firm.

For instance, the trucking part of a business, once spun off, has the incentive to look for new business. And the spin-off in a competitive market environment stimulates innovation. With the prospect of new customers, there needs to be innovation and learning to get and to hold the new clients. The empirical evidence from the successful early reformers (e.g., Poland) points to the crucial role of a vibrant sector of small and medium-sized enterprises (see Johnson and Loveman, 1995).

Role of the Government

This sort of spin-off restructuring is possible now; it does not necessarily require new physical or financial resources. But it does require new initiatives and new mind-sets. It requires the middle managers and the workers in the unit to see that their prospects are brighter and their fate more in their own hands if they do the spin-off into a quasi-separate firm than if they remain part of the 'empire' of the large mother firm. And it requires a change in the top managers of the mother firm to let the 'empire' transform itself into a looser complex of contractually related small and medium-sized firms. Above all, it means moving away from the strategy that bigger is better either in terms of market power or lobbying power with the ministries for subsidies and favors.

If ambitious middle managers have to wait for the top managers to voluntarily agree to a part of their empire to become partly independent, then they might have to wait a very long time. Here is where government support might be crucial. There has to be a pincer action on the top management of the large socialistic dinosaurs to promote the breakaways and spin-offs: middle managers pushing from below and government pushing from above. There might be large discrepancies between top manager's private returns and social returns (which requires the governments assistance to overcome). Governments have many levers of action, such as the threat (or reality) of enforcing tax, utility, and wage arrears as well as promises of any future assistance. Indeed, given the magnitude of such arrears, even governments that have aggressively pushed privatization have this option for encouraging restructuring. Governments cannot and should not allow firms that have outstanding tax obligations or debts to the government-owned banks simply to continue operating as is. In the reorganization that should be a standard part of bankruptcy procedure in the economies of transition, spin-offs of the viable parts of a firm should be a standard option.

Thus there could be a public program, perhaps sponsored by a ministry for promoting small and medium-sized firms, where spin-offs would be fostered in any large firm (say over 1000 workers) which had tax, utility, or wage arrears or which 'required' some form of government assistance, i.e., in most if not all large firms. If the middle managers and the workers in a unit could satisfy certain objective requirements, then the top management in the mother firm would be obliged to negotiate in good faith to arrange the spin-off (or have default terms imposed by law).

In this manner, improvements in the investment climate (like the proverbial 'charity') can start at home. But what about foreign investors? What is important is an openness to knowledge and experience from the successful market economies. One of the most important forms of interchange is a simple business relationship such as exporting a product to a Western firm or making a locally sold product under contract to and using specialized inputs from a Western firm. At first, knowledge will flow in from the Western firm to the Eastern partner. Then the Western firm might fund the purchase of new machinery to improve the product. The payback for the investment could be arranged through the transfer pricing of the business relationship. After the experience of such a successful relationship, then a Western firm might consider a more direct form of investment or 'marriage' with the Eastern firm. If 'investment follows trade' is the more normal sequence, then the government should actively promote foreign trade relationships that might eventually lead to a more direct form of investment.

INSTITUTIONAL CHANGE STRATEGIES

Rethinking Corporate Governance from Scratch

The institutions of corporate governance in the market economies have evolved over this entire century.[16] Expectations that these institutions could simply be transplanted to the transitional economies have been widely disappointed (see Black et al., 1996, followed by Black et al., 2000). In the slow-reforming post-socialist economies, it is best to go back to basics and rethink corporate governance from scratch.

There are two intertwined problems: managers who act in an opportunistic and self-dealing manner as agents of the shareholders, and controlling shareholders who ignore and violate the interests of the other non-controlling minority shareholders.

In the agent–principal relationship between the managers and shareholders, the agent has a fiduciary role to act in the interests of the principal. Ordinarily the agents' actions are hidden from the scrutiny of the principals, and the agents have specialized information not available to the principals. This being the case, there is always the temptation for the agents to exploit their informational advantage and the non-transparency of their actions to step out of their fiduciary role and to engage in self-dealing opportunistic behavior. Sometimes the agency relationships are stacked up in a chain of relationships. In the plan of voucher privatization with investment funds (see Ellerman 1998; 2001) that was preferred by most Western advisers, the principal–agent links in the long agency chain were:

1. the millions of shareholders of voucher investment funds, who are supposed to control;
2. the boards of the funds, which are supposed to control;
3. the fund management companies, which are supposed to control;
4. the boards of their hundreds of portfolio companies, which are supposed to control;
5. the managers of the portfolio companies, who are supposed to control;
6. the middle managers and workers, who are supposed to actually produce something that somebody wants to buy.

In such an agency chain, a minority interest might nevertheless be controlling and there is plenty of room for self-dealing.

In the West, informal norms of managerial behavior and formal institutions of governance have evolved over the 20th century. Financial accounting and auditing standards have been devised, and whole professions of accounting and auditing have developed to maintain the public trust in implementing those standards. That brings a measure of transparency so that principals can better monitor their agents. Corporate law and related criminal law fraud statutes have evolved so that there are more effective sanctions for gross misconduct.

We cannot simply assume that all these institutions are up and running in the post-socialist environment. In that environment, it is best to reduce or collapse the agency chains back to the level where the principals are close to the agents (if not identical with the agents as in the family farm or small owner-operated business). The up-close parties who can better monitor the managers are the parties who have some implicit or explicit contracts with the firm such as the workers, suppliers, creditors, customers, and local government. They are called the 'stakeholders' of the firm, so when the stakeholders are also shareholders, then the up-close principals have both the ability and the incentives to better monitor their agents.

Monitoring needs to be coupled with enforcement. Enforcement of good corporate governance through the whole system of courts, judges, juries, and lawyers is rather inefficient even in the Western economies. When the principals are not just absentee and unrelated shareholders but are up-close principals with a direct relationship with the firm, then there is a more practical means of enforcement. The firm is already embedded in relationships with workers, suppliers, creditors, customers, and the local government, and these relationships provide a forum for discussions of mutual interests and instruments for adjusting those interests (e.g., the terms of all the contracts between stakeholders and the firm). The stakeholders do not ordinarily need to rely on the courts to deliver their messages or protect their interests since they have an on-going relationship of give-and-take with the firm. They, in effect, have 'mutual hostages'. Only in very exceptional cases would the parties need to resort to the courts to adjudicate and enforce the interests of the principals.

'Going back to basics' in agent–principal relationships means having principals who are 'up-close' to the agents (if not identical) for better monitoring, and who are transactionally related so that the principals can use the give-and-take nature of the relationship (ongoing discussions plus bargaining power) as the means of corporate governance. Many decades of evolution were necessary to establish the viability of a system of absentee ownership where the shareholders have no up-close informational relationship and no direct business relationship with the firm aside for the bare ownership of shares. The ongoing debate in the US about shareholder suits is evidence that even then, there are widespread perceptions that the system needs further tuning. It should come as no surprise that these 'advanced' corporate codes transplanted to the post-socialist environment have not provided a basis for adequate corporate governance.

The techniques of restructuring described here (e.g., spin-offs with stakeholders as shareholders) will also increase stakeholder ownership so that corporate governance should at the same time be improved. It should be particularly noted that the idea is not to 'postpone' privatization until some near-ideal corporate governance institution can be somehow created out of the void. The idea is go forward with the forms of privatization (e.g., short agency chains) that can be implemented with the existing and near-future institutions of governance.

Shock Therapy versus Incremental Step-by-Step Change

History offers few 'crucial experiments,' but the contrast between the Russian and Chinese transitions is probably the best one could ask for to contrast a 'institutional shock therapy' or blitzkrieg approach with an incremental, step-by-step, or staged approach to institutional change. The Yeltsin reformers used rather 'Bolshevik' methods to try to storm the ramparts during the few windows of opportunity. In Stiglitz (1999a) and Reddaway and Glinski (2001) this is called 'market bolshevism'. There was also a sort of institutional 'Coase theorem' involved in this change strategy; once the impediments of the socialist past were removed, the 'natural market forces' would emerge to build a market economy. We suspect that history will judge this strategy a failure – particularly in contrast to the incremental strategy used in China.

What is the alternative or counterfactual? In this case, the alternative has long found its sophisticated expression in the work of Albert Hirschman about incremental 'reform-mongering' change driven more by endogenous linkages rather than by exogenous 'carrots and sticks' embedded in IFI loan conditions.[17] The Chinese reform experience represents this incremental approach in practice; crossing the river groping for the stepping-stones rather than jumping over the chasm in one last 'great leap forward'. The point is to find and build step-by-step upon the reform efforts of the past (which requires taking into account past conditions) rather than trying to wipe the slate clean and legislate ideal institutions in one fell swoop. Black et al. (2000) have used the word 'staged' in much the same sense. In Lau et al. (2000), the 'two-track' system of reforms is analyzed where a second track, step, or stage is inaugurated and can then grow to eventually render the earlier stage obsolete. In *Whither Reform?* (Stiglitz, 1999b), the two 'ideal types' were compared as a 'battle of metaphors' (see Table 3.1).

Another part of the incremental approach, also evident in China, is the willingness to allow experiments in different parts of the country and then foster horizontal learning and the propagation of the successful experiments.[18] This is an important part of the alternative to the Bolshevik/Jacobin approach of legislating the brave new world from the capital city to be applied uniformly across the country. The transition from socialism to capitalism had not happened before in history, so the situation clearly called out for experimentation and pragmatism ('It is not important if the cat is black or white, but that it catches the mice' – Deng Xiaoping). Instead the Western assistance institutions succumbed out of their own self-confidence and *la rage de vouloir conclure* (the rage to conclude) to the Bolshevik/Jacobin mentality, with aid and abetment from elite academic advisors (e.g., the Harvard wunderkinder), and supported Moscow legislation to apply the dreamed-up solutions across the whole Russian Federation.

CONCLUSIONS

Sometimes just to know that a competitor has made a breakthrough is enough to spur a company to make the same innovation on its own. Even scientists in one country can be motivated to make a breakthrough knowing only that scientists in another country have already done so. In other words, just knowing that a journey is actually possible sweeps away half the excuses for not making the journey oneself.

Table 3.1 'Battle of metaphors'

	Shock therapy	Incrementalism
Continuity vs. break	Discontinuous break or shock – razing the old social structure in order to build the new.	Continuous change – trying to preserve social capital that cannot be easily reconstructed.
Role of initial conditions	The first-best socially engineered solution that is not 'distorted' by the initial conditions.	Piecemeal changes (continuous improvements) taking into account initial conditions.
Role of knowledge	Emphasizes explicit or technical knowledge of end-state blueprint.	Emphasizes local practical knowledge that only yields local predictability and does not apply to large or global changes.
Knowledge Attitude	Knowing what you are doing.	Knowing that you don't know what you are doing (see Benziger, 1996).
Chasm metaphor	Jump across the chasm in one leap.	Build a bridge across the chasm.
Rebuilding the ship metaphor	Rebuilding the ship in dry dock. The dry dock provides the Archimedean point outside the water so the ship can be rebuilt without being disturbed by the conditions at sea.	Rebuilding the ship at sea. There is no 'dry dock' or Archimedean fulcrum for changing social institutions from outside of society. Change always starts with the given historical institutions.
Transplanting the tree metaphor	All at once transplantation in a decisive manner to seize the benefits and get over the shock as quickly as possible.	Preparing and wrapping the major roots one at a time (*nemawashi*) to prevent shock to the whole system and improve chances of successful transplantation.

Note: See Elster et al. (1998) for the 'rebuilding the ship at sea' metaphor and Morita (1986) about *nemawashi*.

We now know that a successful transition is possible. Within Eastern Europe, Poland, Slovenia, Hungary, and Estonia can be counted as successes, and China is in its own category as a success story. Each country has its own history, its own strengths and weaknesses, but each learned to use its strengths and overcome its weaknesses to make the journey.

We now know that a quick leap across a chasm is unlikely to succeed, and we also know that half-hearted bridge-building attempts will leave only half-bridges going nowhere. With 10 years of transitional experience, there is much to be learned from the successes and failures. Indeed, within the broad expanse of Russia there have been many local success stories, and likewise in neighboring countries. Rather than hatch some new optimal master plan in Moscow, it is a time to promote decentralized experimentation, bench-marking between experiments, and learning from the successes. We can point you to lessons, strategies, and examples that can be the basis for learning, and we have tried to do so here. Transformation can neither be imposed nor given as a gift from the outside; transformation is a do-it-yourself project.

NOTES

1. David Ellerman is former adviser to the Chief Economist and Joseph Stiglitz is former Chief Economist at the World Bank. The findings, interpretations, and conclusions expressed in this chapter are entirely those of the authors and should not be attributed in any manner to the World Bank, to its affiliated organizations, or to the members of its Board of Directors or the countries they represent.
2. To be sure, there are measurement problems, but there are arguments both that the numbers underestimate and overestimate true GDP (see Gaddy and Ickes, 1998). The corroborating evidence – the huge decline in lifespans and the large numbers of individuals in poverty revealed by survey methodologies – corroborates the more pessimistic views of what has happened. On the history of the Russian reforms, see Reddaway and Glinski (2001).
3. See Shleifer and Vishny (1998) and the discussion below of the 'grabbing hand' theory.
4. For instance, would those who grabbed fabulous wealth during the last decade want to fundamentally reform the judicial system so that verdicts could not be 'bought' or would they prefer to keep the current way of 'getting things done'?
5. There is some debate about the critical threshold, with Bruno and Easterly (1995) citing numbers around 40 per cent, and others, such as Barro (1997), citing numbers around 10 per cent. Fischer (1993) shows that while low inflation and small deficits are not necessary for high growth even over long periods, high inflation is not consistent with sustained growth. The problem is that in Russia, and in many of the other economies in transition, cutting inflation was pushed well beyond these numbers.
6. There is no agreement about the reason for the growth of barter, but several of the favored explanations focus on policies that aimed for macro-stabilization, such as tax policies which use the financial system for tax collection and cash flow constraints unmatched by expenditure constraints, which lead to arrears.
7. This point was brought home forcefully by the East Asian Crisis. See, e.g., Stiglitz (2002). For a theoretical discussion of the issues, see, e.g., Greenwald and Stiglitz (1993).
8. These adverse consequences, resulting in the destruction of informational, organizational, social, and reputational capital, may have had particularly severe effects, given the

limitations of this capital at the beginning of the transition and the natural dissolution of some forms of this capital in the process of transition. See Blanchard and Kremer (1997).

9.   Contrast the strategy with that of China, where little privatization occurred, yet the share of non-state enterprises in gross industrial output has risen from 22 per cent in 1978 to 74 per cent in 1997, and all but a small percentage of this rise is accounted for by new enterprises.

10. For a discussion of the issues of corporate governance, see below. For the question why privatization did not really succeed in removing government from enterprise activity, see Stiglitz (1999a; 1999b).

11. Contrast the strategies of privatization in Poland and Hungary with that pursued by Russia.

12. Note that the strategy sometimes argued for by the radical reformers runs counter to this: they argue that if only the government would make business conditions sufficiently attractive, there would be a reversal of the prodigious capital flight and a flow of funds back into the country. Implicitly, they are arguing for a legitimization of the illegitimate privatizations – which would hardly provide the sense of equity and social fairness necessary to rebuild the social contract.

13. This view is sometimes called the 'political Coase theorem': privatize quickly and then the necessary new institutions will automatically arise out of pressure from the new property owners and the market. For example, the Russian privatization program 'de-emphasized corporate governance precisely because the intent was to reduce the damage from government failure rather than from market failure' (Shleifer and Vishny, 1998, p. 11). 'The architects of the Russian privatization were aware of the dangers of poor enforcement of property rights. Yet because of the emphasis on politics, the reformers predicted that institutions would follow private property rather than the other way around' (ibid., p. 11). 'Institutions supporting corporate governance, such as the banking sector and capital markets, are also developing rapidly [sic] in part because of the profit opportunities made available by the privatized firms' (ibid, p. 254, note 4).

14. Or according to an old Chinese proverb: 'Better the head of a chicken than the tail of a horse' (Campos and Root, 1996, p. 62).

15. 'Many of the most economically creative breakaways have this sort of history: individuals, or a few colleagues together, leave their jobs in a large organization and independently reproduce the same fragment of work they had been doing there. Usually their customers are small organizations too. Then the breakaway adds new work to its older work' (Jacobs, 1969, p. 67).

16. See Marshall (1897) for an early statement of the problem, but mainly see Berle and Means (1932) and the huge literature following it. For recent treatments see Roe (1994); Kaufman et al. (1995); Stiglitz and Edlin (1995); Stiglitz (1982; 1985; 1987; 1994); and Dyck (1999).

17. See the 'two basic approaches' in Hirschman (1973, pp. 247–8) where he contrasts an ideological, fundamental, and root-and-branch approach to reform with an incremental, remedial, piecemeal, and adaptive approach.

18. 'The diffusion of innovations in China is distinctive in that it is (1) more horizontal in nature, (2) less dependent upon scientific and technical expertise, and (3) more flexible in allowing re-invention of the innovation as it is implemented by local units. These aspects of decentralized diffusion are facilitated by China's use of such diffusion strategies as models and on-the-spot conferences. The "learning from others" approach to decentralized diffusion in China was adopted officially as a national policy in the national constitution in 1978' (Rogers, 1983, pp. 340–41).

REFERENCES

Akerlof, George, William Dickens, and George Perry (1996), 'The Macroeconomics of Low Inflation', *Brookings Papers on Economic Activity*, **1**: 1–59.

Barro, Robert (1997), *Determinants of Economic Growth*, Cambridge, MA: MIT Press.

Benziger, V. (1996), 'The Chinese Wisely Realized that They Did Not Know What They Were Doing', *Transition*, **7** (7–8 July–August): 6–7.

Berle, A. and G. Means (1932), *The Modern Corporation and Private Property*, New York: Macmillan.

Black, Bernard, Reinier Kraakman and Jonathan Hay (1996), 'Corporate Law from Scratch', in Roman Frydman, Cheryl W. Gray and Andrzej Rapaczynski (eds), *In Corporate Governance in Central Europe and Russia: Insiders and the State*, Budapest: Central European University Press, vol. 2, pp. 245–302.

Black, Bernard, Reinier Kraakman, and Anna Tarassova (2000), 'What Went Wrong with Russian Privatization', *Stanford Law Review*, **52**: 1–84.

Blanchard, Olivier and Michael Kremer (1997), 'Disorganization', *Quarterly Journal of Economics*, **112** (4): 1091–1126.

Bruno, Michael and William Easterly (1995), *Inflation Crisis and Long-run Growth*, NBER Working Paper No. 5209, Cambridge, MA: National Bureau of Economic Research.

Campos, Jose Edgardo and Hilton L. Root (1996), *The Key to the Asian Miracle: Making Shared Growth Credible*, Washington, DC: The Brookings Institution.

Chang, Ha-Joon (ed.) (2001), *Joseph Stiglitz and the World Bank: The Rebel Within*, London: Anthem.

Coase, R.H. (1937), 'The Nature of the Firm', *Economica*, **4**, November: 386–405.

Dyck, Alexander (1999), *Privatization and Corporate Governance: Principles, Evidence and Challenges for the Future*, Washington, DC, World Bank, mimeo.

Ellerman, David (1998), *Voucher Privatization with Investment Funds: An Institutional Analysis*, Policy Research Report 1924, Washington, DC: World Bank. Paper available at: http://www.ellerman.org.

Ellerman, David (2001), 'Lessons from East Europe's Voucher Privatization', *Challenge: The Magazine of Economic Affairs*, **44**, 4 July–August: 14–37.

Ellerman, David and Vladimir Kreacic (2002), *Transforming the Old into a Foundation for the New: Lessons of the Moldova ARIA Project*, Washington DC: World Bank Policy Research Working Paper #2866. Paper available at http://www.ellerman.org.

Elster, J., Claus Offe and Ulrich Klaus (1998), *Institutional Design in Post-communist Societies: Rebuilding the Ship at Sea*, Cambridge: Cambridge University Press.

Fischer, Stanley (1993), 'Role of Macroeconomic Factors in Growth', *Journal of Monetary Economics*, **32** (3), December: 485–512.

Gaddy, C. and B. Ickes (1998), 'Beyond the Bailout: Time to Face Reality about Russia's "Virtual Economy"', *Foreign Affairs*, **77**: 53–67.

Greenwald, Bruce and Joseph E. Stiglitz (1993), 'Financial Market Imperfections and Business Cycles', *Quarterly Journal of Economics*, **108** (1), February: 77–114.

Hirschman, A.O. (1973), *Journeys Toward Progress*, New York: Norton.

Jacobs, Jane (1969), *The Economy of Cities*, New York: Random House.

Johnson, Simon and Gary Loveman (1995), *Starting Over in Eastern Europe: Entrepreneurship and Economic Renewal*, Boston, MA: Harvard Business School Press.

Kaufman, A., L. Zacharias and M. Karson, (1995), *Managers Vs. Owners*, New York: Oxford University Press.

Lau, Lawrence, Ying-Yi Qian and Gerard Roland (2000), 'Reform without Losers: An Interpretation of China's Dual-Track Approach to Transition', *Journal of Political Economy*, **108** (1): 120–43.

Marshall, Alfred (1897), 'The Old Generation of Economists and the New', *Quarterly Journal of Economics*, January: 115–35.

Milanovic, B. (1998), *Income, Inequality, and Poverty during the Transition from Planned to Market Economy*, Regional and Sectoral Studies, Washington, DC: World Bank.

Morita, A. (1986), *Made in Japan*, New York: E.P. Dutton.

Murrell, Peter (1996), 'How Far Has the Transition Progressed?', *Journal of Economic Perspectives*, **10** (2): 25–44.

Reddaway, Peter and Dmitri Glinski (2001), *The Tragedy of Russia's Reforms: Market Bolshevism Against Democracy*, Washington, DC: United States Institute of Peace Press.

Rogers, Everett (1983), *Diffusion of Innovations*, 3rd edn, New York: Free Press.

Roe, Mark J. (1994), *Strong Managers, Weak Owners: The Political Roots of American Corporate Finance*, Princeton, NJ: Princeton University Press.

Shleifer, Andrei and Robert Vishny (1998), *The Grabbing Hand: Government Pathologies and their Cures*, Cambridge, MA: Harvard University Press.

Stiglitz, Joseph (1982), 'Ownership, Control and Efficient Markets: Some Paradoxes in the Theory of Capital Markets', in Kenneth D. Boyer and William Shepherd (eds), *Economic Regulation: Essays in Honor of James R. Nelson*, Ann Arbor, MI: University of Michigan Press, pp. 311–41.

Stiglitz, Joseph (1985), 'Credit Markets and the Control of Capital', *Journal of Money, Banking, and Credit*, **17**, 2 May: 133–52.

Stiglitz, Joseph (1987), 'Principal and Agent', in J. Eatwell, M. Milgate and P. Newman (eds), *The New Palgrave: Allocation, Information, and Markets*, New York: Norton, pp. 241–53.

Stiglitz, Joseph (1994), *Whither Socialism?*, Cambridge, MA: MIT Press.

Stiglitz, Joseph (1998), 'Towards a New Paradigm for Development: Strategies, Policies, and Processes', given as Raul Prebisch Lecture at United Nations Conference on Trade and Development (UNCTAD), Geneva, 19 October. For this and other selected World Bank speeches and papers, see Chang (2001).

Stiglitz, Joseph (1999a), 'Quis Custodiet Ipsos Custodes? (Who is to Guard the Guards Themselves?)', *Challenge*, **42** (6), November/December: 26–67.

Stiglitz, Joseph (1999b), 'Whither Reform?', speech at ABCDE Conference, World Bank, Washington, DC. See Chang (2001).

Stiglitz, Joseph (2002), *Globalization and its Discontents*, New York: Norton.

Stiglitz, Joseph and A. Edlin (1995), 'Discouraging Rivals: Managerial Rent-Seeking and Economic Inefficiencies', *American Economic Review*, **85** (5): 1301–12.

Vahcic, Ales and Tea Petrin (1989), 'Financial System for Restructuring the Yugoslavian Economy', in C. Kessides, T. King, M. Nuti and C. Sokil (eds), *Financial Reform in Socialist Economies*, Washington, DC: World Bank, pp. 154–61.

PART II

The International Context

4. Paradoxes of Globalization

Paul Streeten

INTEGRATION AND INTERDEPENDENCE[1]

We read everywhere that international integration is proceeding rapidly as the result of the increased flow of trade, capital, money, direct investment, technology, people, information and ideas across national boundaries. International integration implies the adoption of policies by separate countries as if they were a single political unit. The degree of integration is often tested by whether interest rates or share prices or the prices of goods are the same in different national markets. Integration, however, can be a term loaded with positive value connotations. Although there may be some objections to the unwanted imposition of uniformity, and although the disintegration of a pernicious system may be desirable, it would generally be regarded as improper to advocate 'disintegration'.

But it is possible for integration to be defined either with or without such value premises. The value premise can be that all members of the integrated area should be treated as equals, either with respect to certain opportunities, such as access to the law, jobs, trade, credit, capital and migration, or with respect to certain achievements, such as a minimum standard of life, education and health services. In this sense of integration, equalizing common taxation and social services are implied. If we omit this particular value premise and confine integration to mean equal economic opportunities, however unequal the initial endowments of members of the integrated area, the world was more integrated at the end of the 19th century than it is today.[2]

Although tariff barriers in countries other than the United Kingdom were higher then (20 to 40 per cent compared with 5 per cent in 1990), non-tariff barriers were much lower; capital and money movements were freer under the gold standard (i.e. without the deterrent to trade of variable exchange rates); and movement of people was much freer; passports were rarely needed, visas were unknown, and citizenship was granted easily. Today, international migration is strictly controlled. Between 1881 and 1890 the average annual rate of immigration into the US was 9.2 per 1,000, reaching over 10 in the first decade of this century. Between 1991 and 1997 the average annual rate of immigration was 3.8 per 1,000 of US population (US Bureau of the Census, 1999, p.2).

If we include the value premise of equal treatment, the world is, of course, even less integrated. International inequalities are today greater than ever before. Dani Rodrik uses the term 'international economic integration' instead of 'globalization' (Rodrik, 2000, pp. 177–8). He does this for two reasons. 'First, while not as trendy, my term has a distinct meaning that will be self-evident to economists. Globalization, by contrast, is a term that is used in different ways by different analysts. Second, the term "international economic integration" does not come with the same value judgments – positive or negative – that the term "globalization" seems to trigger in knee-jerk fashion' (ibid., pp. 177–8).

It will be seen that I disagree with both reasons. 'Integration' is also ambiguous and comes also with or without value judgments. Rodrik illustrates the unparalleled prosperity and integration of today's economy by a chart showing rapid growth of exports. But this, of course, does not show anything of the kind.

Functions of an Integrated International System

The four functions that would be coordinated in an integrated international system designed to promote development are today fragmented (Streeten, 1989a). These are:

1. the generation of current account surpluses by the center;
2. the financial institutions that convert these surpluses into loans or investments;
3. the production and sale of producer goods and up-to-date technology;
4. the military power to keep peace and enforce contracts.

Before 1914 these functions were exercised by the dominant power, Great Britain; between the wars there was no international order, Britain no longer being able and the US not yet willing to accept the functions; for a quarter of a century after World War II they were exercised and coordinated by the US. But today we live in a schizophrenic fragmented world, without coordination. The surpluses were generated in the 1970s by a few oil-rich Gulf sheikdoms, later by Germany and Japan, and today mainly by Japan. The financial institutions have mushroomed all over the world; not only in London and New York, but also in Tokyo, Hong Kong, Singapore, Frankfurt, Amsterdam, Zurich, the Cayman Islands, the Isle of Jersey, the British Virgin Islands, Cyprus, Antigua, Liechtenstein, Panama, the Netherlands Antilles, the

Bahamas, Bahrain, Luxembourg, etc. And the economically strong countries such as Germany and Japan were strong partly because they did not spend much money on the military.

Non-tariff barriers for trade imposed by the OECD countries and restrictions on international migration have prevented fuller global integration. The result is deflation, unemployment, and slow or negative growth in many countries of the South. But the present fragmentation provides us for the first time with the opportunity to coordinate these four functions and to build a world order on equality, not dominance and dependence. It is a challenge to our institutional imagination to design ways of implementing this new order.

It may be objected that there is no reason why different countries or agents, without coordination, should not exercise the four functions. But the historical evidence and theoretical considerations show that coordination is necessary if we are to avoid inflation and unemployment in the North, stagnation and underemployment in the South, and growing inequality and slow growth in the world as a whole. The global public goods of world prosperity, stability, growth and peace cannot be provided by uncoordinated laissez-faire. Without coordination the current account surpluses will be invested in the US and Europe instead of in the capital-hungry South, the financial institutions will be media of speculation instead of productive investment, and the industries, including the potential export industries in the North, will be partly underemployed.

Between 1870 and 1914 the world was integrated unwittingly. By imposing fewer objectives on government policy (such as those mentioned in the next paragraph), and by accepting what later, in retrospect, appeared to be irrational constraints, such as the gold standard, and consequentially fixed exchange rates, and lack of freedom to pursue expansionist monetary policies, and the constraint of balanced budgets, different countries were integrated into a single world economy. It was dominated by one power, Great Britain. Domestic policies were severely constrained by the need to adhere to the gold standard. Today the constraints on national policies consist of the activities of multinational companies and banks. Before 1914 the world had been more integrated than it is today. International integration, however, was no guarantee of peace. It did not prevent World War I.

Later, many objectives of government policy were added to the night watchman state's duty to maintain law and order: among them full employment, economic growth, price stability, wage maintenance, reduced inequality in income distribution, regional balance, protection of the natural environment, greater opportunities for women and minorities, etc. The rejection of constraints on policy such as fixed exchange rates, and limits on the discretion of monetary and fiscal policies, led to greater integration of national economies by permitting policies for full employment and the welfare state; but at the same time they led to international disintegration. Such disintegration is, however, entirely consistent with a high degree of international interdependence. For interdependence exists when one country by unilateral action can inflict harm on other countries. Competitive protectionism, devaluation, deflation, or pollution of the air and sea beyond national boundaries are instances. A nuclear war would be the ultimate form of interdependence resulting from international disintegration. Today global market forces can lead to conflict between states, which contribute to international disintegration and weakened governance.

Interdependence is measured by the costs of severing the relationship. The higher the costs to one country, the greater is the degree of dependence of that country. If a small country benefits more from the international division of labor than a large country, its dependence is greater. If high costs from severing economic links were to be incurred by both partners to a transaction, there would be interdependence.

It is quite possible to have intensive and rapidly growing international relations, without a high degree of interdependence. This would be so if the relations could be abandoned at low costs. There could, for example, be a large and rapidly growing trade in slightly different models of automobiles, produced at similar costs, but there would be not much deprivation or loss if buyers had to substitute home-produced models for imported ones. The index of interdependence would be the consumers' and producers' surpluses, not the volume, value or rate of growth of international trade.

There is a different sense of 'interdependence', according to which 'dependence' means only 'influenced by', without great benefits from maintaining, or costs from severing, the relationship. In this attenuated sense there can be interdependence even though the costs of cutting off relations are low or even negative. But this is not a useful sense for our purposes.

Has International Interdependence Increased?

International interdependence is often said to be strong and to have increased. International trade is taken to be an indicator of interdependence and its high and, with some interruptions, rapidly growing values are accepted as evidence. Between 1820 and 1992 world population increased fivefold, income per head eightfold, world income fortyfold, and world trade five-hundred-and-fortyfold (Maddison, 1995). Sometimes international financial flows are taken as the measure of interdependence. But five important qualifications to the notion that globalization is unprecedented, large and increasing are necessary.[3]

First, if we consider the ratio of international trade to national income, the rapid growth of the postwar decades can be taken to be a return to pre-1914 values after the interruptions of two world wars, the Great Depression, and high levels of protection.[4] The share of world exports in world GDP rose from 6 per cent in 1950 to 16 per cent in 1992. For the industrial countries, the proportion increased from 12 per cent in 1973 to 17 per cent in 1992. For 16 major industrial countries the share of exports in GDP rose from 18.2 per cent in 1900 to 21.2 per cent in 1913 (Nayyar, 1995, pp. 3–4; Maizels, 1963; Maddison, 1989; Bairoch, 1993). This was largely the result of dramatic reductions in transport costs, as well as of the decline in trade barriers such as tariffs and import quotas and of the opening of new markets such as China and Mexico. The comparisons in the ratios are very similar for particular countries.[5]

The total ratios of trade to GDP are, however, misleading. Over the post-war decades the share of services, including government services, in GDP increased enormously. Many of these are, or were until recently, not tradable. If we were to take the ratio of international trade to the production of goods only, it would show a substantial increase not only compared with the interwar period, but also compared with the time before 1913.

The second qualification to the notion that unprecedented globalization is now taking place is that the developing countries, and the groups within these countries that have participated in the benefits from the growing trade (and also from foreign investment, which is highly concentrated on East Asia, Brazil, Mexico and now China) have been few, not more than a dozen, and no poor ones among them. Twelve countries in Asia and Latin America accounted for 75 per cent of total capital flows, while 140 of the 166 developing countries accounted for less than 5 per cent of inflows (López-Mejía, 1999). A large share of foreign investment is made by firms from a handful of countries, in a narrow range of industries (UN Conference on Trade and Development, 1996). The large, poor masses of the Indian subcontinent and of sub-Saharan Africa have (at least so far) not participated substantially in the benefits from the growth of international trade and investment. In fact, the bulk of the international flow of goods, services, direct investment and finance is between North America, Europe and Japan. The group of least developed countries accounted for only 0.1 per cent of total global investment inflows and for 0.7 per cent of inflows to all developing countries. Africa in particular has been almost completely bypassed.[6] More than 80 per cent of world population living in developing countries account for less than 20 per cent of world income (UNDP, 2000).

The third qualification is that direct foreign investment constitutes a smaller portion of total investment in most countries than before 1914. Domestic savings and domestic investment are more closely correlated than they were then, implying that even investment capital is not very mobile. This is explained partly by the fact that government savings play a greater role today than they did in the past, and partly by floating exchange rates that raise uncertainties and are a barrier to long-term commitments. The same point is made by noting that, though gross capital flows are very large, net flows are not. Current account deficits and surpluses are now a much smaller proportion of countries' GDP than they were between 1870 and 1913. Britain ran a current account surplus that averaged 8 per cent of GNP and invested this overseas, compared with 2–4 per cent for the West German and Japanese surpluses (and the American deficit) in the 1980s. But the fact remains that this is surprising in view of the talk of the globalization of capital markets. The bulk of foreign investment has been the capital import of the US and the outflow from Japan.

Foreign capital, mostly loans, financed one-third of domestic investment in New Zealand and Canada in the late 19th century, and one-quarter in Sweden. Today it accounts for 10 per cent in a few developing countries. Today's foreign investment is more broadly based than it was in the 19th century, is more short-term, more speculative and less stable. Nineteenth-century globalization produced greater stability than today's.

The fourth qualification is, as we have seen, that there is much less international migration than in the earlier period. Barriers to immigration are higher now than they were then. As we have seen, passports were unnecessary and people could move freely from one country to another to visit or work. Sixty million Europeans moved to the Americas or to Australia or other areas of new settlement. In 1900 14 per cent of the American population was foreign born, compared with 8 per cent today.[7]

The fifth qualification is the already mentioned fact that it is not the volume or value or rate of growth of trade that should be accepted as an indicator of economic interdependence, but the damage that would be done by its elimination, i.e. consumers' and producers' surpluses. These are difficult to measure. But we know that much trade is conducted in only slightly differentiated goods, which could readily be replaced by similar domestic products without great loss to buyers or great increases in costs.

On the other hand, a small and slowly growing volume of trade could be of great importance and lead to substantial losses if it were cut off. Like a link in a bicycle chain, it could, though small, make a big difference to the working of the whole system. The United States, for example, depends strongly on quite small imports of manganese, tin and chromium. Before World War I, trade was largely conducted in the form of an exchange between raw materials and manufactured products, for which consumers' and producers' surpluses are large. Today the bulk of trade is intra-industry and even intra-firm trade of often similar manufactured products for which these surpluses are much smaller. Indeed, manufactured goods contain parts from so many countries that it is not possible to attribute their origin to any one country.

There are also important differences between globalization now and before World War I:

- First, intersectoral and inter-industry trade, mainly between agricultural and manufactured products, prevailed in the earlier period, whereas now, as we have seen, trade is largely intra-industry and intra-firm.
- Second, before World War I 45 per cent of foreign investment in the Third World and 55 per cent of total investment went into the primary sector. In the second phase these percentages were lowered to 20 per cent and 10 per cent respectively. Capital then flowed to countries rich in natural resources and much went into the construction of infrastructure; today investment is largely in manufacturing and flows to countries with plenty of cheap labor.
- Third, foreign investment in the earlier phase was largely in search of profits, whereas in the present phase short-term capital movements flow largely in search of capital gains.
- Fourth, as we have seen, in the present phase there are many restrictions on the flow of labor. Capital now goes to labor, while in the past it was labor that went to capital. The large-scale migration to North and South America, Australia and South Africa bear witness to this.
- Fifth, the technology has changed out of all recognition, and electronic technology can be said to have made the movement of labor less important.
- Sixth, the principal players then were imperial nation states, whereas now they are multinational corporations and international banks.
- Seventh, whereas in the earlier period the process of globalization was fairly evenly spread, globalization now is much more unevenly spread, leaving out large parts of the South (Nayyar, 1997).
- Finally, eighth, international integration did not conflict with national integration. Members of the present elites in the low-income countries have their medical and surgical treatment in the advanced capital cities of the North. Their children are sent to the schools in the North. They take their vacations there, do their shopping there, and visit relatives who have settled there. They invest their capital on the stock exchanges of the rich countries. As a result, they have no interest in improving the medical, educational and economic facilities in their own countries. Local 'capacity building' is not part of their agenda.

Partial international integration can thus lead to national disintegration.

INTERNATIONAL INTEGRATION AND NATIONAL DISINTEGRATION

There are five reasons for why (partial) international integration can lead to national disintegration:

1. Downsizing, restructuring, 'delayering', and re-engineering have reduced the demand for low-skilled workers in the rich and middle-income countries and maintained downward pressure on the wages of those who succeeded in keeping their jobs.
2. Preventing increases in the brain drain in developing countries and paying professional manpower salaries not too much out of line with those in rich countries makes egalitarian incomes policies impossible.
3. Tax revenues to pay for social services have been reduced, though the need for them has increased.
4. The elites in the low-income countries are opting out of national commitments. This leads to the neglect of essential social services like education and health.
5. The culture of the elites is global and estranged from the culture of the local people.

The process of globalization, according to some definitions, means opening-up to trade or liberalization. In the last decade such liberalization was followed mainly by the ex-socialist countries, which turned away from central planning in order to link up with the world economy, and by the developing countries, which changed from import-substituting indust-rialization to export orientation accompanied by a partial dismantling of the state. This move was not the result of entirely free choices, but was itself a response partly to global forces, partly to pressures by the World Bank, the International Monetary Fund in their stabilization and structural adjustment programs, and the words and doctrines of state minimalism of the rich countries, and partly to the hopes of benefiting from global gains.

Some OECD countries, on the other hand, have put up additional non-tariff barriers such as so-called voluntary export restraints, procedural protection most notably in the form of anti-dumping actions, and specific subsidies to exports of goods and services competing with imports. The Multifiber Arrangement and the Common Agricultural Policy of the European

Union are blatantly protectionist devices. Other barriers have been raised against steel, electronics and footwear.

Trade is, of course, only one, and not the most important, among many manifestations of economic interdependence. Others include the flow of factors of production, capital, technology, enterprise and various types of labor, across frontiers; there is also the exchange of assets, the acquisition of legal rights, of information and knowledge. The global flow of foreign exchange has reached the incredible figure of $2 trillion per day, 98 per cent of which is speculative. The multinational corporation has become an important agent of technological innovation and technology transfer. In 1995 the sales of multinationals amounted to $7 trillion. Their sales outside their home countries are growing 20–30 per cent faster than exports.

As Jeffrey Williamson has shown, another aspect of globalization is the convergence of real wages in different countries.[8] Since the 1950s the gap between American and European wages has shrunk markedly. Similarly, in the second half of the 19th century European wages caught up with American ones. In Europe, some countries closed the gap with Britain, then the Continent's leader. In a later paper Williamson argues that economic integration (rather than, say, better education in the low-wage countries) was the main cause of this narrowing (Williamson, 1996). As a result of the growth of international trade the prices of traded goods became more alike in different countries. The relative prices of the abundant factors of production in each country rose (land in America, labor in Europe), while those of the relatively scarce factors fell (labor in America, land in Europe). A recent study confirms this (O'Rourke et al., 1996). Emigration from Europe to America also helps to explain the rise in wages in Europe and their containment in America.

After about 1895 the losers from international integration began to revolt and the claims for protection and restrictions on immigration became louder. Between the two wars the international order broke down. Today's low-skilled workers in America and other advanced countries may similarly claim that the economic rise in the South is a threat to them. The voices of Ross Perot and Patrick Buchanan in America and Sir James Goldsmith and Jean-Marie Le Pen in Europe gave shape to these alarms. In the developing countries corresponding visions are calling for a reversal of the trend towards globalization. But, in spite of rising unemployment, the political forces of nationalism are losing out against the economic forces of globalization.

In addition to economic interdependence (trade, finance, direct investment) there are educational, technological, ideological, cultural, as well as ecological, environmental, legal, military, strategic and political impulses that are rapidly propagated throughout the world. Money and goods, images and people, sports and religions, guns and drugs, diseases and pollution now move quickly across national frontiers. When the global satellite communications system was established instantaneous communication from any part of the world to any other became possible. It is not only the creation of a 24-hour money market that had become possible, but also the flashing of pictures of statesmen and film stars across the globe, making these faces more familiar than those of our next-door neighbors.[9]

We hear much of the creation of a borderless world and the end of the nation state. It is true that satellites and the Internet have greatly increased the speed at which the communication of cultural and informational impulses is propagated throughout the globe. Americans fly British Airways, drive Japanese cars and drink Russian vodka. A German firm, Daimler-Benz, buys a quintessentially American company, Chrysler Corporation and Michael Gorbachev does Pizza Hut commercials.

But here again, as in trade and investment, vast areas in the poor South are either left out (subsistence farmers are not affected by global forces), or suffer the backwash effects of globalization. The rise of particularism and religious fundamentalism is a sign that many people protest against it. It has become a cliché to say that international interdependence is great, has increased, and will continue to grow. Normally this is intended to refer to trade, foreign investment, the flow of money and capital, and the migration of people. Advances in technology such as the jet, telex, satellite television, container ships, supertankers, super ore carriers and technical progress in transport, travel and, above all, in communication and information have shrunk the world. By reducing the cost of communication, technology has helped to globalize production and finance. Globalization, in turn, has stimulated technological progress by intensifying competition, and competition has forced the introduction of new technology. Globalization has spread its results widely through foreign direct investment. History may not have ended, but geography, if not coming to an end, certainly matters less. And the interaction of technology and globalization has presented new problems.

The international spread of ideological and cultural impulses is at least as important as that of economic impulses. Observe the young in the capitals of the world: from Ladakh to Lisbon, from Maine to Mozambique, from West Virginia to East Jerusalem, from China to Peru, in the East, West, North, and South, styles in dress, jeans, hair-dos, T-shirts, jogging, eating habits, musical tunes, attitudes to homosexuality, divorce, abortion, have become global. Even crimes such as those relating to drugs, the abuse and rape of women, embezzlement and corruption have become similar everywhere. But although American cultural influences are important, there are many other influences and no single dominant power.

'A typical American yuppie', writes Tylor Cowen, 'drinks French wine, listens to Beethoven on a Japanese audio system, uses the Internet to buy

Persian textiles from a dealer in London, watches Hollywood movies funded by foreign capital and filmed by a European director, and vacations in Bali' (Cowen, 2002, p. 4).

'The super-rich are seceding from their nations. So what you have is not a Western or East Asian or Southeast Asian or Chinese model. We are building enclaves of super-privilege. What you're having is not a global village but a series of global ghettoes. The Western elite is not the sole villain,' said Palagummi Sainath, the author of *Everybody Loves a Good Drought*, a critique of government and the establishment in India, based on his reporting from some of the poorest villages in the country.[10] Partial international integration, once again, leads to national disintegration.

> There is a new catchword in the developing world . . . to cover cultural wounds not believed to be strictly Western, Eastern or self-inflicted; the word is globalization. It wraps up all the fears of somehow losing control to foreigners, felt as much by Americans who hate the United Nations and immigrants as it is by Indians or Filipinos who feel threatened by the International Monetary Fund, Kentucky Fried Chicken, Joe Camel or Time Warner. That shrinking world everyone was so proud of a decade or so ago has become a cultural strangler' (Barbara Crossette, 1997, p. 5).

National Breakup and 'Retribalization'

But the impression of global uniformity can be deceptive. Just as trade, foreign investment and the flow of money have affected only a few regions of the world and left the rest comparatively untouched (except for some negative effects), so this globalization of culture is only partial. It is evident in the towns and suburbs, and the more advanced countryside. The poor in the rural hinterlands, in spite of the spread of transistors and television, have been largely bypassed. And in many lands there has been a reaction toward tradition and tribalism. Global integration has provoked national disintegration. Globalization has posed a threat to the rootedness on which community life depends. Ethnic or cultural passions are fracturing societies and regions. We witness Islamic fundamentalism in the Muslim world. Evangelical fundamentalism is spreading not only in the US, but also in East Asia, Africa, and Latin America, often linked to a Calvinistic, entrepreneurial ethics of saving and hard work. Hindu fundamentalism is evident in India and has led to the most horrific bloodletting (though Hinduism cannot, strictly speaking, be fundamentalist because it is a religion without dogma). In Israel, a recent decision of the Knesset, yielding to he pressure of a minority of fundamentalist rabbis, denies the right of Conservative and Reform rabbis to perform valid conversions for those wishing to become Jewish.

Nations have broken up into smaller, ethnic groups. All this is partly a reaction against westernization, the alienating effects of large-scale, modern technology and the unequal distribution of the benefits from industrialization. In the ex-Soviet countries the assertion of ethnic identities is the result of the weakening powers of the state in the face of globalization. The complaint is that development has meant the loss of identity, sense of community and personal meaning. The Taliban in Afghanistan denied women jobs, forced them to dress in a subservient manner and prohibited girls going to school. Algeria's Islamic Army of Salvation, the military arm of the banned Islamic Salvation Front, according to Amnesty International 'executed' 100,000 people since early 1992 when the authorities cancelled a general election in which the radical Islamic party had taken a lead. People in many countries assert their indigenous cultural values. This assertion of indigenous values is often the only thing that poor people can assert. Traditional values bring identity, continuity and meaning to their lives. Between the two opposite forces, globalization on the one hand, and the assertion of peoples' identities on the other, between what Benjamin Barber calls Jihad and McWorld, (Barber, 1995) states have found their base undermined.

But the same trend, the proliferation of states, can also be explained by an opposite tendency. The increase in the number of countries in the last 10 years can be explained, paradoxically, as a result of globalization. In a world united by air travel, the Internet, multinational enterprises and international organizations, ethnic minorities wish to participate directly in the benefits promised by globalization. These people of the new states feel that their old countries had denied them the opportunities to participate in the affairs of the world. But the rise in the violent expression of ethnic tensions cannot be so easily explained. Rwanda, Burundi, Bosnia, Armenia, Azerbaijan, Chechnya, Kosovo, the Kurds, the Palestinians, the Chiapians have manifested degrees of violence after having lived with their neighbors sometimes for generations in peace. Violence has often been the result of the breakdown of a previous order. Democratic elections in countries without the tradition and institutions of democracy such as courts, police, a free press, often led people to have recourse to ethnic violence.

Technology, communications and market forces are unifying the world, while at the same time ethnic, religious and racial tensions are breaking up the world into small tribal fragments. According to Benjamin Barber, Jihad and McWorld are diametrically opposed yet intertwined forces. 'Jihad not only revolts against but abets McWorld, while McWorld not only imperils but recreates and reinforces Jihad.'

What Barber (1995, p. 4) calls 'retribalization' is a violent process where 'culture is pitted against culture, people against people, tribe against tribe, a Jihad in the name of [a] hundred narrowly conceived faiths against every kind of interdependence, every kind of artificial social cooperation and mutuality: against technology, pop culture and integrated markets.'

Globalization makes national government more difficult. Monetary and fiscal policies run up against the impact of global tides as people, international banks and multinational corporations avoid the intended results by sending or spending their money abroad or attracting money from abroad. The obligations of extended families, government and religion disappear as people leave their rural communities to live in large cities. Recently enriched members of the middle class with links to politicians and officials often use their newly acquired powers in corrupt ways that counteract traditional values.

The difficult task is to build modernity on tradition. Japan has succeeded in this. Traditional consumption habits and community loyalties have contributed, until recently, to the fantastic economic growth of the country. Neither all tradition nor all modernity is to be welcomed. The repressive nature of both some traditional values and structures and some modern ones is evident. Tradition can spell stagnation, oppression, inertia, privilege; modernization can amount to alienation and a loss of identity and sense of community. Traditional cultural practices such female genital mutilation, sexual subjugation, attacks on and killing of women with too small dowries, kerosene burning and honor killing, widow burning (sati), child marriage, female infanticide, domestic battering, wife beating, prevention of women's education, female ritual slavery, cannibalism, slavery, exploitative and hazardous child labor, debt bondage, witchcraft, demon worship, ritual sacrifice, punishment of criminals by amputation, and other barbaric habits are objectionable and should not be tolerated. There is no moral case for abstaining from stopping these native customs, however traditional.

All this suggests that the perception is of a greater degree of globalization and integration than has in fact occurred. Foreign investment is a smaller proportion of GNP than it was before 1914. Transnational corporations are more domesticated than some of the literature suggests. Most of them hold most of their assets and have most of their employees in their home country, and conduct the bulk of their research and development there. This is confirmed by the fact that in the second half of the 1980s 89 per cent of US patents taken out by 600 of the world's largest firms listed the inventor as a resident of the home base (Wade, 1996). Hence strategic decisions and innovations come from the home country. This may, however, be replaced by a wider global spread of R&D as a result of telematics, the convergence of computer, communication and control technology.

The movement of people is severely restricted, much more than it was in the 19th century. Although it is true that states are more constrained than they used to be, from above by global economic forces and from below by peoples (minorities, tribes, ethnic groups) asking for rights, participation or independence, reports on 'Sovereignty at Bay' (Raymond Vernon) 'The Twilight of Sovereignty' (Walter Wriston), 'The End of the Nation State' and 'Borderless World' (Kenichi Ohmae and others) are therefore somewhat premature. The illusion of rapidly increasing globalization arises from a short time perspective that looks only at the last 30 or 40 years, at the beginning of which countries were exceptionally closed as a result of the Great Depression and World War II.

Views on the benefits and costs of the global mobility of the different items, such as trade, finance, technology and ideas, differ. In a much-quoted passage Keynes wrote: 'Ideas, knowledge, art, hospitality, travel – these are things which should of their nature be international. But let goods be homespun whenever it is reasonably and conveniently possible; and, above all, let finance be primarily national.'[11] Today it is more fashionable to deplore the 'cultural imperialism' or the 'homogenization' of television and the mass media and the global spread of mass culture, and to attempt to confine culture to local knowledge, activities and products, while advocating free trade in goods and services.

Neo-liberals advocate free trade and a good deal of laissez-faire but not the free movement of people. François Quesnay had added to laissez-faire laissez-passer, but this is forgotten today, perhaps because contemporary liberals fear that it would accelerate population growth (or reduce the pressures to reduce it) in the low-income countries of emigration and therefore not contribute to raising their welfare, or that it would interfere with economic objectives (especially the level and distribution of income), or cultural values, or social stability and cohesion, or security, in the country receiving the migrants. But all these objections also apply to the free movement of goods and services. In any case, there is an inconsistency.

GLOBAL FINANCIAL FLOWS

Global financial flows have enormously increased and now are on an average day about $2 trillion. Forty per cent of these transactions are reversed within two days and 80 per cent within seven days. This represents a ratio of foreign exchange dealings to world trade of nearly 70:1 and equals the world's total official gold and foreign exchange reserves. In 1971 about 90 per cent of all foreign exchange transactions were for the finance of trade and long-term investment, and only 10 per cent were speculative. Today, these percentages are reversed; well over 90 per cent of all transactions are speculative (Eatwell, 1995, p. 277). The enormous growth of these flows is the result of the collapse of the Bretton Woods system of fixed exchange rates in 1973, combined with deregulation and liberalization of capital flows, and the opportunities this has provided for speculation on variable exchange rates.

The 24-hour international capital market has given rise to the fear that the international financial system is unstable. A run on any one country's currency can easily spread to other countries and lead to a collapse of values on stock exchanges, of markets and of whole economies. It has been argued that recent difficulties point to the strength, rather than the weakness, of the international system. The effects of the different crises – the Latin American debt crisis, the American savings-and-loan fiasco, the BCCI scandal, Mexico, Barings, Daiwa, the 1997/99 crisis in Asia and Brazil – did not spread internationally. Many individuals were hurt, including taxpayers, but these were mainly residents in the area and the rest of the world was sheltered. The system did not break down – at least so far. Obviously, this does not mean that it cannot do so in future. The summer of 1998 came near to such a breakdown.

The precariousness of the world economy is plain, and steps should be taken towards a substantial strengthening of the IMF, together with a change in its conditionality, or, better, a global central bank. As lender of last resort and creator of new money it would have to be able to lend freely, with much larger resources than are now at the disposal of the IMF, at penal interest rates, and against collateral. It would reduce the debts of some developing countries and oversee the operations of shaky financial institutions. It would buy the debt of a country in difficulties and perhaps later resell it at a profit. It would be accountable to an enlarged Group of 7, with additional membership rotating between countries like Mexico, Brazil, South Africa, Poland, India, China and South Korea.

The absence of institutions such as a central bank, a Securities and Exchange Commission, the insurance of bank deposits, or safety nets at the global level, while free markets run wild, accounts for the global turmoil in the stock markets of the world. The problem with creating such institutions is that of the leaky roof that never gets repaired. When the sun shines, there is no need, and when it rains, nobody wants to get wet. When all goes well, nobody is interested in creating such an institution, and in a crisis, officials are preoccupied with grappling with it.

Instability and Maldistribution of Capital Flows

The stunning increase in long-term private foreign investment has built roads, airports and factories in developing countries. Private flows to developing countries have increased from \$34 billion in 1987 to \$256 billion in 1997. They have brought much needed capital to these countries and good returns to the investors. But large inflows can be reversed and become large outflows, as Mexico in 1994–95 and the Asian financial crisis in 1997–98 have shown. Moreover, capital mobility in the presence of trade distortions results in a misallocation of capital and a deterioration of the well-being of people in the capital-importing countries. If capital flows freely into a labor-rich country that protects its capital-intensive industries (such as steel and car production), capital will be misallocated, the country's national product at world prices will be reduced and its national income will be reduced further by the payment of returns to the foreign capital. Countries that impose rules and regulations restricting the purchase and sale of currencies, such as China and Chile, have fared best in times of crisis. (Chile, however, eliminated some of these controls in 1998.)

As we have seen, globalization of financial and real flows, as of trade, has been partial; there are hardly any flows to low-income countries; and while private flows to middle-income developing countries have enormously increased, official development assistance has stagnated. The bulk of the flows is between OECD countries; and there is some foreign investment in a selected group of developing countries, mostly in Latin America, East Asia and China. According to the IMF, 95 per cent of private flows to developing countries in 1996 went to just 26 countries; 140 countries shared the remaining 5 per cent (López-Mejía, 1999). And these private flows are highly volatile, tending to be withdrawn at short notice. The intra-OECD flows contradict neoclassical theory, according to which capital should flow from the capital-abundant to the capital-scarce countries. In fact, the USA, one of the capital-richest countries, has attracted most capital, in 2002 nearly $430 billion per year. And among developing countries it is those with substantial human capital and investor-friendly government policies that attract financial capital.

Some pessimists have two contradictory worries: first, that a massive outflow of capital from rich to poor countries will exports jobs; second, that cheap imports from the South will lead to a current account deficit of the North (which must mean a capital flow from the South to the North) and therefore again to job losses. Neither should be a cause for worry in the long run. A current account deficit of the South is more likely now that the Asian crisis has passed, and the resulting expanding markets in the South will create jobs in the North, although these will be different from current ones and this means re-education and redeployment of labor.

In the light of this large increase in financial flows, it is, as already mentioned, a puzzle to find that domestic savings and investment are closer together for most countries than they were before 1914. It follows that net flows are much smaller than gross flows. As we have discussed, many explanations have been offered for this paradox, among them the possible obstacle to long-term real investment and consequential global integration of fluctuating exchange rates. Deregulation and liberalization have accelerated neither investment nor growth, nor resulted in high levels of employment nor in a better income distribution, nor in lower borrowing costs. They have also increased the volatility of asset prices.

Global financial deregulation and liberalization have brought some benefits but also greater risks for investors and the financial system. In the 1980s the task of stabilizing against high inflation, the debt crisis and structural adjustment preoccupied many governments. In the 1990s problems of coping with rapid swings in capital flows had become more pressing, highlighted by Mexico's financial crisis in 1995 and the troubles in South Korea, Thailand, Malaysia, Indonesia and the Philippines in 1997/98. Suddenly government was called upon to bail out the financiers who previously had preached the virtues of free markets. The cause of the East Asian financial crisis, as Robert Wade has said, 'was a structure of financial claims that involved too much short-term debt relative to long-term debt, too much debt relative to equity, too much foreign debt relative to total debt, too much foreign equity relative to domestic equity' (Wade, 1999, p. 485). This raised the question whether a return to control of capital markets is indicated. In developing countries regulations that favor direct foreign investment over purchases of shares, that inhibit short-term flows, and that discourage local firms from accumulating large foreign debts are again being discussed.

There is a need for re-regulation and harmonization of legislation. The more free-enterprise-oriented a country is, the greater the need for official supervision. Deregulation has resulted in higher and less stable interest rates, less stable exchange rates, boom and slump in property prices, gambling on asset values, interest and exchange rates. Excessive deregulation, allowing firms to borrow abroad without any government control or coordination, has led to the run on the currencies. The danger of business and bank failures is high. If we wish not to have to bail out financial institutions, deregulation has to be supported by close and well-coordinated supervision.

The Bretton Woods system was based on the premise that currency convertibility, multilateral trade and stable exchange rates require constraints on international capital mobility. Financial liberalization, carried too far, can damage the more important trade liberalization. For example, when a country should devalue because its prices have risen by more than foreign prices, it may be unable to do so because of speculative short-term capital inflows. Or changes in capital flows can produce large swings in the exchange rate, which are detrimental to trade. One way to slow down short-term capital movements would be the Tobin tax, a small, uniform tax imposed on all short-term international capital flows. There has been a good deal of recent discussion, and a book has been published that discusses the desirability and feasibility of the tax, both for and against it (Haq et al., 1996). More ambitiously, a new global institution has been proposed that would supervise the participants in the global capital market and establish trading, reporting and disclosure requirements.

UNEVEN BENEFITS AND COSTS OF GLOBALIZATION

Globalization has helped to create undreamed-of opportunities for some people, groups and countries. Human indicators such as literacy, school enrolment, infant mortality, and life expectancy have enormously improved in the last few decades. In low- and middle-income countries life expectancy has increased from 46 years in 1960 to 64.4 years in 1998; infant mortality per 1000 live births has fallen in the same period from 149 to 64; adult literacy rates have risen from 46 to 73 per cent; and real GDP per head from $950 to $1,250 (UNDP, 2000). The Cold War has ended and democracy has spread throughout the world and replaced autocratic regimes. Between 1986 and 1996 the portion of the world's states with democratically elected governments jumped from 42 per cent to 61 per cent. Globalization has been particularly good for Asia, for the global growth of production, for profits and for the owners of capital and sophisticated skills (see Balance Sheet of Globalization, p. 73 below).

At the same time, the economic restructuring, liberalization, technological changes and fierce competition, both in the markets for goods and for labor, that went with globalization have contributed to increased impoverishment, inequalities, work insecurity, weakening of institutions and social support systems, and erosion of established identities and values. Liberalization and reduced protection of agriculture, by reducing agricultural supplies, have raised the price of food (compared with what it would otherwise have been), and food-importing countries have suffered as a result.

Globalization has been bad for Africa, and in many parts of the world for employment of those without assets or with rigidly fixed and unadaptable skills. International competition for markets and jobs has forced governments to reduce taxation and with it social services that had protected the poor, and cut public services and regulations that had protected the environment, has forced governments and firms to 'downsize', 'restructure' and 're-engineer' and has made necessary all kinds of steps to ensure that the cost of labor is low.[12]

Between 1972 and 1986, for developing countries as a whole, social expenditure as a proportion of total government expenditure declined from 35 per cent to 27 per cent and for industrial market economies from 58 per cent to 56 per cent (World Bank, 1988). Between 1980 and 1993, in the Philippines health expenditure declined from 4.5 per cent to 3.0 per cent, and in Kenya from 7.8 per cent to 5.4 per cent (World Bank, 1995). In Latin America, despite some recovery of social expenditure in 1991, expenditure per head on health and education was lower than in 1980–81 (IDB, 1996, p. 47).

At the height of the welfare state, in the quarter century after World War II, when it was thought that a government can steer the economy to full employment and keep it there, national integration had been accompanied by international disintegration. Though people had expected full employment to remove the case for trade restrictions, there were at least four (not equally good) reasons for trade restrictions and for limiting access of imports of labor-intensive products in conditions of full employment. The first and most obvious reason is the fact that full employment policies (and even more so over-full employment policies) make for stronger inflationary pressures and therefore tend to aggravate balance of payments problems if the country's inflation is greater than the average rate in its trading partners. Balance of payments difficulties resulting from inflation are perhaps not good reasons, but they are often used as excuses for trade and foreign exchange restrictions.

The second reason is that full employment policies were often interpreted (or perhaps misinterpreted) as policies that guarantee particular workers their present jobs. Transitional unemployment was not easily distinguished by its victims and their representatives from lapses from full employment. While it would be clearly a mistake to identify full employment in a growing and changing society with a prescriptive right to existing jobs in particular occupations and regions, it should be remembered that change and transition have social costs. The better off a society is, the more it can afford to forgo extra increases in income and production for the sake of less disruption, particularly if such disruption continues to be called for repeatedly or if its benefits are mainly enjoyed by others than its victims. If full employment policies were interpreted in this way, they presented a new motive against admitting more imports.

The third reason is that, according to the Stolper-Samuelson theorem, labor-intensive imports tend to reduce the absolute incomes of unskilled and semi-skilled workers. This is so because the relative price of the product intensive in this type of labor will fall after trade liberalization. Unless there is a perfect system of compensation, it is understandable that these groups resist the removal of trade restrictions.

The fourth reason is that in conditions of full employment the terms of trade argument for protection, also called the optimum tariff argument, comes into its own. If resources are unemployed, the nation can export more and simultaneously raise everybody's income. But in conditions of full employment national gains may be at the expense of other nations. In particular, it becomes important to keep the prices of imported necessities as low as possible. It is not to be expected that many governments have imposed tariffs in order to improve their terms of trade. In any case, trade restrictions imposed for other reasons must often have led to higher barriers than those indicated by the optimum tariff argument. Nevertheless, there may be conditions in which the restrictions are not above the optimum and then governments are for good reasons reluctant to remove them because this would lead to a deterioration in the terms of trade below the optimum. To wish to avoid a loss is rather different from trying to snatch a gain at the expense of others.

It is for these and similar reasons that in the quarter century after World War II national integration led to international disintegration, in spite of what is regarded in retrospect as a golden age. Now the situation is reversed. After the early 1970s (partial) international integration has led to national disintegration. Beveridge and Keynes had to be dismissed in the face of the pressures of globalization, which weakened the pursuit of national monetary, fiscal and social policies, while at the same time weakening organized labor.

The Zapatista guerrillas held a convention in 1996 in the jungles of Southern Mexico entitled 'The Intercontinental Forum in Favor of Humanity and Against Neo-Liberalism'. The closing session met in a steamy, mudhole amphitheatre and ended with the Zapatistas doing a kind of drum roll and denouncing the most evil, dangerous institution in the world today. To a standing ovation, the Zapatistas declared the biggest enemy of humanity to be the World Trade Organization in Geneva, which promotes global free trade (Friedman, 1997).

But it is not primarily critics from the Left who have pointed to the excesses and threats of globalization, but the capitalists themselves. The 1997 meeting of the World Economic Forum in Davos – the assembly of the world's free-market elite – was devoted to ways of ameliorating the worst consequences of global competitiveness. George Soros, the multibillionaire financier, wrote an article for the *Atlantic Monthly* entitled 'The Capitalist Threat' (Soros, 1997). In Europe, the chief executives of some of the largest companies are voicing doubts about the European Monetary Union.

Income Disparities and Increasing Inequality

As Table 4.1 and Table 4.2 show, the share of the developing countries in the global distribution of wealth has shrunk between 1960 and 1994. Even in the rich countries unemployment, homelessness, crime, and drug abuse have grown. New conflicts have replaced old ones, terrorism is widespread and the US has declared a global war on it, and people's lives have become more insecure. New technologies, new types of organization, low-cost competing imports, and immigrants have made redundant large numbers of semi-skilled workers.

Balance sheet of globalization (Rough approximations)	
Good for:	**Bad for:**
Japan, Europe, North America	Many developing countries
East and South East Asia (until 1997)	Africa (exceptions: Mauritius and Botswana) and Latin America (exceptions: Chile and Costa Rica)
Output	Employment
People with assets	People without assets
Profits	Wages
People with high skills	People with few skills
The educated	The uneducated
Professional, managerial & technical people	Workers
Flexible adjusters	Rigid adjusters
Creditors	Debtors
Those independent of public services	Those dependent on public services
Large firms	Small firms
Men	Women, children
The strong	The weak
Risk takers	Human security
Global markets	Local communities
Sellers of technologically sophisticated products	Sellers of primary and standard manufactured products
Global culture	Local cultures
Global peace	Local troubles (Russia, Mexico, Turkey)
Advocates:	
Businessmen, economists	Environmentalists, working people, consumer rights groups, family organizations, farmers, religious organizations

Table 4.1   Global distribution of wealth: 1960–94

	Industrial countries %	Developing countries %	Former USSR & Eastern Europe %
1960	67.3	19.8	12.9
1970	72.2	17.1	10.7
1980	70.7	20.6	8.7
1989	76.3	20.6	3.1
1994	78.7	18.0	3.3

Source: UNDP database.

Table 4.2   Global distribution of wealth: 1960–94 (excluding the former USSR and Eastern Europe)

	Industrial countries %	Developing countries %
1960	77.3	22.7
1970	80.9	19.1
1980	77.4	22.6
1989	78.8	21.2
1994	81.4	18.6

Source: UNDP database.

In the poor countries poverty, malnutrition, and disease have grown side by side with improvements in living conditions. Nearly one-third of the population in developing countries and more than a half of Africa's live in absolute poverty. In 1992 six million children under five years died of pneumonia or diarrhea. Twenty-three million people are classified as refugees. The dissolution of the old system of the extended family, together with the increasing reliance on market forces and the dismantling of state institutions, has left many victims of the competitive struggle stranded and helpless.

Globalization and the economic progress that goes with it have proceeded unevenly in time and in space. The rise in income per head has differed widely between countries and regions, so that income gaps have widened. Income disparities between the rich and the poor nations have doubled over the last 30 years. Whereas at the end of the 19th century the main agents on the international scene were states, dominated by Britain until 1913, and by the United States for a quarter of a century after World War II, today transnational corporations and international banks have joined states and to some extent replaced them. The world's 37,000 parent transnational corporations and their 200,000 affiliates control 75 per cent of world trade. One-third of this trade is intra-firm (UNRISD, 1995, p. 27). The principle guiding their action is profit. At the same time, very few of these firms are genuinely transnational or even international (Shell and Unilever are the exceptions in being at least genuinely duo-national, British and Dutch). Most other companies that operate in many countries are stamped by the country of their headquarters. As we have seen, the prediction that sovereignty would be at bay and that the nation state, confronted with ever larger and more powerful transnational corporations, would wither away, was, like reports of Mark Twain's death, somewhat exaggerated. Many countries have successfully dealt with, regulated and taxed these firms.

The new technology, combined with deregulation and privatization, has contributed to the uneven impact of globalization. The new and rapidly growing information technology depends on institutions, infrastructure, skills and policies, which generate oases of activity and growth in the midst of desert zones. In addition to states and private companies and banks, there has been a growth of international non-governmental, non-profit organizations and voluntary agencies that form the international civil society. There are also the multilateral institutions such as the United Nations and its agencies, the World Bank, the International Monetary Fund, the regional development banks. The beneficiaries from the activities of the non-governmental organizations and the multilateral institutions have often been not the poorest but the better off among the small entrepreneurs. There has been polarization even within the informal sector. Some enterprises have done very well and graduated into the formal sector, while others have barely survived.

Finally, there are the international labor unions, which are weak compared with national unions. Globalization that relies solely on market forces further weakens the power of both national and international labor unions. It does not follow that developing countries would have been better off had they closed themselves off from the process of globalization and tried to become autarkic. Joan Robinson said that there is only one thing that is worse than being exploited by capitalists, and that is not being exploited by them. The same goes for participation in globalization. Those with skills and assets take advantage of the opening up to globalization, those without them get left behind. But there are better options than to allow these people to become the victims of the blind forces of globalization. Measures such as social safety nets, guaranteed employment schemes and training provisions to cushion poor people in low-income countries against being battered by these forces, should be built into the system of international relations. This is necessary not only for political stability, but for reasons of our common humanity.

NOTES

1. I am grateful to Ajit Bhalla, Al Berry, Louis Emmerij, Hans Singer and especially to Ronald Dore for helpful comments on earlier drafts.
2. It is the non-historical touting of the current trend to globalization that has led critics to call it globaloney.
3. See Paul Streeten (1989), pp. 1153–86. For a more recent skeptical treatment of the claim of globalization, see Robert Wade (1996).
4. It is often said that globalization is irreversible. But the history of the two wars and the interwar period shows that it is highly reversible. After having reached a peak in the late 19th century, it retreated until after World War II.
5. This increase in the trade/GDP ratios occurred in spite of a general increase in tariff protection between 1870 and 1913. It was therefore not the result of trade liberalization. In the pre-1913 period of globalization the role of the state increased, not declined. See Paul Bairoch and Richard Kozul-Wright, 'Globalization Myths' (undated).
6. TEP: The Technology/Economy Programme (1992, p. 233).
7. On the other hand, electronic technology has made labor mobility much less important than it once was.
8. Jeffrey Williamson (1995). The comparisons of real wages are in terms of purchasing power equivalents.
9. Anthony Giddens (1995). As Mark Blaug has pointed out, there has been no similar globalization in economic theory. 'Almost all Italian economists know everything there is to know about Sraffa and yet one can travel far and wide in the United States without ever meeting an economist that has even heard of Sraffa. Such is the insularity of academia!' (Blaug, 1998, p. 1926).
10. Quoted by Barbara Crossette (1997).
11. J.M. Keynes (1933, p. 237). As Dani Rodrik (1997, p. 72) points out, the rest of the paragraph is not quoted as often: 'Yet, at the same time, those who seek to disembarrass a country from its entanglements should be slow and wary. It should not be a matter of tearing up roots but of slowly training a plant to grow a different direction.'
12. It should, however, be remembered that downsizing in companies such as AT&T, Nynex, Sears, Philip Morris and Delta Airlines cannot be attributed to international competition. Businessmen like to blame global forces for actions for which they should bear responsibility.

REFERENCES

Bairoch, Paul (1982), 'International Industrialization Levels from 1750 to 1980', *Journal of European Economic History*, **11** (2), Fall: 269–334.

Bairoch, Paul and Richard Kozul-Wright (undated), 'Globalization Myths: Some Historical Reflection on Integration', *Industrialization and Growth in the World Economy*, UNCTAD/OSG/DP, 113.

Barber, Benjamin (1995), *Jihad vs. McWorld*, New York: Times Books, Random House.

Blaug, Mark (1998), review of Giovanni Caravale (ed.), *Equilibrium and Economic Theory*, *Economic Journal*, **108** (451), November: 1924–6.

Cowen, Tyler (2002), *Creative Destruction*, Princeton, NJ: Princeton University Press.

Crossette, Barbara (1997), 'The Unreal Thing. Un-American Ugly Americans', *The New York Times Week in Review*, 11 May, Section 4: 1.

Eatwell, John (1995), 'The International Origins of Unemployment', in J. Michie and J.G. Smith (eds), *Managing the Global Economy*, New York: Oxford University Press.

Friedman, Thomas L. (1997), 'Roll Over Hawks and Doves', *New York Times*, 2 February, Section 4: 15.

Giddens, Anthony (1995), 'Affluence, Poverty and the Idea of a Post-Scarcity Society', United Nations Research Institute for Social Development, Discussion Paper DP 63, May.

Haq, Mahbub ul, Inge Kaul and Isabelle Grunberg (eds) (1996), *The Tobin Tax: Coping with Financial Volatility*, New York: Oxford University Press.

Inter-American Development Bank (IDB) (1996), *Economic and Social Progress in Latin America – 1996 Report*, Washington, DC, November.

Keynes J.M. (1933), 'National Self-Sufficiency', *Yale Review*, Summer, and *New Statesman and Nation*, 8 and 15 July 1933, in Donald Moggeridge (ed.) (1982), *Collected Writings of John Maynard Keynes*, vol. 21, [1933] Activities 1931–39, London: Macmillan and Cambridge University Press.

López-Mejía, Alejandro (1999), *Large Capital Flows: A Survey of the Causes, Consequences and Public Responses*, IMF Working Paper 99/17.

Maddison, Angus (1989), *The World Economy in the Twentieth Century*, Paris: OECD Development Centre.

Maddison, Angus (1995), *Monitoring the World Economy*, Paris: OECD Publications.

Maizels, A. (1963), *Industrial Growth and World Trade*, Cambridge: Cambridge University Press.

Nayyar, Deepak (1995), *Globalisation: The Past in Our Present*, Presidential Address to the Seventy-Eighth Annual Conference of the Indian Economic Association, Chandigarh, 28–30 December.

Nayyar, Deepak (1997), 'The Past in Our Present', *Third World Economics*, **168**: 7–15.

O'Rourke, Kevin, Alan Taylor and Jeffrey Williamson (1996), 'Factor Price Convergence in the Late Nineteenth Century', *International Economic Review*, **37** (3): 499–530.

Rodrik, Dani (1997), *Has Globalization Gone Too Far?* Washington, DC: Institute for International Economics.

Rodrik, Dani (2000), 'How Far Will International Economic Integration Go?', *Journal of Economic Perspectives*, **14** (1), 177–86.

Soros, George (1997), 'The Capitalist Threat', *The Atlantic Monthly*, **279** (2), February: 45–55.

Streeten, Paul (1989a), 'International Cooperation', in Hollis Chenery and T.N. Srinivasan (eds), *Handbook of Development Economics*, vol. 2, Amsterdam: North Holland.

Streeten, Paul (1989b), 'The Judy Trick', in Lionel Orchard and Robert Dare (eds), *Markets, Morals and Public Policy*, Annandale, NSW: Federation Press.

TEP: The Technology/Economy Programme (1992), *Technology and the Economy: The Key Relationships*, Paris: OECD.

United Nations Conference on Trade and Development (1996), *World Investment Report*, New York: United Nations.

United Nations Development Programme (UNDP) (2000), *Human Development Report*, New York: Oxford University Press.

UNRISD (1995), *States of Disarray; The Social Effects of Globalization*, Geneva: UNRISD.

United States Bureau of the Census (1999), *Statistical Abstract of the United States*, Washington, DC: US Government Printing Office.

Wade, Robert (1996), 'Globalization and its Limits: Reports of the Death of the National Economy Are Greatly Exaggerated', in Suzanne Berger and Ronald Dore (eds), *National Diversity and Global Capitalism*, Ithaca and London: Cornell University Press.

Wade, Robert (1999) 'National Power, Coercive Liberalism and "Global" Finance', in Robert Art and Robert Jervis (eds), *International Politics: Enduring Concepts and Contemporary Issues*, Addison Wesley Longman.

Williamson Jeffrey (1995), 'The Evolution of Global Labour Markets since 1830: Background Evidence and Hypotheses', *Explorations in Economic History*.

Williamson Jeffrey (1996), 'Globalisation, Convergence and History', *Journal of Economic History*.

World Bank (1995), *World Development Report*, Washington DC: World Bank.

5. Globalization and Financial Crises: A Proposal for a New Approach to Macroeconomics[1]

Nahid Aslanbeigui

INTRODUCTION

In his classic essay on *The Nature and Significance of Economic Science*, Lionel Robbins declared economics to be a study of 'human behaviour as a relationship between ends and scarce means which have alternative uses' (Robbins, 1935, p. 16). According to Robbins, economics assumes that 'human beings have ends in the sense that they have tendencies to conduct which can be defined and understood', but it does not take any position on them. Investigations of ultimate values, or anything concerning 'what should be', rest on 'speculations whose very nature no philosopher since the beginning of time has succeeded in making clear'. They are not verifiable, scientifically intelligible, and are best left to ethics or aesthetics (see Robbins, 1927, pp. 176–7; 1935, p. 24). In contrast, the science of economics investigates how people's 'progress towards their objectives is conditioned by the scarcity of means' (Robbins, 1935, p. 24), i.e., it describes 'what is', or 'what can be'. Its propositions are 'deductions from a series of postulates, the chief of which are almost universal facts of experience present whenever human activity has an economic aspect' (ibid., pp. 99–100).

Authors of introductory economics textbooks embrace Robbins's dicta on the scope and method of economics. Economists, Stiglitz and Walsh tell students, 'study how individuals, firms, and governments within our society make choices. Choices are unavoidable because desired goods, services, and resources are inevitably scarce' (2002, p. 21). In 'applying the principles of economics to questions about the real world', say Boyes and Melvin (2002), it is important to use positive analysis: 'avoid imposing your opinions or value judgments on others'. Normative analysis does not *'advance one's understanding of events'* (ibid., p. 8; emphasis in the original).

The 'scientific' method consists of identifying a problem, making simplifying assumptions, constructing a model, and finally testing it (ibid.). Models do not capture every nuance of the empirical reality, but they do capture its essence. They are used to 'study how the economy works and to make predictions about what will happen if something is changed. A model . . . is designed to mirror the essential characteristics of the particular phenomena under study' (Stiglitz and Walsh, 2002, p. 22).

As the arguments in this chapter demonstrate, there is a great chasm between what authors of macroeconomics textbooks preach and what they practice. Macroeconomics is neither a value-free science that studies human behavior conditioned by scarcity, nor does it reflect the 'essential characteristics of the particular phenomena under study'. In this chapter, I propose a structural adjustment program for macroeconomics textbooks that includes recommendations for revising the introductory chapter on scope and method, and suggestions for incorporating analyses of globalization and financial crises, essential features of the global economy. A portion of what follows will use Charles Perrow's normal accident theory to analyze financial crises as an inherent risk of globalization. The Asian crisis of 1997–98 will serve as a case study.

RESTRUCTURING MACROECONOMICS TEXTBOOKS

Method and Scope

Embracing the Robbinsian definition of the scope and method of economics creates many inconsistencies in macroeconomics textbooks. In the introductory chapter, students are advised to limit themselves to establishing the necessary conditions for reaching optimal solutions, or equilibria, given scarce resources. As scientists, they are to avoid attaching 'a penumbra of approbation' round an equilibrium position. 'Equilibrium', as Robbins said, 'is just equilibrium' (1935, p. 143).

Since the 1960s, philosophers of science have systematically demonstrated that value-free science is impossible, and that scientists are far from dispassionate producers of hypotheses and tests. It is not necessary to review Sellars (1963), Popper (1965), Kuhn (1970), or Feyerabend (1975; 1978) to see why. Macroeconomics texts provide ample evidence. As an end, economic growth is deemed as clearly superior to stagnation. People 'are made better off by economic growth' because it 'increases the number of jobs and draws people out of poverty and into the mainstream of economic progress' (Boyes and Melvin, 2002, p. 107). Because it raises 'living standards', a high-level equilibrium is 'a fundamental macroeconomic goal'

(Stiglitz and Walsh, 2002, p. 102). A low-level equilibrium, economic stagnation, is undesirable because it 'throws the relatively poor out of their jobs and into poverty' (Boyes and Melvin, 2002, p. 107). Joblessness can 'deal a powerful blow' to the self-respect of the unemployed, force them 'to choose between poverty and the bitter taste of government or private charity', break up families, and alienate the youth enough to drive them to 'antisocial activities such as crime and drug abuse' (Stiglitz and Walsh, 2002, p. 102).

Macroeconomic concepts are also loaded with 'unscientific' elements. The gross national/domestic product (GNP/GDP), consumer/producer price index, and index of leading economic indicators require aggregation. To aggregate, economists must assign weights. In the national product accounts, for example, a dollar spent by Bill Gates has the same value as a dollar spent by a vagabond who spends his or her nights in New York City's Central Park. The explicit or implicit assignment of such weights includes value judgments, or 'conventional elements' (Robbins, 1935, p. 63). So does the interpretation of these concepts. Positivists eschew distributive investigations because they involve taking positions on 'what should be'. But statements about growth are no less value laden. The GNP of 2001 is consistent with prices in 2001, which partly determine the distribution of income in 2001. The GNP of 2002 may be higher but it is associated with a different set of prices and a different distribution of income. To declare that the economy is better off in 2002 due to higher GNP or growth rates is tantamount to ignoring such distributive changes, itself a value judgment.

Mainstream economists are often narrowly trained and lack enthusiasm for the humanities and other social sciences. As such, it is not obvious that they should venture into philosophy of science. However, if they feel compelled to do so, they should not neglect over four decades of systematic work that has proved the poverty of positivism as 'the' method of scientific inquiry. At the very least, students should learn that knowledge is produced by scientific communities, members of which import their values at various stages of scientific inquiry: collection of data, testing hypotheses, and interpreting results. Moreover, different paradigms produce different truths. Such an approach is more suitable for understanding macroeconomic debates among classical, Keynesian, monetarist, supply-side, or new classical economists, which are discussed in macroeconomics texts with some detail.[2]

The introductory chapter of a macroeconomics textbook announces a scarcity focus. A great portion of the text itself, however, is dedicated to the study of economic fluctuations and underutilization of resources (Stiglitz and Walsh, 2002, p. 115), with an eye toward devising policies that raise people's living standards, elevate them above poverty, improve their self-respect, and reduce alienation and antisocial behavior (see Stiglitz and Walsh, 2002, p. 102; Boyes and Melvin, 2002, p. 107). Academic honesty requires that the discrepancy between what the authors preach and what they practice be eliminated. This can easily be achieved by redefining economics in the pre-Robbinsian fashion: 'a scientific study' of people's 'social actions', which 'may lead, not necessarily directly or immediately, but at some time and in some way, to practical results in social improvement' (Pigou, 2000 [1932], p. 4). In the post-positivist literature in development (Sen 1982; 1999; Nussbaum, 2000), economics is about enhancing people's capabilities to 'live a healthy and full life, be free of abuse, enjoy art and literature, hold property, and make decisions concerning labor force participation and reproduction' (Aslanbeigui and Summerfield, 2001, p. 8). Both sets of literature can inform a discussion of the scope of economics in an introductory macroeconomics text.

Globalization is an 'essential characteristic' of the global economy, a phenomenon with profound implications for human welfare and capabilities. Introductory macroeconomics fails to 'mirror' this important feature of the empirical reality. Of the two textbooks examined for this chapter,[3] the first completely ignores globalization and contagious financial crises (Boyes and Melvin, 2002). The only sources of economic instability are business cycles, which are caused by domestic monetary and fiscal policies, politicians' agendas, or real shocks (e.g., changes in tastes and technology, labor strife, climate) (ibid., pp. 365–8). Boyes' and Melvin's approach presumes the institutional setting at the time of the Bretton Woods conference: strong nation states and weak international linkages. Their model does not explain the financial and economic crisis that began in Thailand, engulfed Indonesia, South Korea, the Philippines, and Malaysia and affected South Africa, Brazil and Russia. Neither does it predict the consequences of such crises: a 72 per cent depreciation in Indonesia's currency, a 13.7 per cent decline in South Korea's real GDP, and the impoverishment of more than 50 million people in the region (Aslanbeigui and Summerfields, 2001, p. 9).

Stiglitz and Walsh do define globalization, link it to financial crises, and provide a brief account of the Asian crisis and its 'devastating economic consequences' (2002, pp. 489–92; also see pp. 418–19). However, their approach is problematic in many ways. First, their brief discussion of global financial crises is relegated to the last few chapters (17 and 20), which instructors often do not assign to students. Second, their analysis of globalization is not systematic. The book begins with expenditure and income determination in a closed economy followed by monetary and fiscal policy. When the economy is opened to trade (and, by implication, finance), there is no significant change in results, except that monetary policy becomes more effective and fiscal policy less so. Uncontrollable financial crises, and stabilization policies that produce more instability and massive involuntary unemployment, are not mentioned as risks generated by globalization.

Globalization and financial crises are only linked in the final chapter, 'Development and Transition' (ibid., p. 487), creating the impression that global crises affect developing nations more because they have high unemployment, limited entrepreneurship, scarce capital, and 'a hard time controlling' volatile capital flows (ibid., pp. 487–9). This impression is magnified if the plight of poor countries is juxtaposed with the fortunes of more developed economies that experience fewer and milder recessions because of reduced reliance on manufacturing, improved management of inventories, and better success in policy-making (ibid., pp. 379–81). In these economies, unemployment is voluntary; labor markets do not adjust because of sticky wages, which compel employers to seek adjustment mechanisms other than price, e.g., layoffs (ibid., pp. 261–2).[4] Given such pronouncements, it is hard to explain how Europe was faced with a 'global financial crisis' in 1992, when the United Kingdom, Italy, and Sweden were forced to abandon pegged exchange rates and 'several other members of the European Monetary System [had] to devalue their currencies' (ibid., p. 418).

Every introductory macroeconomics textbook precedes its theoretical discussion by introducing basic concepts that include the production possibilities frontier, specialization on the basis of comparative advantage, and trade. This is a highly selective subset of essential concepts for today's world. Given the highly integrated nature of the world economy, there is no reason to neglect, or relegate to the end of the book, a discussion of globalization and its consequences.[5] From the outset, students should understand that 'The World Around You' (Boyes and Melvin, 2002, p. 2) is a global one.

Placing the domestic economy in the context of global markets sets the stage for incorporating global financial (and economic) crises in later chapters. Currently, introductory macroeconomics texts treat business cycles as primarily originating in domestic problems: changes in aggregate expenditure due to animal spirits, domestic policy, politicians' agendas, or real shocks. In the following section, I recommend that this treatment be modified to include global financial crises as system-produced risks. The catastrophic consequences of the Asian crisis will shed light on the importance of incorporating financial crises in a textbook that is focused on human capabilities and well-being.

Globalization and Financial Crises

The meaning and degree of globalization at the turn of the 21st century are debatable (see Streeten, this volume), but its characteristic features are not. New markets (foreign exchange), technology (information, communications, transportation), actors (multilateral institutions, multinational corporations, and nongovernmental organizations), and rules (agreements on trade and the environment) have produced a highly integrated global economy. The ensuing data are illustrative. In the 1990s, $1.5 trillion were exchanged in currency markets on a daily basis (1998); about one–fifth of the world's annual production of goods and services were traded (1999); 250,000 African professors worked in Europe and the United States (1998); the world population spent 70 billion minutes on international telephone calls (1996); less than one-third of television programming in Latin America originated in the region (1998); cross-border mergers and acquisitions approximated sixty billion dollars (1998); and the number of international nongovernmental organizations equaled 28,900 (UNDP, 1999, pp. 1–44).

The actual and potential benefits of globalization are undeniable. Global output has grown ninefold in the past 50 years. Between 1975 and 1997, an added 11 per cent of the world's population enjoyed medium human development, and the number of those who fell in the low human-development category was cut by half (ibid., p. 25). Technological breakthroughs make it possible for micro-enterprises to find distant markets for their products without the help of intermediaries, and expert doctors can run training programs for their peers in remote areas of the world through video links (Spar, 1999, p. 349). Finally, increased transparency makes discrimination, cronyism or human rights violations more costly for governments around the world.

The same forces that have the potential to create astounding levels of wealth also produce risks with unpredictable and disastrous consequences. The most noted of these risks are environmental disasters such as nuclear meltdowns, oil spills, or global warming (see Beck, 1992; 1999).[6] Another set of risks, the focus of this chapter, is global financial crises, which result in economic, social, and sometimes political crises. In the context of this chapter, risk implies uncertainty: 'the unknowability of the timing, duration, extent, or impact of such crises' (Aslanbeigui and Summerfield, 2001, p. 9).

Although financial and economic crises are not new phenomena – the last 25 years of the 20th century alone experienced 80–100 crises (Stiglitz, 2000, p. 1075) – the magnitude and frequency of these crises have increased. The 1990s, for example, witnessed three major crises. During the last quarter of 1992 a speculative attack on Finland's currency spread to the UK, Italy, Sweden, and Norway, also affecting Spain, Portugal, and Ireland in 1993. In late 1994, the Mexican Peso was subject to a speculative attack, which spread to Argentina, Brazil, Peru, and Venezuela. The 'Tequila' attacks also created short-term attacks on the currencies of Thailand, Hong Kong, the Philippines, and Hungary (FRBSF, 1998, pp. 1–3).

The 1990s ended with the Asian crisis, which serves as a case study for the arguments in this chapter. The crisis began when a speculative bubble in the Thai asset markets (property and stock) ruptured shortly before July 1997. Foreign banks, which had made short-term, unhedged foreign-exchange loans to that country's borrowers, recognized that these loans were not covered by Thai reserves. Expecting that the currency peg would be lifted, they pulled their funds out of Thailand. The prophecy was self-fulfilled, and the government was forced to float the bhat in early July 1997 (Wade, 1998, p. 699). Within days, the Philippines and Malaysia followed suit as investor perception about the region changed and financial panic spread. When the IMF signed its 14 August bailout package to Thailand, Indonesia floated its currency as well. The panic spread to East Asia, when the government of Taiwan unexpectedly devalued its currency in October, creating the expectation that Hong Kong and South Korea would soon adopt similar measures. Before South Korea floated its currency in December, shockwaves had spread to the US and European financial markets and reverberated in Latin America (Kawai et al., 2001, pp. 13–14).

The Asian crisis had disastrous consequences. Table 5.1 shows significant declines in exchange rates, real GDPs, and trade for crisis-ridden economies of Asia in the 1996–98 period. With the exception of the Philippines, improvements in current accounts were achieved through drastic declines in imports. Bankruptcies swept the region – 435 firms in Malaysia over a nine-month period – and real wages dropped significantly (40 per cent in Indonesia). Unemployment tripled in Korea, and more than 50 million people in the region became poor. All countries reported increased rates of street crime, domestic violence, and suicide (UNDP, 1999, p. 40; IMF, 2000, p. 65). Existing social tensions intensified (Stiglitz, 2000).

The international community of scholars and policy-makers are in agreement that the Asian crisis exemplified historic volatility, contagion, and costs. However, there is a vigorous debate on what forces or actors primarily caused the crisis. The IMF blamed various actors in Asian economies: the private sector that borrowed vast sums of unhedged, short-term foreign exchange without appropriate risk assessment; Asian governments that failed to establish a strong financial structure with adequate regulation and supervision, espoused crony capitalism and lack of transparency, tolerated high debt-equity ratios, and allocated loans on the basis of connections; banks that excessively exposed themselves to corporations; and investors who used most of the short-term loans that flowed into Asia in the early to mid-1990s for speculative or low-quality projects (Lane et al., 1999, pp. 17–19).

Those opposing the IMF criticized the international financial institutions, particularly the IMF, for putting pressure on Asian countries to liberalize their financial markets and capital accounts. Table 5.2 demonstrates that most of the resulting private capital flows were short-term and speculative. Financial liberalization had two consequences for Asian economies. Lack of regulation made countries vulnerable to wide swings in financial flows, exchange rates (see Tables 5.1 and 5.2) and interest rates. It also made these swings contagious. Once 'lenders' perceptions' of risk changed, there was massive capital flight from the region (Stiglitz, 2000, p. 1080; Taylor, 1998).

Table 5.1 *Percent changes in macroeconomic variables for countries most affected by the Asian crisis*

Country	Exchange rate (2/6/97–24/3/98)	Real GDP (1998)	Exports (96–98)	Imports (96–98)
Indonesia	-72	-13.0	-1.9	-36.3
Malaysia	-31	-7.4	-6.4	-25.6
Philippines	-29	-0.6	44.1	-7.7
South Korea	-36	-6.7	2.0	-38.0
Thailand	-36	-10.2	-2.3	-40.6

Sources: Wade (1998, p. 694); Greene (2002, pp. 4, 7).

Table 5.2 *Net capital flows for crisis countries in Asia (billions of dollars), 1994–98*

Type of Capital Flow	1994	1995	1996	1997	1998
Net private capital flows	33.6	53.9	67.4	-15.6	-28.2
Net private direct investment	6.5	8.8	9.8	9.8	10.3
Net private portfolio investment	12.0	18.8	25.5	8.4	-8.2
Other net private capital flows	15.1	26.3	32.0	33.8	-30.4
Net official flows	0.6	0.7	-6.1	15.7	19.5
Change in reserves*	-6.1	-18.5	-5.6	39.5	-47.0

Note: *A negative number signifies an increase.

Source: IMF (2000, p. 65).

The IMF was also criticized for failing to predict the crisis in Asia. A document prepared for IMF's executive board in December 1998 reported 'deep seated' weaknesses in financial systems and a 'long history' of government mismanagement (Lane et al., 1999, pp. 19, 17). Yet, three months before the crisis overtook South Korea, the IMF was full of adulation for Korea's high growth rates and fiscal responsibility. It did not identify weak financial structures, crony capitalism, or government misallocation of loans as problems that could induce a financial crisis (Sachs, 1997, p. 2).

The IMF made many mistakes in managing the crisis once it occurred. It underestimated the extent of the economic downturn in a region where almost 50 per cent of trade is intra-regional. The miscalculation had two reasons: (a) the IMF's staff assumed that the Fund's programs would restore confidence; and (b) they chose to err 'on the side of optimism in part because of concerns that realistically pessimistic forecasts would have exacerbated the situation further' (Lane et al., 1999, p. 45). By now it is well known that IMF's programs were also faulty. Tight monetary policy, which in some cases increased interest rates to above 100 per cent, made exchange rates more, not less, volatile (World Bank, 1999b, p. 88). Closing 16 banks in Indonesia reinforced the sense of panic among depositors, whose deposits were not insured. Cutbacks in government expenditure, high interest rates, and panicky capital flight stifled investment, increased bankruptcies, reduced GDPs, and increased unemployment and poverty.[7] The 'slowdown in economic activity was dramatically different from that assumed in formulating the [IMF's] programs, and its magnitude, once appreciated, prompted revisions in economic policies'. According to the IMF, the 'large revisions in projections were detrimental to credibility', making the situation worse (Lane et al., 1999, p. 45).

The IMF or Asian governments are presumed to have played the most significant role in the Asian crisis. However, scholars have identified many other contributory factors. Governments of more developed nations – particularly the United States – supported the IMF's pursuit of indiscriminate financial liberalization, which significantly contributed to paroxysmal movements in financial markets and the contagion of the crisis from Thailand to other countries and regions. Financial institutions of more developed countries exhibited herd-like behavior, lending to Asian countries feverishly and without risk assessment when optimistic, and pulling out irrationally and in droves when pessimistic (Singh and Zammit, 2000, p. 125). Western financial innovations such as hedge funds and derivatives, and round-the-clock trading, courtesy of information technology, made financial markets significantly interdependent (Kregel, 1998). Finally, crisis countries witnessed shrinking export markets after the mid-1990s, thanks to a depreciating yen, declining terms of trade mostly because of competition from China, and a stagnating Japanese economy, a major trading partner for the region (see Wade, 1998, pp. 697–8).

The debate on the causes of the Asian crisis does not establish which factors or group of factors were responsible for its creation. The IMF continues to believe that weak financial structures and government mis-management were the primary causes of the crisis, although it does not deny the role played by contracting export markets or herd-like behavior on the part of investors. Critics of the IMF admit that the Asian economies suffered from structural weaknesses, but they insist that the push for financial liberalization was responsible for the crisis. Finally, neither the IMF nor its critics belittle the importance of declining terms of trade or overvalued exchange rates. In what follows, I use Charles Perrow's normal accident theory to argue that no single factor or player can alone be blamed. Financial crises are endemic to the global economy, arising from complex interactions in a tightly coupled environment.

Normal Accident Theory: A Framework for Analyzing Global Financial Crises

Normal accident theory, developed by sociologist Charles Perrow (1999), is used to analyze high-risk technologies such as nuclear power and petrochemical plants, aircrafts and airways, and dams. High-risk technologies have the potential to produce catastrophic accidents. The 1986 Chernobyl nuclear accident, for example, impacted over 8.2 million people immediately, close to 350,000 of whom had to be relocated. Today, 5.75 million people, including more than one million children, still live in the contaminated areas of Belarus, the Ukraine, and the Russian Federation. In some areas of Belarus, the incidence of thyroid cancer among children has increased more than a hundredfold. The aggregate economic loss of this accident for the Ukraine is estimated to be $100 billion (United Nations General Assembly, 2001, pp. 3–4).

The characteristics of high-risk technologies – complexity and tight coupling – make accidents inevitable regardless of the number or quality of built-in safety devices. A system is called complex when its components interact in a non-linear fashion, producing 'unfamiliar . . . or unplanned and unexpected sequences', which are 'either not visible or not immediately comprehensible' (Perrow, 1999, pp. 78–9). Understandably, operators/ overseers of these systems have difficulty comprehending the nature of failures once they occur.

A system is tightly coupled or interconnected if there is 'no slack or buffer or give between' its components (ibid., p. 90). In such a system, there is no room for delays; malfunctions must be attended to immediately, otherwise they spread, bringing down part of, or the entire, system. The structure of a tightly connected system does not allow for creative, on-the-spot solutions (ibid., pp. 91–6); contingencies, and ways to address them, must be thought out in advance and built into the system.

Normal accidents are inevitable products of systems that are both highly complex and tightly connected. Perrow describes how these accidents might occur:

Since nothing is perfect – neither designs, equipment, operating procedures, operators, materials and supplies, nor the environment – there will be failures. If the complex interactions defeat designed-in safety devices or go around them, there will be failures that are unexpected and incomprehensible. If the system is also tightly coupled, leaving little time for recovery from failure, little slack in resources or fortuitous safety devices, then the failure cannot be limited to parts or units, but will bring down subsystems or systems. These accidents then are caused initially by component failures, but become accidents . . . because of the nature of the system itself . . . (ibid., p. 330).

Accidents are labeled normal not because they occur frequently, but because they are inevitable (ibid.).

The world economy can be viewed as a system that has become highly complex and tightly coupled. Many factors explain the increased complexity of the global economy. First, the components of global markets interact in a more complex fashion because the 'rate of production of new financial instruments [e.g., derivatives and hedge funds], each with its own associated rules and regulations has increased dramatically'. Each new financial instrument increases the level of market sophistication, requiring that 'the average market participant . . . know more and more just to know what is considered common knowledge' (Mezias, 1994, p. 184).

Second, there are many more players on the international scene. Toward the end of World War II, representatives from 45 governments negotiated the establishment of the IMF and the World Bank in New Hampshire; today, the membership of these organizations stands at 183. The termination of the Cold War, the fall of the Berlin Wall, and the market reforms in China, integrated an additional 1.7 billion people into global markets (UNDP, 1999, p. 28). Many developing nations have wooed foreign direct investment, multinational corporations, and export promotion strategies hoping to achieve higher growth rates. As conditions for financial assistance from the IMF and the World Bank, or membership in the World Trade Organization (WTO) and the Organization for Economic Co-operation and Development (OECD), other countries have privatized state-run enterprises, allowed a higher degree of foreign ownership, and liberalized trade and finance. In 1998 world exports equaled $7 trillion. By 1997 foreign direct investment exceeded $400 billion, a sevenfold increase from the 1970s; India's average tariffs had dropped to 30 per cent (from 82 per cent in 1990) and Brazil's had declined to 12 per cent (from 25 per cent in 1991) (UNDP, 1999, pp. 25, 29).

Third, the complexity brought about by high levels of integration among people, countries, and markets is exacerbated by the diversity in legal, economic, social, and political structures. Table 5.3 demonstrates some of this diversity for nations that were most affected by the Asian crisis. Economic indicators (GDP per capita, unemployment, and inflation) vary significantly from one country to another. Four of the five countries are former colonies of the UK, the US, the Netherlands, and Japan respectively; Thailand has never been colonized. Not surprisingly, the legal systems of these countries vary significantly. Differing degrees of ethnic and religious diversity have produced substantial variations in development strategies. Indonesia and Malaysia, for example, have experienced ethnic unrest and riots that South Korea has not had to contend with. The economic policies of both Indonesia and Malaysia have included significant redistributive measures in favor of their poor, indigenous populations (see Wahid and Ikhsan, 1997; Chowdhury, 1997; Jomo, 1998).

Increasing complexity makes it progressively more difficult to predict how policies and/or events interact; which measures, policies or institutions could prevent crises; or what the nature or magnitude of crises will be as they unfold. The case of South Korea is illustrative. For nearly three decades (early 1960s to early 1990s), the South Korean government pursued a high-investment, high-growth development strategy, implemented through five-year plans. Selective industrial policy acted as a coordination mechanism that prevented 'excessive competition' (Chang et al., 1998, p. 740). Chaebols were preferentially treated as a group, but no individual conglomerate had a distinct advantage over others. High interest rates and low profitability did not harm the corporate sector because the government ensured that 'the income appropriated by the financial sector was recycled to the manufacturing corporate sector' (ibid., p. 742). High debt-equity ratios of Korean corporations provided effective and '"patient" long-term investment' (ibid., p. 744).

The liberalization of the financial sector in the early 1990s increased the amount of short-term debt significantly. Leading among the debtors were the newly created, inexperienced, and unsupervised merchant banks; 64 per cent of these banks' debts were short-term, but 85 per cent of their lending was long-term. In conjunction with liberalization, the abolition of five-year planning led to over-investment, excess capacity, and major corporate failures. Crony capitalism became worse; in the absence of a five-year plan, it was much easier for specific chaebols to seek and receive undue favors from the government (ibid., p. 640). By the time of the crisis in Thailand, the dismantling of the traditional mechanisms of generating and coordinating long-term investment' (ibid., p. 745) had produced significant weaknesses in the South Korean economy, which was easily brought down by the panicky flight of capital from the region.

The IMF misunderstood these complex interactions and their un-predictable results. A case of overinvestment was characterized as a balance-of-payments problem and excessive consumption (Wade, 1998, p. 700). It is,

Table 5.3 Social, economic and political diversity among Asian countries

Country	Ethnic groups	Independence	Legal system	GDP per capita (PPP) ($US)	Unemployment rate (%)	Inflation (%)
Indonesia	Javanese 45% Sudanese 14% Madurese 7.5% Coastal Malays 7.5% Other 26%	27/12/1949 (legal) from the Netherlands	Based on Roman-Dutch law, substantially modified by indigenous concepts	2,900	15–20 (1998)	9 (2000)
Malaysia	Malays & other Indigenous 58% Chinese 27% Indian 8% Other 7%	31/8/1957 from the UK	Based on English common law	10,300	2.8 (2000)	1.7 (2000)
Philippines	Christian Malay 91.5% Muslim Malay 4% Chinese 1.5% Other 3%	4/7/1946 from the US	Based on Spanish and Anglo-American law	3,800	10 (2000)	5 (2000)
South Korea	Homogeneous except for 20,000 Chinese	15/8/1945 from Japan	Combines continental European civil law, Anglo-American law, and Chinese classical thought	16,100	4.1 (2000)	2.3 (2000)
Thailand	Thai 75% Chinese 14% Other 11%	Never colonized	Based on Civil Law System, influenced by common law	6,700	3.7 (2000)	2.1 (2000)

Source: CIA (2001).

therefore, not surprising that the IMF's stabilization and structural adjustment did not restore confidence, contributed to panic, weakened the exchange rates further, increased bankruptcies, and diminished output even more (Aslanbeigui and Summerfield, 2000, pp. 84–5).[8]

Because the world is also tightly coupled, unanticipated malfunctions cannot be contained and a global financial crisis, a normal accident, might ensue. Several factors explain the increasing interdependence among countries. The most noteworthy are developments in the world of finance. In the 1970s, $10 to $20 billion was exchanged in foreign exchange markets on a daily basis. In 1998, that figure was $1.5 trillion (UNDP, 1999, p. 25). Most of these transactions are short-term and speculative: 40 per cent of these flows are reversed in one day, 90 per cent in one week (Tobin, 2000, p. 1101). The explosion in financial transactions is due to financial liberalization, high-speed and round-the-clock transactions, creation of new financial instruments, and a homogenization of the activities of different sectors of the financial industry (Mezias, 1994, p. 185).

The unimpeded and continuous flow of funds around the world makes all countries susceptible to instability as well as contagion. The Asian crisis is a clear illustration that portfolio interdependence proliferates shocks as 'international commercial banks [try] to reduce exposure in other countries to protect the quality of their portfolios' (Kawai et al., 2001, p. 22). Large capital losses in one country lead to sell-offs in holdings in other markets 'in an effort to raise cash to meet investor redemptions' (World Bank, 1999b, p. 48). More important is herd-like behavior. Financial panics ensue if institutional fund managers copy other investors' behavior 'to protect themselves from being blamed' for potential losses due to not following trends, or if they view the region's stocks as an 'asset class' (ibid.).[9]

No individual phenomenon or event can alone be held responsible for system-produced accidents. Economic histories of countries and regions are replete with cases where the free flow of funds, overvalued exchange rates, or unfavorable terms of trade have failed to produce global financial crises. Weaknesses in Asian financial systems were 'deep seated' and government mismanagement had a 'long history' (Lane et al., 1999, pp. 19, 17), but Asia did not experience a financial crisis until 1997–98. 'Crony capitalism' is not unique to Asia or the developing world. Enron and its dubious connections to American politicians and policies, and Arthur Anderson's creative accounting practices, which go back to the early 1980s (see Mezias, 1994, p. 187), are vivid examples of high-level corruption in the United States, the most powerful economy in the world. They may have contributed to the sluggishness in the American economy but have not resulted in a global financial crisis. Finally, the IMF's template of stabilization and structural adjustment programs has been able to arrest crises in some cases, albeit at the cost of creating severe recessions.

Financial Crises and Macroeconomic Policy

If global financial crises are viewed as system-produced risks, then it would be a mistake to blame their causation on a particular component – developing nations, international financial institutions, or more developed countries. Liberalization of financial markets and capital accounts has as much responsibility as does cronyism, government mismanagement, or investors' herd-like behavior.

In a perfect world, the collective nature of crises would be apparent to all world actors, who would accept responsibility for their consequences. Given the world's existing power structure, however, the distribution of costs is anything but equitable. Countries that were seriously affected by the Asian crisis received large financial packages. In return, they had to adopt stabilization and structural adjustment policies. As stated earlier, cutbacks in government budgets reduced social expenditures on health, nutrition, and education; interest-rate hikes choked consumption and investment; further liberalization and privatization increased bankruptcies; and depression-level unemployment and poverty ensued. They also had to undertake measures for improving regulation, transparency, accountability, and governance in various sectors of the economy (World Bank, 1999b, p. 91; Lane et al., 1999).

Other actors that contributed to the crisis did not face similar demands. The international financial institutions, especially the IMF, were not held accountable for their mistakes in predicting or managing the crisis. Nor were lenders punished for irresponsible lending or herd-like behavior. In fact, if the case of Long Term Capital Management (Edwards, 1999) is any indication, they were rescued when threatened by bankruptcy.

Developing nations are expected to bear a disproportionate burden of the costs of global financial crises. Within these countries, the distribution of costs follows the same pattern.[10] There is evidence that crises do not affect the elite as much as they damage the poor and the disadvantaged. People with political and economic power are much better informed and well connected, can export their capital to other countries when necessary, and their debts are likely to be assumed by their governments in times of insolvency. In contrast, the politically and economically disadvantaged groups – the poor, women, children and minorities – bear the brunt of the costs, which affects their well-being and capabilities for life.

Data from the Asian crisis illustrate the diverse nature of the impact of the crisis across the region and within each country. Nonetheless, the disproportionate impact of the crisis on different groups is clear. In Korea, 7.1 per cent of women lost their jobs in the beginning stages of the crisis compared to 3.8 per cent of men. Seventy-five per cent of the discouraged workers were women; so were 86 per cent of the 'retrenched' workers in banking and financial services (World Bank, 2000; Lee and Rhee, 1998). In Thailand, 60 per cent of those who were laid off were women (USAID, 2000, p. 2). In countries where the real wage, not employment, was the main adjustment mechanism, women increased their paid and unpaid work to cushion the impact of the crisis on the household (ibid.). Increased child labor was another means by which households coped with unemployment or reduced incomes (Cameron, 2002). In 1998, Jakarta's red light districts absorbed 2.5 to four times as many prostitutes as they did in 1997 on a monthly basis. Reported cases of domestic violence dramatically increased in Thailand, the Philippines and Korea (World Bank, 1999a, pp. 6–7).

If global financial crises are incorporated into introductory macroeconomics, then students must be exposed to the following facts. First, more-developed nations can often counteract the effects of a recession or depression by adopting expansionary monetary and fiscal policies. Developing countries do not have the same options. International financial institutions direct them to devalue their currencies and adopt contractionary monetary and fiscal policies. In addition to increasing unemployment, these policies increase the cost of food, education, health-care, and medicine. The Indonesian government, for example, cut subsidies on beans, sugar, and flour during the Asian crisis, while their prices escalated by as much as 85 per cent. The Thai government cut its health budget for the poor by 50 per cent (in real terms). In the Philippines, 'immunization programs [were] cut by 27 per cent and preventive health measures for malaria and tuberculosis ... dropped by more than 30 per cent' (White and Sharma, 1999, pp. 5–6).

Second, developing nations' counter-cyclical policies, even if permitted, would primarily help formal-sector workers, leaving out the poor, women, and minorities who are over-represented in the informal sector. As a result, any policy designed to soften the impact of a financial crisis must include nontraditional elements: micro-credit programs that lend more to the poor during crises, public-work programs that employ informal-sector workers (including women), or education scholarships that would keep children (girls and boys) in school.

Finally, more developed countries possess a relatively comprehensive social safety net that can partially restore lost incomes through unemployment compensation or welfare assistance. In contrast, the social safety net in most developing nations is either nonexistent or is very primitive and focuses on the formal sector of the economy (Lane et al., 1999, p. 115). The strengthening of the social safety net is crucial for reducing the burden of financial crises on a significant portion of the population in the developing world.

CONCLUSION

Macroeconomics textbooks set out to study human behavior in the context of scarcity, engage in a scientific (positive) analysis of the economy, and produce models that 'mirror' the essential characteristics of macroeconomic phenomena. Currently, macroeconomics textbooks fail to achieve these objectives. Macroeconomics is not about scarcity, its concepts and analyses are replete with normative judgments, and models exclude one of the most essential characteristics of today's economies: globalization and financial crises. A restructuring of macroeconomics along the lines suggested in this paper would produce more honest, realistic, consistent, and useful pedagogy.

NOTES

1. Portions of this chapter are based on a previously published article (Aslanbeigui and Summerfield, 2001). I am grateful to my coauthor, Gale Summerfield, and the *International Journal of Politics, Culture and Society* for permitting me to replicate those arguments here. An earlier version of this paper was presented at the Rethinking Macroeconomics Conference, sponsored by the Global Development and Environment Institute, Tufts University, 20–23 June, 2002. I wish to express my gratitude to the participants of that conference, especially Jonathan Harris, for their helpful comments.
2. For a critique of textbook treatment of positivism, see Aslanbeigui and Naples (1996). The authors also suggest ways by which a paradigm approach can be integrated in both micro- and macroeconomics textbooks.
3. My decision to refer to two macroeconomics textbooks – *Macroeconomics* by William Boyes and Michael Melvin (2002) and *Principles of Macroeconomics* by Joseph E. Stiglitz and Carl E. Walsh – is not arbitrary. Boyes and Melvin were among the first set of authors to emphasize the international sector in each chapter. As the former chief economist of the World Bank during the Asian crisis, Stiglitz is fully aware of the importance of globalization and financial crises.
4. See Naples and Aslanbeigui (1996) for an analysis of textbook treatment of involuntary unemployment.
5. Institutions that try to maintain world political and economic stability (The UN, IMF, the World Bank), and create and enforce uniform rules (WTO), are an important element of such a discussion, their imperfections notwithstanding.
6. Consider, for example, the Union Carbide gas leak in Bhopal, India, in December 1984. Estimates of deaths and permanent disabilities range between 3,800 to 16,000 and 2,680 to 500,000 respectively (see Union Carbide Corporation, 2001; Greenpeace, 2002).
7. See Stiglitz (2002) for a detailed criticism of IMF's policies.
8. See World Bank (1999b) for an unusual criticism of IMF's policies.
9. The herd–like mentality of investors was clear when in late October 1997, Argentina, which does not have many linkages to east Asia, was attacked by speculators because its exchange–rate regime was similar to that of Asian countries (Kawai et al., 2001, p. 22).

10. As early as 1944, Karl Polanyi recognized that the costs of globalized financial markets are imposed on the ordinary people.

REFERENCES

Aslanbeigui, Nahid and Michele I. Naples (1996), 'Positivism versus Paradigms: The Epistemological Underpinnings of Economic Debate in Introductory Textbooks', in Nahid Aslanbeigui and Michele I. Naples (eds), *Rethinking Economic Principles: Critical Essays on Introductory Textbooks*, Chicago: Irwin, pp. 11–27.

Aslanbeigui, Nahid and Gale Summerfield (2000), 'The Asian Crisis, Gender, and the International Financial Architecture', *Feminist Economics*, **6** (3): 81–103.

Aslanbeigui, Nahid and Gale Summerfield (2001), 'Risk, Gender, and Development in the 21st Century', *International Journal of Politics, Culture and Society*, **15** (1): 7–26.

Beck, Ulrich (1992), *Risk Society: Towards a New Modernity*, trans. Mark Ritter, London: Sage Publications.

Beck, Ulrich (1999), *World Risk Society*, Cambridge: Polity Press.

Boyes, William and Michael Melvin (2002), *Macroeconomics*, 5th edn, Boston, MA: Houghton Mifflin.

Cameron, Lisa A. (2002), 'The Impact of the Indonesian Financial Crisis on Children: Data from 100 Village Survey', Washington, DC: World Bank.

Central Intelligence Agency (CIA) (2001), *The World Factbook, 2001*, http://www.cia .gov/cia/publications/factbook/.

Chang, Ha-Joon, Hong-Jae Park and Chul Gyue Yoo (1998), 'Interpreting the Korean Crisis: Financial Liberalisation, Industrial Policy and Corporate Governance', *Cambridge Journal of Economics*, **22**: 735–46.

Chowdhury, Anis (1997), 'Malaysia in Transition', in Abu N.M. Wahid (ed.), *The ASEAN Region in Transition: A Socioeconomic Perspective*, Aldershot: Ashgate, pp. 43–64.

Edwards, Franklin R. (1999), 'Hedge Funds and Collapse of Long-Term Capital Management', *Journal of Economic Perspectives*, **13** (2): 189–210.

Federal Reserve Bank of San Francisco (FRBSF) (1998), 'How do Currency Crises Spread?', http://www.frbsf.org/econrsrch/wklyltr/wklytr98/el98–25.html.

Feyerabend, P.K (1975), *Against Method: Outline of an Anarchist Theory of Knowledge*, London: NLB.

Feyerabend, P.K. (1978), *Science in a Free Society*, London: NLB.

Greene, Joshua E. (2002), 'The Output Decline in Asian Crisis Countries: Investment Aspects', IMF Working Paper, WP/02/25.

Greenpeace (2002), *Toxic Free Asia Tour. Remember Bhopal*, 4 October, http:// archive.greenpeace.org/~toxics/toxfreeasia/rembhopal.html.

International Monetary Fund (IMF) (2000), *World Economic Outlook*, October, Washington, DC: IMF.

Jomo, K.S. (1998), 'Malaysian Debacle: Whose Fault?', *Cambridge Journal of Economics*, **22**: 707–22.

Kawai, Masahiro, Richard Newfarmer and Sergop Schmukler (2001), 'Crisis and Contagion in East Asia: Nine Lessons', Working Paper, World Bank, 27 February.

Kregel, Jan A. (1998), 'Derivatives and Global Capital Flows: Applications to Asia', *Cambridge Journal of Economics*, **22**: 677–92.

Kuhn, T. (1970), *The Structure of Scientific Revolutions: International Encyclopedia of Unified Science*, vol. II, no. 2, 2nd enlarged edn, Chicago: University of Chicago Press.

Lane, Timothy, Atish R. Ghosh, Javir Hamann, Steven Phillips, Marianne Schulze-Ghattas, and Tsidi Tsikata (1999); IMF-Supported Programs in Indonesia, Korea and Thailand: A Preliminary Assessment; review document of design of programs for discussion by executive board in 1998, International Monetary Fund.

Lee, Jong-wha and Changyong Rhee (1998), 'Social Impacts of the Asian Crisis: Policy Challenges and Lessons', prepared for the United Nations Development Programme, Human Development Office.

Mezias, Stephen J. (1994), 'Financial Meltdown as Normal Accidents: The Case of the American Savings and Loan Industry', *Accounting Organizations and Society*, **19** (2): 181–92.

Naples, Michele I. and Nahid Aslanbeigui (1996), 'Is there a Theory of Involuntary Unemployment?', in Nahid Aslanbeigui and Michele I. Naples (eds), *Rethinking Economic Principles: Critical Essays on Introductory Textbooks*, Chicago: Irwin, pp. 109–26.

Nussbaum, Martha (2000), *Women and Human Development: The Capabilities Approach*, Cambridge: Cambridge University Press.

Perrow, Charles (1999), *Normal Accidents: Living with High-Risk Technologies*, Princeton, NJ: Princeton University Press.

Pigou, Arthur Cecil (2002 [1932]), *The Economics of Welfare*, 4th edn, New Brunswick, NJ: Transaction Publications.

Polanyi, Karl (2001 [1944]), *The Great Transformation: The Political and Economic Origins of Our Time*, Boston, MA: Beacon Press.

Popper, Karl (1965), *Conjectures and Refutations: The Growth of Scientific Knowledge*, 2nd edn, New York: Basic Books.

Robbins, Lionel (1927), 'Mr. Hawtrey on the Scope of Economics', *Economica*, **7** (20): 172–8.

Robbins, Lionel (1935), *An Essay on the Nature and Significance of Economic Science*, London: Macmillan.

Sachs, Jeffrey D. (1997), 'IMF is a Power unto Itself', *Financial Times*, 11 December, http://www.stern.nyu.edu/~nroubini/asia/AsiaCrisisSachsViewFT1297.html.

Sellars, Wilfrid (1963), *Science, Perception, and Reality*, New York: Humanities Press.

Sen, Amartya K. (1982), *Poverty and Famines: An Essay on Entitlements and Deprivation*, Oxford: Clarendon Press.

Singh, Ajit and Anna Zammit (2000), 'International Capital Flows: Identifying the Gender Dimension', *World Development*, **28** (2): 1249–68.

Spar, Debora L. (1999), 'The Public Face of Cyberspace', in Inge Kaul, Isabelle Grunberg and Marc A. Stern (eds), *Global Public Goods. International Cooperation in the 21st Century*, published for the UNDP, New York: Oxford University Press.

Stiglitz, Joseph (2000), 'Capital Market Liberalization, Economic Growth, and Instability', *World Development*, **28** (6): 1075–86.

Stiglitz, Joseph E. (2002), *Globalization and Its Discontents*, New York: W.W. Norton.

Stiglitz, Joseph E. and Carl E. Walsh (2002), *Principles of Macroeconomics*, 3rd edn, New York: W.W. Norton.

Taylor, Lance (1998), 'Capital Market Crises: Liberalization, Fixed Exchange Rates and Market Driven Destabilization', *Cambridge Journal of Economics*, **22**: 663–76.

Tobin, James (2000), 'Financial Globalization', *World Development*, **28** (6): 1101–4.

UNDP (1999), *Human Development Report 1999*, New York: Oxford University Press.

Union Carbide Corporation (2001), 'Bhopal', http://www.bhopal.com/review.htm.

United Nations General Assembly (2001), 'Report of the Secretary-General to the UN General Assembly', A/56/447, 10 August, http://www.un.org/ha/Chernobyl/a56–447.pdf.

USAID (2000), 'Working without a Net: Women and the Asian Financial Crisis', *Gender Matters Quarterly*, **2**, January: 1–8, http://www.genderreach.com.

Wade, Robert (1998), 'From 'Miracle' to 'Cronyism': Explaining the Great Asian Slump', *Cambridge Journal of Economics*, **22**: 693–706.

Wahid, Abu N.M. and Mohammad Ikhsan (1997), 'Policy Reforms in Indonesia: A Political Economy Perspective', in Abu N.M. Wahid (ed.), *The ASEAN Region in Transition: A Socioeconomic Perspective*, Aldershot: Ashgate, pp. 25–41.

White, Marceline and Ritu R. Sharma (1999), *The Asian Financial Crisis: Hearing Women's Voices. An Occasional Paper from Women's Edge*, Washington, DC.

World Bank. (1999a), 'Gender Dimensions of the East Asia Crisis', summary of Preliminary Findings, East Asia and Pacific Region, January, Washington, DC: World Bank.

World Bank (1999b), *Global Economic Prospects and the Developing Countries*, Washington, DC: World Bank.

World Bank (2000), *East Asia: Recovery Exhibits Greater Breadth and Depth, but Remains Uneven*, http://www.worldbank.org/eapsocial/inex.html.

6. Institutional Foundations of Economic Growth and Price Stability

Michele I. Naples

The macroeconomic theories of John Maynard Keynes (1964 [1936]), as well as many subsequent analyses, acknowledge the importance of the business climate as facilitator of economic growth. At the micro- and meso-level, institutionalists have outlined the particular profile of financial, industrial, international, or labor-management structures in various periods, identifying those features that were functional or counterproductive for investment and for the stability of such variables as the exchange rate, price level, interest rate, and profitability.

This chapter argues that the macroeconomic and the microeconomic institutional perspectives are linked. Eras characterized by relative profitability, price stability, and economic growth are typically underpinned by a characteristic system of institutions (Bowles et al., 1989; Kotz et al., 1994; Naples, 1998). The institutions are not autonomous islands, but fit together into an articulated whole. Certain common, basic 'rules of the game' inform institutional mechanisms in each sector. The institutional framework represents a paradigm (following Kuhn, 1976), whose axiomatic starting points emerge from a historical process of conflict, experimentation, and negotiation. This institutional paradigm embodies what comes to be perceived as the legitimate and fair approach, reflecting a political as well as an economic consensus.

The crucial role of this system of institutions is to manage conflicts among economic actors in order to minimize any disruptions of economic activity and to orient conflict towards specific legitimate issues. Less disruptive forms of conflict mean increased predictability, which promotes investment and growth. Containing conflict permits a range of issues to be considered settled, or reducible to a common denominator (an income equivalent, e.g., the real wage or the real interest rate). The development of an effective system for conflict management promotes price stability, since real distributional conflicts can be addressed directly, rather than emerging indirectly through wage-price spirals.

This chapter outlines this paradigm approach to macroeconomic stabilization. It applies the approach to the postwar stabilization of international financial and trade relations, and to relations between industry and finance domestically, as they spilled over to the foreign sector. It describes the initial paradigm crisis of the 1930s, the new institutional framework that emerged with its macroeconomic consequences, and its unraveling, then discusses some recent experimentation with new conflict-management mechanisms.

THE INSTITUTIONAL FRAMEWORK FOR MACROECONOMIC STABILIZATION

While many economists treat institutions as a backdrop, institutions are created by conscious human efforts; they are not 'natural'. It takes work and resources to develop institutional mechanisms, so such institutions must have perceived economic benefits in the future. If macroeconomists are to evaluate different historical periods as more or less conducive to investment and economic growth, then macroeconomists must become both sociologists and historians. We must analyze institutions as a set, not as static givens, but as part of a social and systemic whole, with a dynamic and a life cycle that can be studied.

Kuhn's Intellectual Scientific Paradigms

Thomas Kuhn's (1976) influential analysis of the history of natural science provides a helpful analytical apparatus for thinking about institutional history as well. Kuhn described intellectual paradigms as worldviews or conceptual frameworks that focus on certain theories, questions, research apparatus and techniques, while leaving others outside the realm of legitimate science. Each paradigm rests on certain unquestioned axioms that underlie the theory. Normal science involves applying and extending that theory to the task of research, at first addressing the obvious problems.

Over time the theory is applied to more and more areas, and in the regular process of research and discovery certain anomalies or unexpected results emerge. The accumulation of anomalies can present a paradigm crisis, insofar as the established ways of thinking do not seem to work any more. Then scientists experiment with new ideas, and old ideas and methods of research may resurface. This is the most open period intellectually, since there is no single commonly accepted paradigm. Science is diverse, and scientists experiment with new methodologies as well as applying new ideas via their standard research methods. Kuhn emphasized that the history of ideas is nonlinear, since in certain periods previously rejected ideas may be more successful in explaining the anomaly than the most recent paradigm, and may therefore become again more widely accepted.

Kuhn suggested that any consensual new paradigm has to meet several criteria. It has to explain the salient anomalies of the day. It has to be powerful, which means that it is able to explain more information than the previous paradigm, even if it cannot explain every phenomenon that the old paradigm could. A paradigm is more likely to succeed if it is simple, if it provides certain clear overarching themes that distill complex theoretical processes down to basic principles. Once the new paradigm has become accepted (Kuhn describes a process of diffusion that is relatively rapid in supplanting alternative views), those alternatives are not tolerated any more, and their advocates are considered unscientific or out of date.

Institutional Frameworks as Counterparts of Intellectual Paradigms

Kuhn's paradigm framework for understanding scientific revolutions is also helpful for thinking about the kind of institutional revolutions that have characterized certain epochs in US history, in particular the post-Civil War Reconstruction and the depression of 1873–99, and the 1930s New Deal and Great Depression of 1929–41. Consider how characteristics of intellectual paradigms in natural science translate to institutional paradigms for social behavior. First, the idea of paradigm itself as a worldview suggests that given institutions reflect a pattern of thinking about what 'rules of the game' will effectively manage conflicts so as to provide a stable macroeconomic framework. Once a particular paradigm or institutional framework for macroeconomic stabilization (or IFMS) has gained general acceptance, the ensuing normal application of this framework on an expanding scale permits institution-building, conceivably over decades, in accordance with its basic parameters.

As the IFMS matures, certain signs of its limitations in managing conflict emerge; these correspond to Kuhn's anomalies. The institutional framework does not prevent conflicts; rather, it contains them so as to manage them effectively. The logical application of this institutional framework on an expanded scale brings out the inherent limits of the institutions themselves. For instance, the very success of the IFMS leads to economic growth, accumulated wealth, and expansion of the profit-driven market economy to more and more parts of daily life and more parts of the world. Institutional paradigms differ from intellectual paradigms because human beings are not just cogs in the institutional wheel; they are sentient beings who act in their self-interest. As players acting in their own individual or community interest push the limits of the system, the holes and problems in the IFMS emerge.

The institutional framework for macroeconomic stabilization differs from an intellectual paradigm because shifting macroeconomic conditions can impact on the balance of power among categories of economic participants, with implications for the IFMS itself. For instance, as growth raises capital-utilization rates and profitability, fewer businesses and banks fail. This encourages both lenders and borrowers to lower their assessments of the riskiness of debt. Continued growth reinforces the view that there will be no reckoning. Mild recessions, reflecting the success of demand management and financial restructuring through the IFMS, provide an opportunity to clean up balance sheets. Yet 'risk drift' continues, as economic actors become increasingly willing to take on more and more risk, and debt–equity ratios trend upward (Minsky, 1975; Isenberg, 2002).

When failed expectations and crucial miscalculations do cause profitability problems, the initial effort is to buy time and weather the storm. (Examples include the 1970 suspension of the Bretton Woods international financial system, the 1978 Bankruptcy Reform Act which permitted companies to file for Chapter 11 protection from creditors, and the 1980 deregulation of the Savings and Loans [S&Ls]). The profit squeeze forces companies to find ways to cut costs, including costs associated with funding institutional mechanisms (e.g., the early 1980s reluctance to fund any S&L clean-up). The initial efforts to dismantle regulatory institutions may be functional for the individual financial institution, company, sector or country, because it is a temporary reprieve from economic distress. The dysfunctional consequences of unregulated conflict will only appear over time. So the success of the institutional framework in contributing to economic growth can bring about its opposite, the unraveling of the IFMS and a long-wave economic slowdown or downturn.

There are other avenues whereby an institutional framework for macroeconomic stabilization can unwind. As Kuhn recognized, no scientific paradigm can explain every natural phenomenon; similarly, the IFMS is a paradigm, but not a cure-all. The institutional framework may not succeed in containing conflict, which explodes out of the box, outside the rules that had hitherto been established. Alternatively, the IFMS may succeed in containing conflict, but in doing so economic actors increasingly sense their institutionalized powerlessness, lack of due process, or unequal access to these conflict-resolution institutions. As a consequence, the institutions themselves can become delegitimized. Or new terrains of conflict may appear, as when companies seeking new markets run into conflict with traditional societies not previously within the paradigm's reach. The failure of the institutional framework for macroeconomic stabilization to contain these conflicts may undermine the functionality of its institutions more generally.

During a widespread institutional or paradigm crisis, as Kuhn suggested, the accumulated anomalies force a re-examination of received ideas. With respect to institutions, the old rules do not work any more the way they were intended to. It takes financial and human resources to manage conflict effectively. If the resources prove inadequate, the mechanisms do not work as well, and eventually they may be consciously dismantled through 'deregulation'.

As Keynes perceived with respect to saving, there can be unintended negative macroeconomic consequences from behaviors that are individually rational. For instance, institutional breakdown expands the range of outcomes, so that any expected result has a lower probability. It becomes more likely that companies will guess wrong about future trends, and bankruptcy becomes more probable. Thus the paradigm crisis expands to an economic crisis.

During the crisis phase, previously ignored regulatory ideas become legitimate to discuss, and older views resurface (e.g., the policy discussions about banks' moral hazard and the need to limit deposit insurance in the early 1990s[1]). This may be less about open-mindedness than about inertia and anxiety: without a new paradigm, many will hold on to the old ways, fearful that 'anarchy' or open conflict would be worse. While rhetoric asserting political coherence may hold sway, in practice diversity of opinion prevails as to how the economy works, and how and how much it should be deregulated or restructured. This increased diversity of views and de facto tolerance are the preconditions for experimentation. Without a clear roadmap as to how to proceed, policy-makers are more willing to try out novel ways of doing things. Often the smaller political regions take precedence over the international or federal level in terms of policy formation, as when President Clinton threw welfare policy into the states' laps and explicitly asked them to provide the federal government with some innovative alternatives on which to base new policy.

Furthermore, contractual innovations may pave the way for new institutional mechanisms or controls. For instance, traditional institutional arrangements permitted small banks to lend their excess reserves to large regional correspondent banks at 0 per cent interest, in exchange for certain services the large banks could provide for them, e.g., inviting them to participate in syndicated loans. The high interest rates of the late 1970s and early 1980s led small banks to chafe at this arrangement, and a private institution called the federal funds market was born. All banks could lend excess reserves to other banks overnight or for a short period, and pay the federal-funds rate. That rate was determined by the supply and demand of excess reserves. It became clear in the early 1980s when the Fed was tightening the money supply that this put pressure on the federal-funds market, shrinking the total amount of reserves in the system and therefore raising the federal-funds rate. A new Fed indicator and target was born.

Initially, those with the most power may hold sway in the rule-setting process. But ultimately the disenfranchised may hit rock bottom and protests may destabilize the system – consider the 1930s union drives and sit-down strikes, the 2001 anti-IMF riots in Argentina, and 2002 conflict and attempted coup in Venezuela.

The next sections examine the rise of the institutional framework for macroeconomic stabilization that developed during the 1930s and was applied on an expanded scale through the 1950s to early 1970s, its dismantling and continued breakdown through the 1980s, and attempts at restructuring into the early 1990s. The focus will be on international financial relations, and domestic financial events and conflicts that had international dimensions or consequences.

THE HISTORICAL DEVELOPMENT OF INSTITUTIONAL FRAMEWORKS

The Breakdown of the Institutional Framework between the World Wars

The 1930s–40s were a time of economic and international political crisis. The international economic malaise of the 1930s led to beggar-thy-neighbor trade barriers which contributed to a collapse in world trade over the period 1931–33, with associated large multiplier effects in reducing GDP. The breakdown of international trade relations appears to have been a major factor in turning the recession of 1929–31 to the depression of 1931–33.

In 1931 the New York Fed acted in the interest of the money-center banks by raising the discount rate in an effort to attract foreign capital and prevent US suspension of convertibility to gold, knowing Britain would be hard-pressed not to suspend convertibility. Should the US sustain convertibility, New York banks could potentially supplant London banks as lenders to the world since the US currency unit would be perceived as a more stable currency unit (especially as the unit of account for debt) than the British pound. This was largely a successful strategy: the US suspended convertibility briefly, then returned to a fixed exchange rate with gold (although to be honored on more limited basis than previously). This financial success, however, had an economic price: high interest rates in New York forced the interest rate up throughout the US, contributing to the economic decline.

In large part as a result of economic instability, the early 1930s were politically unsettled times. Experimentation at the federal level in the US took the form of the New Deal; in parts of Europe, socialists and fascists came to power. There was a revolution off the US coast in Cuba in 1934. World war broke out in Europe, then in the Pacific. Britain and Germany were both theaters of war, and by 1944 the US had emerged as the clear political and economic victor.

The Emergent Institutional Framework

The financial regulatory framework developed in the 1930s is well known. It included the creation of bank-deposit insurance and firewalls between different financial sectors (S&Ls would handle home mortgages, commercial banks could not speculate in the stock market, there would be no inter-state banking, etc.). A series of regulations sought to reduce speculative behavior (high margins for stock purchases) and maintain the viability of the structure (for example Regulation Q's ceiling on deposit interest to protect Savings and Loan institutions, which lent long-term at low rates, from having to pay high rates on deposits).[2] Discount lending was expanded to include loans against all good collateral, not just the previous limited categories. The Federal Reserve Bank was given a governing body, the seven-member Board of Governors, who aided the Fed chair in policy decisions and improved Fed legitimacy. The 12-member Open-Market Committee provided the New York Fed with a voice but not control, as four of the other regional Fed chairs and the governors also would vote on regular Fed policy. It was hoped that this new structure would overcome the historic problems of strong regions and a weak central Fed.

A paradigm for international economic relations emerged from negotiations at Bretton Woods, New Hampshire in 1944 (see Block, 1977). The US was able to translate its political and economic strength into the Bretton Woods system, which made the US dollar both the unit of account for international loans and also the means of payment for settling such debts. Simultaneously, the New York money-center banks became lenders of dollars to the world.

Keynes's outline for international trade favored national autonomy, to effectively isolate a nation's macroeconomic policy from countervailing international forces by maintaining trade barriers. The Americans successfully promoted 'free trade' or the reduction of import tariffs and quotas; in the 1950s the first rounds of the General Agreement on Tariffs and Trade (or GATT) were negotiated. Such negotiations were revisited for decades, and the GATT achieved a gradual reduction in the trade barriers that had been built at the onset of the depression.

Economists in 1946 predicted a sharp collapse as had happened after World War I, but the crisis was averted in part because the parameters for the new institutional framework for macroeconomic stabilization had been identified. The emerging consensus served to rally resources around institution-building and conflict containment.

Aspects of the US restructuring of the domestic financial sector had international ramifications. In 1946, the Fed's mandate was expanded beyond its original charter, which had required it to ensure the health of the banking system in order to protect savers' deposits. The 1946 Employment Act required the Fed to fight both unemployment and inflation. In 1952 the Fed-Treasury Accord promised that the Fed would buy Treasury debt and maintain a stable, low interest rate as long as any expansionary fiscal policy was non-inflationary (Epstein and Schor, 1995). This Accord institutionalized an accommodating central bank whose policy would be to maintain economic growth by not permitting fiscal policy to crowd out private investment.[3]

In addition to avoiding a recurrence of depression, the new institutions were initially successful at preventing inflation. All economics students know that inflation characteristically hurts those on fixed incomes. Most learn that lenders, to the extent that long-term loans are made at fixed interest rates, are the primary fixed-income industry of the economy, and face major profitability problems in the face of accelerating inflation. Bondholders are doubly damaged, insofar as they sought liquidity through purchasing bonds rather than making long-term loans. In addition to their returns failing to keep up with inflation, the current value of their holdings will fall. An increase in the inflation rate will force market interest rates up as new bond-purchasers build in the expected erosion of their nominal returns by inflation. A higher interest rate means any bonds currently held by Wall Street (brokerage houses, bond-dealers, insurance companies, cash managers for large corporations) will have a lower nominal market price, while the loans on banks' balance sheets still retain their nominal value. Bondholders' real net worth drops.

The combination of international economic stability and domestic restructuring of the financial sector to promote stability for the most part averted the problems both of inflation and of depression, creating the conditions for the extraordinarily healthy period of the 1950s to the early 1970s. Both business failures and bank failures almost disappeared, running at the lowest levels in the 20th century. As this environment was sustained, banks and financial institutions became more and more willing to extend credit with lessening fear of default risk.

THE POSTWAR INSTITUTIONAL FRAMEWORK EXPANDS AND ERODES: 1950s–70s

Financial Developments

The sustained growth of the 1940s and 1950s turned to a boom in the 1960s, in part because of the impetus from expenditures on the Vietnam War. During the 1960s, two financial innovations provided the means for banks to circumvent Fed restrictions, reducing the Fed's power to control the US money supply. In 1962, negotiable certificates of deposit (NCDs) were created, for large denominations (at least $100,000). These NCDs permitted companies to lock in the current market interest rate, while providing some liquidity before the term of the CD. A five-year CD could be cashed in after three years for a fee if another company seeking a two-year CD was willing to take it over. This innovation benefited banks because it helped them to compete with the otherwise more liquid bond market in placing CDs.

Banks also favored CDs because typically the Fed did not require any reserve requirements to be held against such long-term savings, allowing the bank to lend out the full amount. This provided banks an avenue to expand their lending capabilities via liability management. Banks could effectively change the average reserve requirement they were subject to by getting customers to change the form of their deposits from checking to short-term savings to long-term savings. They could offer toasters or coffeepots as extra inducements to customers to open savings accounts when they sought to make more loans but the Fed was tightening reserve requirements. So this institutional innovation undermined the effectiveness of the postwar IFMS.

The second innovation developed in the 1950s, but was not important in magnitude until the middle 1960s. The Eurodollar market was born of British banks' desire to continue to engage in international lending, despite the dollar's importance after the Bretton Woods Agreement. London banks created dollar-denominated accounts that were CDs, and in turn kept their reserves as CDs in large New York banks. The balance they lent out as dollar-denominated loans. Because these were not checkable deposits, they did not have to deal directly with the US Federal Reserve System. Since they were dollar deposits, they were not subject to regulation by British authorities.

In 1967, when the Fed tried to tighten the money supply, the availability of the Eurodollar market meant that US banks and their customers moved their NCDs and lending overseas to the bank's London subsidiary. In this way they escaped regulations, and the effect of the Fed's tight-money policy was seriously dampened. The Fed ended up stepping away from tight money as the booming US economy induced companies to continue to seek loans for their projects, and banks to try to find some way to lend to them.

While the Bretton Woods system had created a mechanism to permit countries with overvalued or undervalued currencies to devalue and revalue in a predictable manner, the system was not designed to handle a devaluation for the currency of account, i.e., the dollar. In 1970 the US suspended convertibility of the dollar at a fixed peg to gold, even for foreign governments. The dollar was allowed to float in foreign currency markets, meaning that its exchange rate would be determined by market forces. The Fed continued to intervene to prevent wide swings in the exchange rate. This was called a 'dirty' float. Subsequent inflationary pressures were an expression of the weakening of the IFMS's success in managing conflict over the income distribution, but were initially abated by wage and price controls until 1974.

Trade Developments

The success of the postwar institutional framework for macroeconomic stability led to sustained growth internationally from the 1950s through the early 1970s. After World War I, the Allies had forced Germany to pay reparations to reimburse them for the cost of the war. Arguably this external debt was the foremost cause of the hyperinflation experienced by Germany in the early 1920s. Keynes had warned that the best way to secure the peace was to integrate Germany into the European economy through the expansion of trade based on Germany's economic recovery, not growth-hampering debt. After World War II, the Allies followed Keynes's earlier proposal, and contributed towards reorienting the German and Japanese economies towards peacetime production, including providing aid through the Marshall Plan.

In the 1950s Japan exported cheap light-manufacturing goods. By the 1980s Japan had emerged as a technology giant. German automobiles were already starting to compete with the American 'big three' in the 1960s. American manufacturers' market shares, and institutionalized oligopolistic pricing practices, were steadily eroded, both domestically and in the world market, by the economic rise of Germany and Japan. By the 1980s–90s, new competition appeared from the so-called newly industrializing countries (NICs), or four tigers (Taiwan, South Korea, Hong Kong, Singapore).

The US before-tax profit rate peaked in the middle 1960s, declining partly as a result of increasing foreign competition. Thereafter, US companies increasingly borrowed to maintain expenditure levels, and debt–equity ratios rose steadily from their postwar lows, after adjusting for each recession's balance-sheet restructuring.

In the early 1970s a new raw-materials cartel was formed in an effort to cooperate in charging high prices. Most such cartels are short-lived, given the pressures from competition, but the Organization of Petroleum Exporting

Countries (OPEC) had a major advantage: one producer (Saudi Arabia) met 40 per cent of world demand. By organizing as a group of countries rather than companies, OPEC could play on nationalist sentiment in the Middle East. When OPEC quadrupled the price of a barrel of oil in 1973, US oil companies were able to benefit from the oil-price increase, prompting discussions of a windfall profits tax.

OPEC raised oil prices again in 1977–78, which further contributed to a burst of oil-exploration activity. Discoveries in Mexico, Venezuela, and in the North Sea fueled new lending to oil-rich countries. Continued high raw material prices in other sectors, together with accelerating US inflation in the late 1970s, encouraged further investments in developing countries exporting primary products in high demand. As the US profit rate declined, US bankers looked to other sources for borrowers, and increasingly lent to foreign companies and/or governments for economic-development projects.

By the early 1980s four of the top 10 US banks (Chase, Manufacturers Hanover, Chemical, and Citibank) had lent more than 100 per cent of their net worth to clients in a handful of Latin American countries (Brazil, Argentina, Venezuela, Mexico) that were at risk of defaulting on their loans. Both government regulations and financial prudence prevented banks from lending more than 1 per cent of the net worth to any single borrower. However, the fact that the borrowers were grouped in such a small number of economic domains exposed the banks to both the default risk and exchange-rate risk that emerged with the shift in US monetary policy in 1979.

THE END OF THE POSTWAR FED-TREASURY ACCORD AND ITS INTERNATIONAL CONSEQUENCES

After the US suspended the dollar's convertibility to gold in 1970, the market decline in the dollar's exchange rate made imports more expensive. By cheapening US exports abroad, the dollar's decline permitted US companies to raise their dollar-prices while lowering their foreign sales prices. These factors exacerbated the ongoing inflationary pressures from the relatively low unemployment associated with Vietnam War expenditures. The Nixon administration implemented wage and price controls in an ad hoc temporary effort to cut short a wage-price inflationary spiral. The imbalances generated were already inducing political pressures to suspend the controls when OPEC catapulted oil prices upward in 1973–74. While the drop in industrial production as the US pulled out of Vietnam reduced inflationary pressures, the return of relatively rapid economic growth after the counter-cyclical tax cut in early 1975 meant that inflation returned.

President Carter appointed an industrialist (William Miller) to head the Fed. Miller's accommodation of the highest inflation rates that the US had experienced in the modern era signaled the end of the Fed-Treasury Accord. The innate conflict of interest between finance and industry over real interest rates would become open conflict. The immediate impact was that corporate debt was lightened by the accelerating inflation, and economic growth continued, albeit at a slower pace than during the Vietnam War.

However, lenders who saw their balance sheets and profits being inflated away became less and less sanguine about making dollar-denominated loans. The real rate of interest (i_{real}) is

$$i_{real} = (i_{nominal} - P*)/(1+P*)$$

where $i_{nominal}$ is the nominal or market interest rate, and P* is the rate of change of prices or the rate of inflation. In the late 1970s the real interest rate fell into the negative range for Saving & Loans Institutions, since they were charging fixed nominal rates of 4–6 per cent on existing home mortgages they held. Inflation in the producer price index exceeded 6 per cent from 1978 through 1981, peaking at 12.8 per cent in 1979 (US Council of Economic Advisors, 1999, p. 406). By 1979 large international loans were actually being calculated in terms of a basket of currencies, a weighted share of Deutschmarks, yen, British pounds, French francs, and US dollars. The principle was to protect lenders' asset-values by hedging risks, presuming that if the dollar continued to depreciate, the yen or Deutschmark or other currency would appreciate, so the total real value represented by the loan repayments would remain unchanged. Fear of an impending depreciation of the dollar as a result of accelerating inflation prompted a panicked flight from dollar-denominated assets.

Accelerating inflation in the late 1970s was an expression of the breakdown of the institutional framework for macroeconomic stabilization, which in turn further undermined that framework. Uncontained conflict over income distribution (between employers and workers, between finance and industry) contributed to inflation, as each set of economic actors tried to avoid real-income losses by passing on cost increases to others. Given a finance-sector institutional framework premised on relative price stability, the late 1970s inflation caused substantial dislocations in that postwar financial structure. It was in this period that Savings and Loan institutions began to face bankruptcy, since their nominal rates on deposits exceeded their fixed nominal rates earned from mortgages.

Tight Money, High Interest Rates, and the Strong Dollar

In the effort to restore confidence, the banks succeeded in lobbying for a new Fed chair who would represent their interests. Paul Volcker was known as a monetarist, and entered vowing a drastic reduction in the money supply. While the exigencies of presidential politics, and an effort not to be blamed for Carter's failed reelection, induced a temporary respite from the monetary contraction in 1980, by 1981 monetary policy was so tight that the prime interest rate (charged to the best corporate borrowers) hit 21 per cent. Since this translated to a real interest rate of 9 per cent, the swing in the rates realized by banks and financiers from the late 1970s was a span of 13 real percentage points. There had been a shift in policy influence from industry to finance, since industry now had to pay these higher rates. The end of the Fed-Treasury Accord was expressed in this more open warfare between the two sectors.

The high interest rates put many savings and loans (S&Ls) in effective bankruptcy, since their assets consisted of long-term mortgages at fixed lower rates. In 1980 Congress had doubled federal deposit insurance to cover $100,000 worth of deposits, which helped mollify larger depositors concerned about the health of the thrifts; but it also meant these highly leveraged financial institutions could gamble without exposing themselves to bank runs, since insured deposits meant less depositor scrutiny. A 1982 law made it easier for S&Ls to diversify into non-traditional assets, effectively dismantling this part of the IFMS. By taking down some of the firewalls between S&Ls and other savings institutions, the hope was that S&Ls could restore profitability.

The Federal Savings and Loan Insurance Corporation (FSLIC) did not have enough resources to finance the cost of shutting down all the marginal S&Ls, and the Reagan administration's focus on increasing defense spending did not allow space for channeling money down the black hole of S&L insolvency. So banking regulators had to revise their notions of what collateral could count as part of a bank's net worth (which regulations set at 6 per cent of total assets). They determined that a bank's or S&Ls 'good will', which referred to established marketing relationships with depositors and borrowers, could count as up to one-half of the institution's net worth. Previously 6 per cent of total assets would act as a buffer against failure, and a drop to 3 per cent would put a bank on a problem-bank list; now effectively a net worth of 3 per cent beyond good will was being deemed healthy, providing very little capital cushion against bank failure. This policy of 'forbearance', which was meant to buy time for the S&Ls, in fact increased the scope for and incentive to gamble in risky assets in the hope of winning big returns and avoiding the otherwise probable failure.

High real interest rates provided incentives for resources to shift from real to financial investment. Capital flows into stock market and real estate rather than real investment were self-reinforcing, fueling a speculative bubble by the mid-1980s. The economic recovery out of the 1982–83 depression-level unemployment was consequently slow.

The run-up in interest rates had international as well as domestic implications. Foreign financiers were attracted to the opportunity to earn high real interest rates in the US, and capital inflow increased; in parallel, capital outflows were reduced since pension funds and insurance companies had no reason to seek opportunities abroad when domestic options were so profitable. Both of these results contributed to an increase in the US exchange rate, or 'strengthening' of the dollar.[4] From late 1979 to mid-1981 the US exchange rate rose 80 per cent, despite 12 per cent inflation. (Inflation would normally tend to depreciate a currency, each inflated dollar being able to buy less.)

Financial interests benefit from a strengthening dollar. Speculators and arbitrageurs recognize that if they make financial investments in dollar-denominated accounts, they will gain doubly: they will earn interest on, for instance, Treasury bills, and they will capture the benefits of the dollar's appreciation when they return to their home currency. Anyone who bought dollar-denominated assets in 1980 and sold them in mid-1981 reaped a 55 per cent annual return over and above any interest earnings.

The extraordinarily expensive dollar (overvalued from the perspective of US trade) had negative consequences for US industrialists and the unemployed as well: it became very difficult for US manufacturers to export their products, or to compete with imports that had suddenly dropped to almost half of their former prices. Because import/export contracts are often made a year or two in advance, it took time for the full impact to be felt. While the US exchange rate continued to rise through 1985, real US exports fell 25 per cent from their high in 1980 (when they were 8 per cent of GDP) to their low in 1983 and 1985 (when they were 5 per cent of GDP). Real imports also peaked in 1980 (when they were almost 9 per cent of GDP), and fell with the economic recession; but the low in their real value in 1985 was only 15 per cent lower than their peak, and their share of GDP was therefore only slightly lower, having only fallen to 8 per cent. This decline in exports and relative rise in imports contributed to the steep depression-level unemployment of 1982–83, and was particularly bad in the relatively more unionized manufacturing sectors. It spurred efforts already underway to decertify existing unions. Congressional protectionist legislation was only blocked by presidential veto.

The heightened capital inflow generated a demand for financial services, and Wall Street boomed. Foreign companies and countries complained that their domestic capital flight was having excruciating consequences. In Spain in 1982, where unemployment measured 22 per cent, a political poster vented, 'que dolores nos dan los dolares!', or 'what pains dollars give us'. This redirection of short-term funds to the US played an important role in a liquidity crunch and a series of defaults on foreign loans by Third World countries in 1982–83. The high exchange rate itself was the primary cause, since banks had sought to protect themselves from exchange-rate risk by passing that risk to the borrowers. That is, when the US exchange rate strengthened precipitously, the exchange rates of other countries fell precipitously. So for these countries' companies to repay fixed dollar-denominated amounts required generating almost twice as much domestic income as usual, hardly feasible in the context of a global economic downturn. In 1982 Mexico threatened default, and Brazil, Argentina, and Venezuela were also financially vulnerable. Many of the top US banks were immediately implicated, since they had lent funds extensively in these countries. Other money-center banks that had made loans to developing countries were also threatened. Ironically, the high interest rates consequent upon the breakdown of the Fed-Treasury Accord ended up indirectly damaging the banks.

Business Failures and Bailouts

There were several significant US financial shock 'events' in this period (Wolfson, in Dymski et al., 1993, pp. 141–3; Wolfson, 1994). In 1980, the third largest US automaker, Chrysler, had difficulty raising funds. Congress invoked the 'too big to fail' doctrine and guaranteed a $1 million loan for Chrysler, which it ultimately repaid. In 1984 Continental Illinois, the eleventh largest US bank, was also deemed too big to fail. Government regulators guaranteed all of the bank's liabilities; finding no purchasers of its assets and liabilities, the government ran the bank for two years, effectively nationalizing it. It was ultimately divided into pieces and sold to several buyers.

While for most of the postwar period bank and business failures had been almost nonexistent, business and bank failures accelerated after 1979. For the first time the Federal Deposit Insurance Corporation (FDIC) started to consider payout a viable option for liquidating a failed bank. In principle, the FDIC guarantees only the first $100,000 of any deposit. While for most individuals that is adequate coverage, for most businesses it is not. As was true for Continental Illinois, if some other bank or banks will purchase the bank's assets and assume the bank's liabilities (called 'purchase and assumption'), then all deposits are de facto insured. In 1974 when Franklin National Bank had faced financial difficulties, the Fed extended discount loans to tide the bank over until a purchaser could be found. Then not only domestic deposits, but also Eurodollar deposits in Franklin's London branch were effectively protected, despite the fact that only domestic deposits pay deposit insurance.

In the 1980s, when it became apparent that banks and S&Ls caught short by the interest-rate run-ups had liabilities far in excess of their assets, the FDIC moved to 'payout', primarily for smaller banks (Dymski, in Dymski et al., 1993, p. 125). Under payout, depositors were given their $100,000 immediately, and the government insurer gradually liquidated other assets, ultimately returning as many of the deposits as they were able. But large depositors were not fully covered, and took losses. Notice that no interest accrued during the delay either.

The financial volatility in the US left a relative vacuum in international lending. Japanese companies' search for offshore production facilities contributed to Japan's increase in foreign direct investment through the 1980s, especially in South Korea, Taiwan, Hong Kong and Singapore (the NICs). Japan quickly became the leading world net exporter of capital, primarily through its banks and financiers buying foreign financial assets, including US Treasury bills. Net outflows rose from $3 billion in 1977 to almost $137 billion in 1987 (Zarsky, in Epstein et al., 1993, p. 270).

This period of international realignment of economic power and associated 'free-market' unleashing of open conflict within the US gave way to new, creative ways of rethinking how to manage international economic relationships, and domestic financial problems. The next section summarizes these experiments, with their mixed record of successes and failures.

EXPERIMENTS WITH A NEW INSTITUTIONAL FRAMEWORK: 1970s–90s

The period from the late 1970s to the present has been characterized by paradigm crisis and experimentation international financial and industrial interests promoted efforts to continue to manage exchange rates despite the end of Bretton Woods. In 1975, representatives of the G6 nations (the US, UK, West Germany, France, Italy, and Japan) met in France to develop mechanisms to deal with exchange-rate adjustments despite floating exchange rates. The US invited its North American neighbor, Canada, to join in 1976. The goal of economic cooperation in the interests of international stability was realized with respect to coordinated demand-management and agreement to reduce trade barriers (the Tokyo Round) in 1978.

But successful international Keynesian coordination fell apart in the face of US President Reagan's and UK Prime Minister Thatcher's free-market initiatives. The domestic lifting of restrictions on market processes meant reckonings previously forestalled came home to roost. As the United States began to recover from the 1982–83 recession, it became clear that permitting the dollar to continue to rise would have permanent consequences for US competitiveness. Once American consumers started to buy Japanese imports, their brand loyalties would realign, and US car companies faced permanent erosion of their market; the same was true in other industries. The US business failure rate reached depression levels in 1986 and 1993 (Naples and Arifaj, 1997), but even more deleterious was the fact that it was now large brand-name companies that were failing, with associated contractionary economic pressures (Naples, 1997).

In 1985 the new Treasury Secretary, Jim Baker, promoted a return to G7 (G6 plus Canada) cooperation on economic policy, this time with respect to reducing the overvalued dollar in an orderly fashion. The Humphrey-Hawkins bill of 1978 had required the Fed chair to make biannual presentations and answer questions on its policies. This move towards a more transparent Fed policy was given further impetus by Baker's public and international approach to US monetary policy. Since the international dollar drain had also meant fewer domestic financial resources in other advanced countries, Baker's proposal was adopted, and a cooperative effort to reduce the value of the dollar was announced by G7 finance ministers in 1985 at the Plaza Hotel (the Plaza Accord). In some sense the Executive, i.e., the Treasury Secretary, was taking over the prerogatives of the Fed chair for exchange-rate management usually achieved by buying and selling foreign currencies. But he was also selling the desired US Fed policy to other central banks.

Any financier with dollar-denominated investments stood to lose from a drop in the value of the dollar. But by providing coordination among central banks, and advance notice of the chosen policy, the G7 permitted financiers to hedge their financial risks. The predictability of ensuing events dramatically narrowed the scope for speculative activity, with its potentially destabilizing influence, and helped to prevent financial panic. By early 1987, when the finance ministers announced in Paris that the dollar had reached its appropriate level, its trade-weighted value was about two-thirds of its previous level.

This administered depreciation averted a repeat of the 1979 international crisis of confidence, when foreign financiers had dumped dollars. However, the substantial decline in the value of the dollar may have contributed to the stock market crash later in 1987. The run-up in stock prices was initially fed by the search for dollar-denominated assets to serve as stores of value for foreign capital inflows. There ensued a self-propelling bubble of inflating stock values whose momentum must have been drained by the reduced capital inflow after the Plaza Accord.

A second contributor to the extraordinary stock-market gains in the mid-1980s was modern buying on margin: leveraged buyouts (LBOs). While regulations prohibited speculation in individual stocks with less than 50 per cent down, individuals could speculate on the rise in value of an entire company by borrowing to buy the company, on the promise to improve performance or to cash in assets so effectively that stockholders would benefit. It has been estimated that the demand for money for financial transactions during the stock-market boom was many times the demand for current real transactions. As Pollin (1997, p. 324) recognized, relative illiquidity in the financial sector would follow from such borrowing to finance asset purchases just as much as from borrowing to finance real investment. This non-goods transactions demand for money also contributed to perceived volatility in money velocity, and made the Fed's job of projecting demand much harder.

The brokerage house Drexel Burnham Lambert made the market for junk bonds, buying and selling the high-interest rate debt with low credit ratings associated with LBOs.[5] They served as intermediary to secure refinancing for problem loans during the 1980s, until their own liquidity crisis in 1989 forced them into bankruptcy, and the LBO market evaporated as a source of funds.

The October 1987 crash was almost twice as large as the 1929 one-day drop (22 per cent vs 12 per cent). The day after the crash, there were no buyers of stock, but plenty of offers to sell. With such disproportions the New York Stock Exchange (NYSE) faced the prospect of having to close the exchange to give traders time to 'appreciate the fundamentals' and identify bargains to buy. But the 1980s had also witnessed the rise of offshore stock exchanges. Markets for US stocks and bonds were being made in Hong Kong, Tokyo, London, and Zurich, among others. To the extent that the regulatory environment in the advanced countries can be circumvented by trades abroad, the NYSE was already on the defensive in a world reporting round-the-clock changes in stock values, and international opportunities for arbitrage and speculation. Maintaining the stature of the NYSE served the interests of both the major industrialists who sat on the exchange and the financiers who made trades every day. The incentive for US financial and industrial interests to work together prompted an unusual intervention by the Federal Reserve.

In this environment the Fed chair, Alan Greenspan, expanded his job description. In cooperation with the Securities and Exchange Commission (SEC), and NYSE, he went out on the floor of the stock exchange and persuaded large US corporations to buy back their cheapened stocks and put a floor under the stock-market collapse. They did, and the NYSE did not have to close. More in keeping with his traditional purview, he also promised to act as lender of last resort to area banks and financial institutions, and to provide plenty of liquidity. In so doing he helped contain the ensuing depression-magnitude collapse in asset values, such as real estate, to the adjacent states (New Jersey, New York, Connecticut), and staved off nationwide depression.

In 1986 Republic Bank Holding Company, based in the southwest US, had failed. It had not even been on the comptroller of the currency's problem bank list, and yet threatened a quarter of the FDIC fund. The financial ill-health of the savings and loans continued, and state insurance funds for savings banks ran out of funds and there were bank runs in Ohio and Maryland in 1986. But it was not until after the stock market crash that people like Danny Wall, head of the Federal Home Loan Bank Board, got Congress's attention.

In 1989 the Financial Institutions Reform, Recovery, and Enforcement Act (FIRREA) was passed in an effort to address S&L and FSLIC insolvency. Congress initially allocated $50 billion to finance the closing of the failed S&Ls. (Some two-thirds of the S&Ls would ultimately fail; the newly created Resolution Trust Corporation that took over failed S&Ls became the largest financial institution in the country.) S&Ls were once again limited on their asset side to home mortgages. Deposit insurance was restructured from a series of autonomous institutions to one overarching FDIC, including a commercial bank fund (BIF) and savings insurance fund (SAIF) under its umbrella. The FIRREA also mandated new risk-based capital requirements for both savings and commercial banks. For the latter, capital requirements had to rise from 6 to 8 per cent by 1992.

This 33 per cent increase in capital requirements would be difficult to meet by raising the numerator of the net-worth ratio, that is, convincing new investors to buy into a bank with no new expansion plans, and thereby diluting current bank-owners' stock. The more feasible approach was to contract bank assets by extending fewer loans. New loans would be made to a narrower customer set, and involve less default risk. The magnitude of the potential credit contraction was draconian for a three-year period – *ceteris paribus*, a 25 per cent decline in the money supply.[6] Fed efforts to maintain liquidity and low short-term Treasury bill rates helped mitigate the problem. Yet in early 1993, when President Clinton arrived in office, corporations complained widely about the credit crunch.

Numerous banks did not make the cut. From 1989 through 1990, about 10 per cent of US commercial banks failed, beyond those that had been acquired or had merged. This quantitative difference from the Great Depression, when one-third of commercial banks failed, had qualitative implications: there was no Depression, but a managed destruction of capital. Centralization of control, and concentration of financial power in the hands of a few large banks, accelerated. Because the reformed FDIC needed the resources provided by 'purchase and assumption', inter-state banking limitations were relaxed, feeding concentration in the financial industry. The FDIC faced a 'liquidity crunch' in this period, which was not publicly called insolvency. The FDIC Improvement Act of 1991 recognized the problem and allowed the FDIC to borrow from the Treasury to remain viable; it also raised deposit insurance rates. With the Depositor Preference Law (embedded in the 1993 Tax Act), Congress required the FDIC to rely on payout or purchase and assumption and ended the 'too big to fail' premise that had led to the temporary nationalization of Continental Illinois and tiding over of Franklin National. It made non-deposit liabilities strictly second in line for deposit insurance, and only as subject to the bank collateral available.

With the FIRREA's realignment of net-worth ratios and therefore the money supply, Congress inadvertently usurped a place traditionally reserved for the central bank. Was this set of legislation, as in the 1930s, the basis of a new institutional framework? Certainly, in the late 1980s to early 1990s the US addressed the issue of bankrupt financial institutions, where Japan has yet to face up to similar problems. In fact, Japanese banks have been financially fragile since the 1997 Asian Crisis, with so many associated defaults. This may have long-run competitive advantages for US financial institutions. Or it may be that when once again large financial institutions are the ones facing bankruptcy, the US will have to relearn the lessons of the Great Depression.

CONCLUSION

The macroeconomy is most stable and predictable when an institutional framework to manage conflicts over income distribution has been established. This history of one strand of the IFMS addresses systems to contain conflicts between industry and finance, domestically and globally, and so to promote macroeconomic stability. In particular, this history differentiates the late 1940s–60s period of relative employment and price stability, where a paradigmatic institutional framework prevailed, from the 1970s–90s period when deregulation and paradigm crisis contributed to economic uncertainty, employment volatility, and accelerating inflation.

While the United States' 1980s experience with economic duress helped it achieve some institutional innovation ahead of other countries, this is not yet a basis for renewed macroeconomic stability and growth. Much as state-level innovative policies in the 1930s could not secure national stability, national policies in the 1990s have not secured international macroeconomic stability. Globalization continues to undermine the effectiveness of national regulation, much as the emergence of national markets undermined state or provincial policies in an earlier period.

The 1990s creation of regional trading areas (NAFTA, Pacific Rim) was a step towards super-national organization, especially for the European

Community. But it also moved away from international organizations and generalized global tariff reductions. Recent regionalizations may serve as a basis for greater international coordination, or for the kind of global territorialization that preceded previous world wars. Historically, successful institutional frameworks for macroeconomic stabilization have prevailed only when one hegemonic power (Britain in the 19th century, the US in the 20th century) set the terms for conflict-management through a national state, and imposed them internationally. It is unclear whether competing nations can achieve that coherence through super-national mechanisms.

Unlike these regional organizations for trade and economic policy, the G7 process promises inter-regional coordination. However, G7 meetings did not anticipate the threatened Mexican default in 1993 nor the Asian Crisis of 1997. The former was only contained by massive US financial aid, and the economic consequences of the latter are still rippling through the international system. And the G7 mechanism itself supplants broader-based UN initiatives with decisions by a coterie of powerful economic players.

The evidence suggests that recent ad hoc and partial stabilization efforts have not got to the root of global economic instability. The large US trade deficit and debt overhang (see Eatwell and Taylor, this volume) continue. Many developing countries remain saddled with large debts they cannot repay; Japanese banks' insolvency threatens their economy and therefore the region. Such symptoms of serious economic vulnerability and fragility do not presage a stable economic future without more far-reaching reforms and global institution building to manage conflicts during the necessary economic restructuring.

NOTES

1. The concept of moral hazard refers to institutional structures that provide incentives for socially damaging or destructive behavior. For example, unlimited deposit insurance encourages banks to take riskier investment positions, while their depositors can remain secure in the knowledge that the government will bail them out should the investments fail.
2. From the 1930s until 1970, the Federal Reserve Board's Regulation Q placed interest rate ceilings on large certificates of deposit. The elimination of this regulation allowed banks to attract more deposits by offering higher interest rates, but placed Savings and Loan banks at risk due to their dependence on long-term fixed interest mortgages.
3. Isenberg (2002, p. 9) argues that the IFMS 'leashed finance to industry and gave industry control of the leash', in part because of the contribution of the commercial banks to the Great Depression. This Accord recognized the long-term commonality of interest between finance and industry in promoting economic growth.
4. The rhetoric of foreign exchange is indicative of the conflict of interest between finance and industry. Financial interests advocate a 'strong' dollar, while industrial interests seek a 'viable' dollar. No financier advocates an 'unrealistically overvalued' dollar, no industrialist promotes a 'weak' dollar.

5. To 'make a market' means to have the necessary liquidity and inventory of the relevant asset (e.g., shares of stock) to be able to meet demand or purchase supply at any time. This permits stock prices to reflect longer-term influences rather than daily market conditions.
6. 6%*(current bank assets)/x = 8% implies x =75% of current bank assets.

REFERENCES

Block, Fred L. (1977), *The Origins of International Economic Disorder; A Study of United States International Monetary Policy from World War II to the Present*, Berkeley, CA: UCLA Press.

Bowles, Samuel, David M. Gordon and Thomas Weisskopf (1989), 'Business Ascendancy and Economic Impasse: A Structural Retrospective on Conservative Economics, 1979–1987', *Journal of Economic Perspectives*, **3** (1): 107–34.

Dymski, Gary A., Gerald Epstein and Robert Pollins (eds) (1993), *Transforming the US Financial System; Equity and Efficiency for the 21st Century*, Armonk, NY: M.E. Sharpe.

Epstein, Gerald A., Julie Graham and Jessica Nembhard for the Center for Popular Economics (1993), *Creating a New World Economy; Forces of Change and Plans for Action*, Philadelphia, PA: Temple University Press.

Epstein, Gerald A. and Schor, Juliet B. (1995), 'The Federal Reserve-Treasury Accord and the Construction of the Postwar Monetary Regime', *Social Concept*, **7** (1), July: 7–48.

Isenberg, Dorene (2002), 'The National Origin of Financial Liberalization: The Case of the United States', paper presented at the Conference on Globalization, Regionalization and Growth, Cambridge University, April.

Keynes, John Maynard (1964 [1936]), *The General Theory of Employment, Interest and Money*, New York: Harcourt, Brace. (Originally London: Macmillan.)

Kotz, David M., Terrence McDonough and Michael Reich (1994), *Social Structures of Accumulation: The Political Economy of Growth and Crisis*, New York: Cambridge University Press.

Kuhn, Thomas (1996), *The Structure of Scientific Revolutions*, Chicago: University of Chicago Press.

Minsky, Hyman P. (1975), *John Maynard Keynes*, New York: Columbia University Press.

Naples, Michele I. (1997), 'Business Failures and the Expenditure-Multiplier, or How Recessions Become Depressions', *Journal of Post Keynesian Economics*, **19** (4): 511–23.

Naples, Michele I. (1998), 'Technical and Social Determinants of Productivity Growth in Bituminous Coal Mining, 1955–1980', *Eastern Economic Journal*, **24** (3): 325–42.

Naples, Michele I. and Arben Arifaj (1997), 'The Rise in US Business Failures: Correcting the 1984 Discontinuity', *Contributions to Political Economy*, **16**: 49–60.

Pollin, Robert (ed.) (1997), *The Macroeconomics of Saving, Finance, and Investment*, Ann Arbor, MI: University of Michigan Press.

US Council of Economic Advisors (1999), *Economic Report of the President*, Washington, DC: US Government Printing Office.

Wolfson, Martin H. (1994), *Financial Crises; Understanding the Postwar US Experience*, 2nd edn, Armonk, NY: M.E. Sharpe.

PART III

Employment, Distribution, and Equity

7. The Micro-Foundations of High Unemployment in Developed Countries: Are Labor Market Rigidities the Problem?[1]

David R. Howell

INTRODUCTION

By the early 1990s, unemployment throughout much of Europe had risen to unprecedented levels and concern over the economic well-being of less-skilled workers appeared at the top of the policy agenda. At about the same time, a broad consensus had been reached about the source of this decline: global forces had generated a protracted imbalance in demand and supply in the labor market, a mismatch caused mainly by computerization in the workplace (Bound and Johnson, 1992, pp. 210–32; Krueger, 1993, pp. 33–60). As Paul Krugman put it, 'the growth of earnings inequality – and quite possibly therefore much of the rise in structural unemployment in Europe – has been the result of technological changes that just happen to work against unskilled workers' (Krugman, 1994, p. 70).

Variously characterized as the 'Unified Theory' and the 'Trans-Atlantic Consensus,' this account has been enormously influential in policy circles for all the obvious reasons – the story is simple, it is consistent with the economist's supply/demand model of the labor market, and the policy implications are clear (Blank, 1977; Atkinson, 1998). In our computerized global economy, vastly higher cognitive skills are required of a large fraction of the US workforce and far greater labor market flexibility is needed in Europe. The belief in free market solutions became the orthodoxy of the 1990s.

A central plank of this orthodoxy was that high unemployment in the developed (OECD) countries could be explained largely by the labor market rigidities that follow from Welfare State regulations and institutions. This simple, textbook account of the European unemployment crisis as a labor market problem caused by government policy interventions is held by economists of wide-ranging political persuasions. For example, the liberal American economist, Robert Haveman, poses the issue as a choice between wage stagnation ('the US model') and double-digit unemployment ('the European model'): 'a European-style policy package comprises generous and accessible social benefit programs, high minimum wage levels, and relatively stringent labor market regulations and constraints. It is accompanied by high unemployment and joblessness, slow employment growth . . .' (Haveman, 1997, p. 3). Similarly, Horst Siebert, a conservative German economist, attributes the unemployment problem in Europe to 'an array of institutional arrangements that form a complex web of incentives and disincentives on both sides of the (labor) market.' The solution can only be to 'undertake major reforms of the institutional setup of the labor market' (Siebert, 1997, p. 53).

Several dimensions of this claim can be addressed with the available evidence: (1) because of the rigidities imposed by European welfare states, the European unemployment experience should be clearly differentiated from that of the US over a substantial period of time; (2) if downward wage rigidities are at the heart of the unemployment problem, as the orthodox view contends, we should observe a clear tradeoff between earnings inequality and unemployment (and employment) rates across countries – relatively high wages for the less skilled will price them out of jobs; (3) since most labor market institutions are designed to protect the least skilled from the most damaging effects of labor market competition, the rise in European unemployment should have been driven by the less skilled, with declining unemployment rates for the more highly skilled (for whom demand has risen); and (4) statistical tests should show convincingly that unemployment is accounted for in large part by 'employment unfriendly' labor market institutions.

This chapter assesses the evidence for this widely accepted Labor Market Rigidity explanation for persistent high unemployment in many OECD member countries. The main conclusion of the chapter is that supportive evidence has remained remarkably thin, particularly given its widespread acceptance. The simple trends suggest numerous anomalies: trends across the OECD are far from uniform; the US did not show distinctively lower unemployment until the late 1980s, and European unemployment rates have lately shown strong convergence towards US levels; the evidence for a tradeoff between unemployment and inequality is ambiguous at best; where unemployment has risen, it has done so across skill groups, not just for the least skilled; and unemployment rates across countries are not impressively accounted for in regression tests by the usual welfare state suspects (e.g., union density, employment protection laws, and the generosity of unemployment benefits) – the results in the literature are widely acknowledged to be extremely fragile, and our simple regressions show no explanatory power.

This absence of compelling empirical support for the Unified Theory challenges the current policy orthodoxy: that high European unemployment must be addressed with a strong dose of the American model of labor market deregulation, and that any attempt to address high wage inequality in the US with labor market institutions will only produce European levels of unemployment. This review of the evidence suggests that the continued status of the Unified Theory as conventional wisdom can be explained less by the compelling nature of the evidence than by the power of the simple demand/supply vision of the labor market. This vision, in turn, has discouraged research into alternative accounts. I suggest that high earnings inequality in the US and high unemployment in many parts of Europe reflect substantial pro-market ideological shifts on both sides of the Atlantic, which have eroded institutional protections for lower skill workers in the US and constrained the growth in job opportunities in Europe.

'EUROPEAN' UNEMPLOYMENT AND THE DISTINCTIVENESS OF THE US

How similar are national levels, trends, and sources of unemployment across Europe? If there is significant heterogeneity in the unemployment experience, a handful of countries with entirely country-specific explanations for rising unemployment may have played a major role in driving up the average unemployment rate for the entire region. Further, to the extent that there are similar levels of unemployment across European economies, this may reflect more the economic integration of the continent than the similarity of labor market institutions and their effects. As Stephen Nickell points out, 'while it is sometimes convenient to lump all the countries of western Europe together in order to provide a suitable contrast to North America, most of the time it is a rather silly thing to do' (Nickell, 1997, p. 55).

Figures 7.1a and 7.1b show a wide range of unemployment rates across Europe. Indeed, there is no obvious grouping of European nations in either of these bar charts. In the 1983–88 period, Sweden, Norway, Switzerland, and Austria had rates that were much closer to those of Japan (less than 3 per cent) than such close European neighbors as Denmark, France, the Netherlands, and Belgium (9–12 per cent unemployment). The same holds true for the more recent 1989–94 period, as Figure 7.1b shows: several European nations with highly developed welfare states – Austria, West Germany, Sweden, and Norway – had unemployment rates that averaged

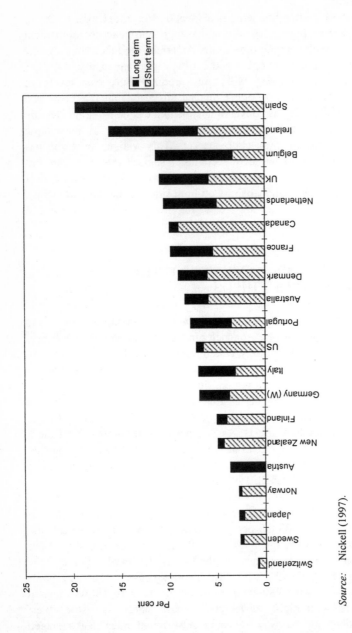

Source: Nickell (1997).

Figure 7.1a   Unemployment in the OECD, 1983–88

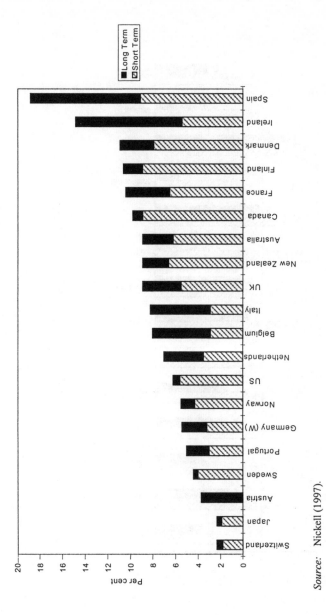

Source: Nickell (1997).

Figure 7.1b   Unemployment in the OECD, 1989–94

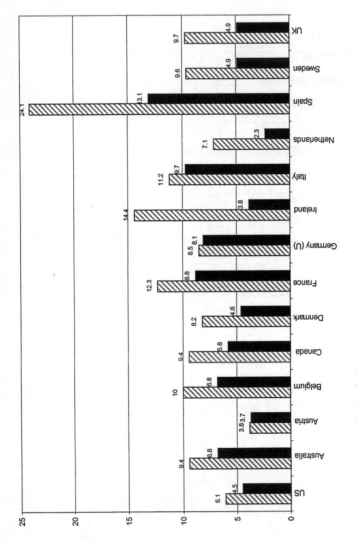

Source: US Bureau of Labor Statistics.

Figure 7.2 Standardized Unemployment Rates, 1994 and 2001 (April)

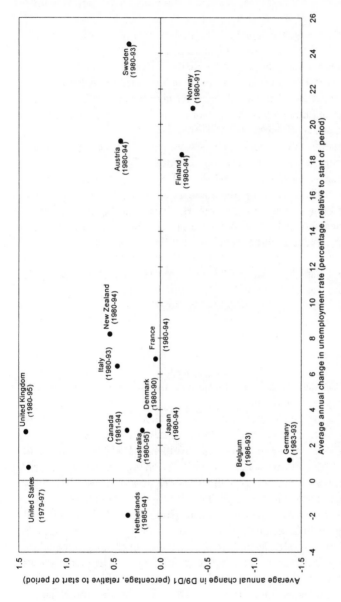

Source: D9/D: OECD, *Employment Outlook* (1996). D9/D1 for United States: L. Mishel, J. Bernstein, J. Schmitt, *The State of Working in America, 1998–99* (1999): D9/D1 for United States. Unemployment rate: OECD, *Economic Outlook*, no. 64 (1998).

Figure 7.3   Unemployment rate and earnings inequality average annual change (relative), 1979–97

between 4 and 6 per cent, while Ireland and Spain had rates of about 15 and 19 per cent. Clearly, the European unemployment varies enormously across, and in some cases – for instance, the UK, Germany, and Italy – within countries.

These figures also suggest that the US experience is less distinctive than commonly believed. Several European countries with strong labor market institutions had lower unemployment rates than the United States in both the 1983–88 and the 1989–94 periods. These included Sweden, Austria, West Germany, Switzerland, and Norway. At least through the early 1990s, the US was not the outlier in unemployment the way it was for both real wages (low) and inequality growth (very high).

It is also notable that recent data show a marked convergence in unemployment rates across the developed world. Figure 7.2 compares unemployment rates in 1994 and 2001 for 14 OECD member countries. Apart from Austria (3.8 per cent), the standard measure of unemployment was lowest in the US (6.1 per cent) in 1994. But by the first quarter of 2001, six of the countries shown here shared with the US the distinction of rates below 5 per cent. Indeed, three countries achieved unemployment rates substantially below the 4.5 per cent US rate: Austria (3.7 per cent); Ireland (3.8 per cent); and the Netherlands (2.3 per cent). By late 2001, Sweden's unemployment rate was also below that of the United States.

DO THE DATA SHOW INEQUALITY-UNEMPLOYMENT TRADEOFFS?

In the conventional view, strong egalitarian institutions and social policies produce unemployment by promoting wage rigidity and by reducing incentives for effective job search. Societies can choose more jobs or more equality. But the statistical facts tell a more complicated story. Figure 7.3 shows a plot of the change in earnings inequality (D9/D1, or ninetieth percentile divided by tenth percentile) against the change in unemployment for 16 OECD member countries over the 1979–97 period. These data show no simple tradeoff. There are two high inequality growth countries (the US and UK), two low inequality growth countries (Belgium and Germany), and many countries with little inequality growth but widely varying changes in unemployment. For example, despite similar increases in earnings inequality, the Netherlands experienced declining unemployment, Denmark shows modestly rising unemployment, and France and Sweden experienced relatively high increases in unemployment. To view it from another angle, with substantial declines in earnings inequality, Belgium and Germany experienced smaller increases in unemployment than the UK, Canada,

Austria, and New Zealand, countries with at least some increase in earnings inequality.

Another way to examine the tradeoff hypothesis is to compare earnings inequality with unemployment inequality – the ratio of the unskilled unemployment rate to the skilled rate. Protective labor market institutions that produce wage rigidity and limit the incentives for job search lead to adjustments on the employment side. On the other hand, less skilled workers in flexible labor markets respond to shocks mainly through wage adjustments and should therefore have unemployment rates not greatly dissimilar to those of high skilled workers. Thus, faced with the same shocks, the US should show rising earnings inequality and European welfare states should show rising unemployment inequality. More generally, across countries that vary in labor market rigidity we should observe a tradeoff between relative wage inequality and relative unemployment inequality.

If anything, the data show the reverse. Figure 7.4 shows earnings inequality (D9/D1) and unemployment inequality (the ratio of low to high skill unemployment rates) for male workers in selected years over the 1979– 93 period for the eight OECD member countries for which data were available. The US appears in the upper right with the highest earnings inequality and the highest unemployment inequality. Canada experienced comparable levels of earnings inequality but lower unemployment inequality, while France, the UK, Germany, Australia, and Italy were all superior on both dimensions of inequality.

Figure 7.5 also compares these two measures of inequality, but does so for all workers (male and female) using a different measure of unemployment inequality for the early 1990s.[2] The pattern is similar. Again, the US had the highest levels of both earnings and unemployment inequality, about twice those of Germany and Sweden. Compared to ratios of about 4.5 in the US, the earnings and unemployment ratios in France were far smaller, around 3.4 for earnings and 2.5 for unemployment. *This evidence directly challenges a fundamental tenet of the conventional wisdom; it shows that countries with lower earnings inequality also tend to have lower unemployment inequality.*

EUROPEAN UNEMPLOYMENT AND SKILL-BIASED DEMAND SHIFTS

At the center of the conventional wisdom is a story about a demand shift away from the less skilled of such magnitude that it is frequently referred to as a 'collapse' in the literature. It is also widely recognized that the severity of the unemployment problem in many countries is due to its long-term nature, and the persistence of unemployment may reflect not only wage

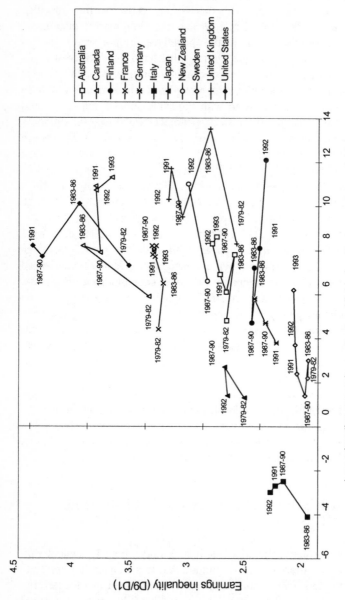

Source: See Howell and Huebler (2003).

Figure 7.4 , Earnings inequality and relative unemployment rates by education level, male workers, 1979–93

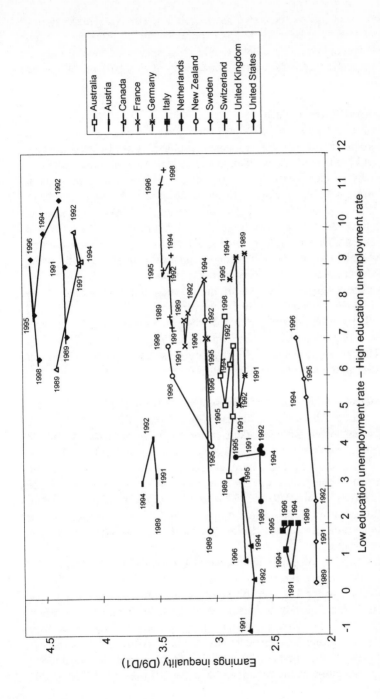

Legend:
- □ Australia
- ▲ Austria
- ▲ Canada
- ✕ France
- ✱ Germany
- ■ Italy
- ● Netherlands
- ○ New Zealand
- ◇ Sweden
- ▲ Switzerland
- + United Kingdom
- ◆ United States

Low education unemployment rate – High education unemployment rate

Earnings inequality (D9/D1)

Source: See Howell and Huebler (2003).

Figure 7.5 Earnings inequality and relative unemployment rates by education level, all workers, 1989–98

rigidity and disincentives for active job search, but also the deterioration of the skills of those out of work for long periods. For these reasons, in this account the unemployment problem should be concentrated among the least skilled. This section addresses three dimensions of this part of the Unified Theory.

Unemployment Rates by Skill

If an important part of the unemployment problem is skill-biased demand shifts in rigid labor markets, we should see at least two empirical patterns. Across countries, unemployment among the least skilled should be greatest relative to those with higher skills in those countries with the most rigid labor markets. After all, workers in countries like the US have, supposedly, adjusted to the new economy with wage cuts. Within countries, if skill-biased technological change is the fundamental problem, we should observe a rising ratio of low-skilled to high-skilled unemployment over time, caused by rising low-skill rates and stable or declining high-skill rates.[3]

Evidence pertaining to the first of these predictions has already been presented. Figures 7.4 and 7.5 show that the probability of being unemployed for low-skilled workers relative to their high-skilled counterparts is greatest in the US, widely regarded as the country with the most flexible labor markets. This result appears to directly contradict the demand shift/rigid labor markets prediction. Other data confirm this result. For example, the OECD *Jobs Study*, perhaps the most authoritative voice of the conventional wisdom, compares white-collar and blue-collar unemployment rates from the mid-1970s through the early 1990s for eight nations (OECD, 1994). The report finds that lower skilled workers in the US have consistently had far higher unemployment rates relative to skilled workers than has been the case in France or most other northern European nations. The blue- to white-collar ratio remained unchanged from 1982 to 1991 in France (at 1.51) while increasing slightly from 1979 to 1990 in the US (2.08 to 2.28). Given the growth in US earnings inequality by skill group over this period, the unemployment ratio should have declined rather than increasing, according to conventional wisdom.

Like the results for blue- and white-collar workers, the unemployment rate for poorly educated workers was far higher relative to that for highly educated workers in the US than in any other OECD nation examined save the UK, whose labor market is on the US side of the flexibility spectrum. Despite substantial downward adjustments in wages, low-skilled US workers appear worse off in unemployment relative to high-skilled workers than in most other major OECD nations. Depending on the measure, this unskilled–skilled ratio was either stable or worsened in the US over the 1980s. (ibid., table 1.16). These data offer no support for the conventional view; in contrast to Europe, wage flexibility should have protected low-skilled US workers from relatively high unemployment.

Nor does the evidence support the related prediction, that the unemployment problem is driven by the less skilled. While the OECD *Jobs Study* concludes that 'the labour market situation for low-skilled workers, as measured by educational attainment, declined over the 1980s relative to that of more skilled workers' (ibid., p. 41), the same data show that high-skilled unemployment rates also increased over the 1980s for every nation they consider except Japan, for both men and women. For example, the unemployment rate for high-skilled ('upper secondary or higher') workers in France increased from 2.6 in 1979 to 4.1 per cent in 1990; in Germany, the increase in this rate was even sharper, from 1.8 in 1978 to 5.0 in 1987 (ibid., table 1.16).

There is even less support in the more comprehensive data for male workers assembled by Nickell and Bell. Seven of the eight nations for which they present data do not even show an increase in the ratio of low- to high-skilled unemployment over the 1979–93 period, and where low-skill unemployment increased, so did high-skill unemployment (Nickell and Bell, 1996, table 1). France shows an upward trajectory in the skill ratio through 1990 and in the low-skilled unemployment rate over the entire period. But even here, in the rigid labor markets of France, the level of low-skilled unemployment is comparable to or below the rates of the more flexible markets of Canada, the UK, and the United States (the high overall unemployment rate in France is due to exceptionally high rates for women).

Of course, as Glyn and Salverda emphasize, low-skilled workers are undoubtedly made worse off relative to high-skilled workers when both experience increasing unemployment rates, since the probability of getting a job for low-skilled workers becomes much lower (Glyn and Salverda, 1999). But this fact does not support the conventional view that the unemployment problem is due to rigidities in low-skilled labor markets. Comparing unemployment rates by education level, an International Labor Organization (ILO) report concluded that

> While it is true that unemployment affects the least skilled workers disproportionately, it is difficult to attribute this phenomenon to a shift in the demand for labour towards higher skills, for if this were so the rise in unemployment of the unskilled should have been accompanied by a real shortage of skilled labour. But this has not been in evidence, since the rise in unemployment of skilled workers has also been observed . . . *Skill shortages do not appear to have contributed significantly to the rise in unemployment* (ILO, 1997, pp. 52–3, emphasis added).

In sum, while the least skilled have borne the brunt of rising unemployment, the trends by skill level do not, by themselves, demonstrate that a 'collapse in demand' for low skilled workers is at the heart of the European unemployment problem. Countries with rising unemployment tend to also experience substantial increases in high-skilled unemployment. As Stephen Nickell has concluded: 'Overall, therefore, there is no evidence that these skill shifts have made a substantial contribution to the rise in European unemployment . . .' (Nickell, 1997, p. 55). Indeed, the data are perfectly consistent with an alternative story, recently advanced by the International Labor Organization, that 'in an environment of widespread unemployment, trained workers apply for jobs for which they are overqualified and, given the choice, firms recruit them first, with the natural outcome that unemployment is transferred to the least skilled workers' (ILO, 1997, p. 53).

Employment Rates by Skill

Drawing conclusions from changes in unemployment rates can be misleading because, faced with worsening job prospects, workers may drop out of the labor force altogether. For this reason it may be more revealing to evaluate the demand shift/rigid labor markets hypothesis by comparing the growth in employment-population rates by skill across countries. Employment rates should be lowest among the least skilled, which is generally true and not something particularly new. But the demand shift/rigid labor markets prediction is different: it suggest that the less-skilled will tend to have the lowest employment rates, and the gap in employment rates between the least and most skilled will tend to be the greatest in countries with labor market institutions that prevent downward wage flexibility. The reasoning is, again, that without wage adjustments, the least skilled will be priced out of their jobs.

Comparing employment rates by skill across different OECD countries using different methodologies, both Nickell and Bell and Card, Kramarz and Lemieux found little support for this fundamental prediction of the conventional wisdom. Comparing growth in employment rates for 'skill' groups defined by age and education for the US, Canada, and France, Card et al. leaves no doubt about the lack of support for the conventional view: 'Taking the evidence for the United States, Canada, and France as a whole, we conclude that it is very difficult to maintain the hypothesis that the 'wage inflexibility' in Canada and France translated into greater relative employment losses for less-skilled workers in these countries' (Nickell and Bell, 1995, pp. 40–62; Card et al., 1995, p. 3). Similar results have been found for Germany and Sweden (Edin et al., 1996). Indeed, Krueger and Pischke point out that 'If demand fell for less skilled workers, we would expect to find employment declining most among the lowest wage groups; instead, there appears to be little relationship' (Krueger and Pischke, 1997, p. 13).

These studies attempt to compare skill groups using educational attainment levels, a difficult task – after all, how comparable is a 'high school degree' in France, the UK, Sweden, Germany, and the US? To deal with this problem, Andrew Glyn has examined employment rates for different quartiles of the education distribution. Again, the employment rate gap between the most and least educated should be greatest in the most rigid labor markets. Glyn's (2001) analysis of employment differences using this measure of skill shows that for 25–64-year-old men, the employment rate skill differential (the most skilled quartile rate less the least skilled rate) for the US was 14.6 percentage points in 1999, lower than that for France (19.3 points in 1998) and the Netherlands (17.7 points in 1998), but higher than Switzerland (11.9 in 1998), Sweden (13.4 in 1997) and West Germany (14.3 in 1996). Usually placed at the flexible end of the spectrum, the UK shows a much higher employment rate gap than many European welfare states (23.2 in 2000).[4] In sum, Glyn's results show that, while the employment rate for the less educated is relatively high in the US, it is also quite high for the most educated workers, and there seems to be little association across countries between employment rates by 'skill' and the strength of protective labor market institutions.

EUROPEAN UNEMPLOYMENT: THE WELFARE STATE AS CULPRIT

Central to the conventional wisdom is the view that what distinguishes the US unemployment experience from the European is the relative rigidity of the European labor market. This rigidity is blamed on 'labor market institutions' that reduce the demand for less skilled labor and reduce the incentives of less-skilled workers to search for jobs. As Blanchard and Wolfers note, 'With the persistence of high unemployment for now more than two decades, explanations based on adverse institutions ('labor market rigidities') have become steadily more popular' (Blanchard and Wolfers, 2000).

A critical problem with the simple rigidities account is that most countries suffering high unemployment in the 1980s and 1990s had these adverse institutions back in the 1960s, when unemployment was well below that of the United States. The solution in the mainstream literature has been to explain the general evolution of unemployment over time by shocks (e.g., the productivity slowdown, oil price hikes, and declining labor demand due to skill-biased technological change), while 'cross-country variation' in unemployment rates is accounted for by 'employment-unfriendly' labor market institutions. In the language of mainstream economics, the European welfare state 'adversely affects the dynamic responses to economic shocks and to increasing turbulence in the economic environment' (Lungqvist and Sargent, 1998, p. 517).

Given the focus of this chapter, I only note here that the 'shocks' part of this conventional wisdom is not entirely convincing. Perhaps the biggest problem concerns timing. Why did productivity and energy price shocks that took place in the 1970s not translate into a US–Europe unemployment gap until the late 1980s and early 1990s? Indeed, German and Swedish unemployment rates were below the US rate until well after German unification and the Swedish macroeconomic crisis of the early 1990s.

Taking into account a variety of shocks to the developed world, has the case been made that differences in employment performance since the early 1980s are attributable to institutions that interfere with competitive market processes? Not only should these adverse labor market institutions account for the cross-national pattern of unemployment, but they should do so over the course of the last two decades of high unemployment, including the late 1990s convergence (see Figure 7.5). The conventional wisdom answers this in the affirmative. As a major OECD report puts it, 'Developments in structural unemployment over the 1990s to a large extent reflect the progress made in implementing the OECD Jobs Strategy' (OECD, 1997a, p. 12). At the core of the Jobs Strategy is the adoption of the 'American model' of highly competitive labor markets.

Absent a prior belief in the labor market rigidity story, the empirical case against 'employment-unfriendly' labor market institutions as the source of the unemployment problem seems remarkably unconvincing. As noted above, Figures 7.1a and 7.1b show a number of central and northern European nations with highly developed welfare states (Sweden, Austria, Switzerland, West Germany, and Norway) with lower average unemployment rates than the US in both the 1983–88 and the 1989–94 periods. And Figure 7.2 shows the US improved its position in the mid-1990s, but by 2001 Sweden, the Netherlands, Austria, and Denmark again had similar or lower unemployment levels than the United States. This comparable or superior employment performance in these European welfare states took place despite collective bargaining coverage rates between 77 to 90 per cent in the early 1990s (the US had an 18 per cent rate), unemployment benefit duration rates between 1.2 to 4 years (US: 0.5 year), and employment protection scores that ranged from 11 to 16 on a scale of 20 (US score: 1).[5] To take just one example, apart from four years in the mid-

1990s, the US has consistently shown higher unemployment levels than the Netherlands.

There is an extensive literature that has attempted to link unemployment levels statistically with measures of various labor market institutions. The results appear quite impressive, with nearly all variables statistically significant with the right signs (effects are in the correct direction). For example, in a recent paper, Fitoussi et al. are able to account for 65 per cent of the variation in unemployment (1983–88) across 19 developed countries with the following variables (coefficient and t-statistic in parentheses): unemployment benefits replacement ratio (.12, 2.95), duration of unemployment benefits (.79, 2.13), union density and coverage (.08, 1.68), union coordination (-3.06, 2.35), employer coordination (-3.95, 3.46), and labor market expenditure (-.09, 2.14) (Fitoussi et al., 2000, table 6). While other measures, such as employment protection and taxation have been employed in some studies, both the theoretical justification and the empirical results for them are rather weak.[6]

It is worth noting that these kinds of tests are used in the literature to support the position that once the shocks pushed unemployment up, the persistence of high rates has been accounted for by 'adverse' labor market institutions. But in fact, much of the strength of these regressions – their explanatory power – is due to institutions that *reduce* unemployment. This can be seen above in the last three variables listed above. Institutions that promote coordination and help train workers and provide job search assistance are costly interventions in the labor market, but they tend to *lower* unemployment. The literature that uses empirical tests of this sort tend to conclude that welfare state institutions can provide a good explanation for observed cross-country patterns of employment performance on the grounds that 'bad' institutions explain the persistence of high unemployment, but do not distinguish the 'good' from the 'bad' institutions! For example, in the Fitoussi et al. test reported above, only the results for the two unemployment benefits measures lend support to the conventional institution-as-culprit story.

Second, the key measure of wage rigidity – union density and coverage – is not statistically significant, a common result. According to an OECD study, 'evidence presented in this chapter does not show many statistically significant relationships between most measures of economic performance and collective bargaining' (OECD, 1997a, p. 64). Other institutions can compress wages (reduce wage inequality) but there is little evidence that they have detrimental impacts on employment. For example, in cross-country tests, OECD researchers have concluded that minimum wage levels appear to have no effect on young adult employment, and while they find small negative effects on teenage employment, there is no evidence of any association with unemployment. Since the greatest employment effects should be felt by youth, the conclusion regarding employment rates is telling:

> It is important to note that these estimated effects are relatively insignificant in terms of explaining the large decline that has occurred in the teenage employment-population ratio in some countries . . . the substantial difference across countries in teenage employment trends can only be marginally attributed to differences in the evolution of minimum wages . . . (OECD, 1998, p. 48).

If wage rigidity were as important as claimed by the conventional wisdom, unemployment and its change over time ought to be strongly negatively associated with earnings inequality, unit labor costs, and wage shares (in total income). In fact, as discussed above (Figures 7.3 and 7.4), the data shows no clear tradeoff between changes in unemployment and changes in earnings inequality. Nor is there a negative association for levels. For example, for 17 countries, the simple correlation coefficient between a standard measure of earnings inequality (D9/D1) and unemployment rates for the early 1990s was .101, a statistically insignificant relationship. Substituting an alternative inequality measure, the ratio of median earnings to the 10th percentile level (D5/D1), shows an even lower association (.085). Nor have aggregate wage costs been rising: wage shares in nearly all countries have been on a downward trend since the early 1980s (OECD, 1997, figure 10).

The two unemployment insurance variables are key measures of 'employment-unfriendly' labor market institutions. While the replacement rate and benefit duration variables are usually found to be statistically significant in the published literature, their importance and robustness are open to question. Table 7.1 presents simple OLS regression results for different measures of unemployment over the course of the last decade or so. Panel A shows results for 1989–94 for 20 countries. The institutional variables are the standard ones with one exception. The usual duration measure is subjectively defined, from 0 to 4. Spain provides an example of the difficulty of constructing such a measure. The standard Nickell-Layard data set assigns Spain a benefit duration value of 3.5 years. But as Munoz de Bustillo comments,

> The 3.5 years of duration considered is only the maximum, subject to strict eligibility criteria and associated with a much lower benefit replacement ratio. In fact 40% of the unemployed receiving unemployment compensation have benefit duration of 1 year or less. On the other hand 44% qualify for a benefit duration from 1.5 to 2 years . . . (Bustillo, 2001).

This suggests that perhaps a 1.5 value would be more appropriate. Separate results are shown for a duration variable in which Spain's value has been changed from 3.5 to 1.5.

Panel A of Table 7.1 shows a fairly similar pattern to the Fitoussi et. al. results reported above. Union density is insignificant for both total and long-term unemployment. Coordination tends to reduce unemployment, but is insignificant for long-term unemployment. Active labor market policies also show the standard negative effect, but again the effects are not reliably measured (low t-statistics). Typically, the two unemployment insurance benefits (UIB) measures have the expected positive effects on total unemployment. The replacement rate is insignificant for long-term unemployment. A key result for our purposes appears in columns 2 and 5, where Spain's duration measure has been changed from 3.5 to 1.5. The coefficient, 't' statistic, and adjusted R squared all drop, with a substantial decline in the explanatory power of the total and long-term equation (over 10 percentage points in each case). As would be expected, the declines are slightly smaller if a value of 2 is used (not shown). Clearly, the results are highly sensitive to judgments about what duration value to attach to each country.

Panel B shows results for tests of the same equation for unemployment in 1995 and 2001, and for young female unemployment in 1995. For 1995, the standard institutional variables perform poorly. Our alternative duration measure is not significant at the 10 per cent level for 1995, and neither duration measure is statistically significant for young female unemployment in 1995 or for total unemployment in 2001. The predictive power of this key institutional measure declines sharply between the early and late 1990s.

But even in the 1980s and early 1990s, when the benefits duration measure appears to have been most strongly associated with unemployment, and ignoring questions concerning the construction of this variable, the evidence for this lynchpin of the conventional story is less convincing that at first glance. Emphasizing the centrality of this disincentive for job search, Layard et. al. write that 'It is noticeable ... that all the countries where long-term unemployment has escalated have unemployment benefits of some kind that are available for a very long period, rather than running out after 6 months (as in the USA) or 14 months (as in Sweden)' (Layard et al., 1994, pp. 59–62) This is certainly one way to view the data. But their figure can also be read to show that the nine countries with 'indefinite benefits' have widely varying propensities for long-term unemployment, with the share of the unemployed out of work for over a year ranging from 20 per cent (Finland) to over 70 per cent (Belgium). Through this lens, the fit between benefits and long-term unemployment in the mid-1980s does not look very close. Then, of course, there is the problem of causation. It would be

142   *New Thinking in Macroeconomics*

perfectly sensible for countries to make benefits available for longer periods the greater the long-term unemployment problem, particularly in the absence of other safety net programs. The extensive literature review and the regression results reported by Baker et al. (2003) strongly confirm the fragile nature of the cross-country evidence linking institutions to poor employment performance.

Table 7.1   Regression results for alternative measures of unemployment, 1989–2001 (t-statistics in parentheses)

Panel A

	Unemployment 1989–94			Long-term unemployment 1989–94		
	(1)	(2)	(3)	(4)	(5)	(6)
Union density, 1988–94 (%)	.029 (.73)	.022 (.46)	.035 (.72)	-.025 (.91)	-.033 (1.0)	-.021 (.69)
Union/employer coord (2–6)	-1.03 (1.7)	-1.14 (1.67)	-1.19 (1.76)	-.045 (.09)	-.154 (.29)	-.077 (.16)
Active labor mkt 1991 (% GDP)	-.078 (1.2)	-.08 (1.1)	-.079 (1.1)	-.015 (.34)	-.014 (.29)	-.019 (.4)
UIB duration (years)	1.53 (3.3)			1.14 (3.66)		
UIB duration (years): Spain = 1.5		1.36 (2.41)	1.16 (1.98)		1.1 (2.9)	.89 (2.4)
UIB replacement (%)	.09 (2.0)	.104 (2.0)	.11 (2.17)	.016 (.48)	.029 (.81)	.029 (.85)
High agric. share (dummy)	5.13 (3.7)	5.7 (3.5)	5.0 (2.9)	3.84 (4.0)	4.36 (4.0)	3.6 (3.2)
20–24 pop. share, 1990 (%)			.7 (1.15)			.683 (1.73)
Adj R^2	.586	.47	.483	.579	.477	.552
N	20	20	20	19	19	19

Panel B

	Unemployment 1995		Young female unemployment 1995		Unemployment 2001	
Union density, 1988–94 (%)	-.031 (.61)	-.036 (.62)	-.197 (1.3)	-.194 (1.2)	-.056 (1.4)	-.056 (1.3)
Union/employer coord (2–6)	-.53 (.7)	-.66 (.8)	1.03 (.47)	.76 (.34)	.42 (.72)	.34 (.55)
Active labor mkt 1991 (% GDP)	.054 (.68)	.051 (.58)	-.08 (.34)	.073 (.3)	.04 (.63)	.038 (.57)
UIB duration (years)	1.44 (2.54)		2.02 (1.2)		.74 (1.65)	
UIB duration (years): Spain = 1.5		1.18 (1.7)		1.29 (.69)		.54 (1.0)
UIB replacement (%)	.076 (1.4)	.088 (1.4)	.026 (.16)	.035 (.2)	-.011 (.26)	-.006 (.1)
High agric. share (dummy)	7.64 (4.5)	8.1 (4.1)	17.9 (3.6)	18.2 (3.4)	3.1 (2.3)	3.31 (2.2)
Adj R^2	.518	.41	.316	.265	.122	.02
N	20	20	20	20	20	20

Explanatory variables:
Union density and union/employer coordination (Nickell and Layard, 1997, table 3);
UIB duration and replacement; active labor market policies (Nickell and Layard, 1997, table 6);
20–24/25–59 population share, 1990 (Women in Statistics Database, Version 4: United Nations Department of Economic and Social Affairs, Statistics Division); High agricultural share, 1980 (ILO, 1999).

Sources: Unemployment: unemployment 1989–94 and long-term unemployment 1989–94 (Nickell and Layard, 1997, table 13); unemployment, 1995 (OECD, 1998, Statistical Annex table A, p. 190); female youth (15–24) unemployment, 1995 (OECD, 1998, Statistical Annex table C, pp. 200–202; unemployment 2001 (bls.gov/pub/special.requests/foreignlabor).

EUROPEAN UNEMPLOYMENT: AN ASSESSMENT

This review of the evidence suggests that the conventional labor market rigidity explanation of the European unemployment problem is not strongly supported by the data. The preoccupation by economists with labor market rigidity explanations has inhibited research that takes alternative explanations seriously. While the principal aim of this part of the chapter is a critical assessment of the mainstream account, here I briefly outline an alternative, potentially more convincing story.

Since unemployment increased dramatically and nearly universally across developed countries between the mid-1970s and mid 1980s, it is hard to imagine that productivity and energy price shocks did not play central roles. Faced with rising inflation, countries responded with tight fiscal and monetary policies, and most agree that these contributed to the high unemployment of the early 1980s. Relying on a vision of a textbook competitive economy, the standard story is that these shocks temporarily raised the 'natural' rate of unemployment (or NAIRU – the non-accelerating inflation rate of unemployment), which would have returned to its pre-shock levels but for adverse labor market institutions. As Ball puts it, 'the conventional wisdom holds that the NAIRU is unaffected by aggregate demand, and thus that demand does not influence long-run unemployment trends' (Ball, 1999, p. 189). Ball argues to the contrary, that the aggregate demand matters for both short- and long-run movements in the unemployment rate:

> In some countries, such as the United States, the rise in unemployment was transitory; in others, including many European countries, the NAIRU rose and unemployment has remained high ever since. I argue that the reactions of policymakers to the early-1980s recessions largely explain these differences. In countries where unemployment rose only temporarily, it did so because of strongly counter-cyclical policy . . . In countries where unemployment rose permanently, it did so because policy remained tight in the face of the 1980s recessions . . . labor market policies are not important cases of the unemployment successes and failures since 1985 (ibid., pp. 190–91).

It is increasingly recognized that, in sharp contrast to US policy, under the leadership of the German Bundesbank and then the European Central Bank an increasingly integrated Europe was saddled with contractionary fiscal and monetary policy for much of the last two decades. Studies by Ball (1999) and Baker and Schmitt (1999) find empirical support for substantial aggregate demand effects on the cross-national pattern of unemployment. While the conventional account relies on adverse labor market institutions to explain the persistence of unemployment since the early 1980s, a more convincing explanation might point to these policy-induced differences in aggregate demand, supplemented by the adverse timing of employment restructuring across sectors and demographic shifts, and country-specific idiosyncratic factors.

After the productivity and energy price shocks of the 1970s, the developed world experienced de-industrialization in the 1980s, but regions with large shares of agricultural employment (e.g., Spain, Portugal, Ireland, Italy, and France) were also faced with de-ruralization (Esping-Andersen, 1999, p. 102–3). At the same time, they experienced a late demographic bulge from the baby boom. The regression results summarized in Table 7.1 show that a high agricultural share of employment was significantly associated with high unemployment in every test – five of the 20 countries had far higher agricultural shares than the rest: Spain, Portugal, Ireland, Finland, and Italy.

While the demographic variable in these tests – the ratio of the 20–24-year-old population to the 25–59 population – approached statistical significance only for 1989–94 long-term unemployment, it consistently had the right sign (the higher the young adult population share, the higher the unemployment). Part of the reason for its weakness in these tests may be that there is a notable overlap between countries with a high agricultural share of employment and those with a high youth share of the population. In addition, countries with high agricultural shares show relatively small declines in the youth share over this decade: while the ratio of 15–19 to 25–59-year-olds dropped dramatically in the US from 21.2 per cent to 14.6 per cent between 1980 and 1990, Ireland saw a decline from 25.4 per cent (1980) to just 23.4 per cent (1990), Spain's teen ratio fell from 20 per cent to 19.3 per cent, Italy's from 17.8 per cent to 16 per cent, and France's from 17.9 per cent to 16.4 per cent.[7]

In a simple regression for unemployment in 1997 (not shown), three demographic and demand variables accounted for over half (54 per cent) of the unemployment variation across 20 countries: the 1990 young adult share of the population (positive and significant), the 1990–97 real interest rate (positive and significant), and the 1990–97 change in investment spending (negative and significant).[8] No combination of labor market institution variables came close to this explanatory power for the 1997 unemployment rate. An adequate accounting of unemployment levels and changes over time would also have to include country-specific events, such as the economic and political restructuring of Spain after Franco's death, German unification, the Swedish fiscal crisis, and the effects of the Soviet collapse on Finland.

In sum, the empirical evidence surveyed above, coupled with the fact that there has recently been a dramatic decline in unemployment rates across Europe to levels approaching or even below that of the US (Figure 7.2), points to the need to move beyond the simple labor market rigidity story. Of course, labor market institutions may have had adverse employment impacts, but the available evidence offers little support for the conventional wisdom among economists and many policy makers that high unemployment in the OECD countries can be explained by labor market rigidities.

NOTES

1. This is a revised version of parts of 'Increasing Earnings Inequality and Unemployment in Developed Countries: Markets, Institutions and the 'Unified Theory' (Howell, 2002). I thank Friedrich Huebler for his outstanding research assistance.
2. Figure 7.4 uses unemployment data by skill for males from Stephen Nickell and Brian Bell, who define skill categories differently for different countries (e.g., across educational attainment categories in some cases, across high and low skill occupations in others). In contrast, Figure 7.5 covers all workers and uses skill categories defined consistently across countries by educational attainment from the OECD.
3. Since the problem is held to lie in the labor market as a result of skill-biased demand shifts and institutional rigidities that work against the least skilled, we should not see rising unemployment rates for skilled workers. Indeed, a queuing story (see Thurow, 1997; ILO, 1997) is perfectly consistent with a rising ratio of low- to high-skilled unemployment even if a downward demand shift afflicts some group of high skilled jobs. If displaced high-skill workers get preferential treatment in competition for lower skilled jobs, 'bumped' lower-skill workers may be left to bear the brunt of the unemployment. Consequently, unambiguous empirical support for the demand-shift story requires not just evidence of a secular rise in the ratio of low to high skill unemployment rates, but a rise generated from rising low-skill rates in the presence of stable or declining high skill unemployment.
4. See Glyn (2001). In addition, it is likely that part of the high employment rate gap in many European countries stems from a generous pension system that encourages retirement before age 60. If this generosity has a greater impact on the employment rates of the less skilled, as I would suspect, limiting the data to those under 60 would tend to reduce the employment rate gap in the strong welfare state countries, leading to some convergence towards US levels.
5. These data come from various OECD documents and appear in Tables 1 and 2 of Howell et al. (1998).
6. As Blanchard and Wolfers (2000, C13) note, 'employment protection both decreases flows of workers through the labour market, and increases the duration of unemployment . . . the effect of lower flows and higher duration on the equilibrium rate itself is ambiguous'. According to an OECD study employment protection legislation 'has little or no effect on overall unemployment, but may affect its demographic composition' (OECD, 1999, p. 50). As for taxation, we again cite Blanchard and Wolfers (2000, C13): 'Taxes which by their nature apply equally on the unemployed and the employed, such as consumption or income taxes, are likely to be roughly neutral. And if the unemployment insurance system tries to achieve a stable relation of unemployment benefits to after-tax wages – a reasonable assumption – even payroll taxes may not matter very much.'

7. Calculated by the author from the UN's Women in Statistics database, generously provided by John Schmitt.
8. The investment and interest rate data come from table 8 of Stanford, 'Canadian Labour Market Developments in International Context: Flexibility, Regulation, and Demand', manuscript, CSLS Conference, Ottawa Canada (April 1999).

REFERENCES

Atkinson, Anthony (1998), 'The Distribution of Income in Industrialized Countries', paper presented at the symposium 'Income Inequality: Issues and Policy Options', the Federal Reserve Bank of Kansas City, Jackson Hole, Wyoming, 27–29 August.

Baker, Dean and John Schmitt (1999), 'The Macroeconomic Roots of High European Unemployment: The Impact of Foreign Growth', Washington, DC: Economics Policy Institute.

Baker, Dean, Andrew Glyn, David Howell and John Schmitt (2003), 'Labor Market Institutions and Unemployment: A Critical Assessment of the Cross-Country Evidence', in David R. Howell (ed.), *Unemployment and the Welfare State: International Perspectives on the Limits of Labor Market Deregulation*, New York: Oxford University Press; available at www.newschool.edu/cepa.

Ball, Laurence (1999), 'Aggregate Demand and Long-Run Unemployment', *Brookings Papers on Economic Activity*, 1.

Blanchard, Olivier and Justin Wolfers (2000), 'The Role of Shocks and Institutions in the Rise of European Unemployment: The Aggregate Evidence', *Economic Journal*, 110, March: C1–C33.

Blank, Rebecca (1977), 'No Easy Answers: Comparative Labor Market Problems in the United States Versus Europe', Northwestern University/University of Chicago Joint Center for Poverty Research Working Paper No. 188.

Bound, John and George Johnson (1992), 'Changes in the Structure of Wages in the 1980s: An Evaluation of Alternative Perspectives', *American Economic Review*, 82 (3), June: 201–32.

Bustillo, Munoz de (2001), 'Spain and the Neoliberal Paradigm', Manuscript, Center for Economic Policy Analysis, New School University.

Card, David, Francis Kramarz and Thomas Lemieux, (1995), 'Changes in the Structure of Wages and Employment: A Comparison of the United States, Canada, and France', Industrial Relations Section, Princeton University Working Paper #355. 3.

Edin, Per-anders, Anders Harkman and Bertil Holmlund, (1996), 'Unemployment and Wage Inequality in Sweden', mimeo, Uppsala University.

Esping-Andersen, Gosta (1999), *Social Foundations of Postindustrial Economics*, Oxford: Oxford University Press.

Fitoussi, Jean-Paul, D. Jestaz, E. Phelps and G. Zoega (2000), 'Roots of the Recent Recoveries: Labor Reforms or Private Sector Forces?', *Brookings Papers on Economic Activity*, 1.

Glyn, Andrew (2001), 'Inequalities of Employment and Wages in OECD Countries', manuscript, Department of Economics, Oxford University.

Glyn, Andrew and Wiemer Salverda (1999), 'Employment Inequalities', unpublished paper presented at the Levy Economics Institute, May.

Haveman, Robert H. (1997), 'Equity with Employment', *Boston Review*, Summer.

Howell, David R. (2002), 'Increasing Earnings Inequality and Unemployment in Developed Countries: Markets, Institutions and the "Unified Theory"', *Politics & Society*, **30** (3), June: 193–244.

Howell, David R. and Friedrich Huebler (2003), 'Unemployment and Earnings Inequality in OECD Countries: Demand Shifts, Labor Market Institutions and the Unified Theory', in David R. Howell (ed.), *Unemployment and the Welfare State: International Perspectives on the Limits of Labor Market Deregulation*, New York: Oxford University Press, available at www.newschool.edu/cepa.

Howell, David R., Margaret Duncan and Ben Harrison (1998), 'Low Wages in the US and High Unemployment in Europe: A Critical Assessment of the Conventional Wisdom', Center for Economic Policy Analysis Working Paper No. 5, New School for Social Research (February).

International Labor Organization (ILO) (1997), 'Chapter 3: Industrial Countries: Reversing the Drift From Full Employment', *World Employment 1996/97*, Geneva: ILO.

International Labor Organization (ILO) (1999), *Key Indicators of the Labor Market* (on CD), Geneva: ILO.

Krueger, Alan B. (1993), 'How Computers Have Changed the Wage Structure: Evidence From Micro Data', *Quarterly Journal of Economics*, February: 33–60.

Krueger, Alan, and Jörn-Steffen Pischke (1997), 'Observations and Conjectures on the U.S. Employment Miracle', NBER Working Paper No. 6146, Cambridge, Massachusetts.

Krugman, Paul (1994), 'Past and Prospective Causes of High Unemployment', in *Reducing Unemployment: Current Issues and Policy Options*, Kansas City, KS: The Federal Reserve Bank of Kansas: 49–80.

Layard, Richard, Stephen Nickell and Richard Jackman (1994), *The Unemployment Crisis*, New York: Oxford University Press.

Lungqvist, Lars and Thomas J. Sargent (1998), 'The European Unemployment Dilemma', *Journal of Political Economy*, **106** (3): 514–50.

Nickell, Stephen (1997), 'Unemployment and Labor Market Rigidities: Europe versus North America', *Journal of Economic Perspectives*, **11** (3), 55–74.

Nickell, Stephen and Brian Bell (1995), 'The Collapse in Demand for the Unskilled and Unemployment Across the OECD', *Oxford Review of Economic Policy*, **11** (1): 40–62.

Nickell, Stephen and Brian Bell (1996), 'Changes in the Distribution of Wages and Unemployment in OECD Countries', *American Economic Review*, **86** (2), May: 302–8.

Nickell, Stephen and Richard Layard (1997), 'Labour Market Institutions and Economic Performance', Discussion Paper, Centre for Economic Performance, Oxford University.

OECD, (1994), *OECD Jobs Study, Evidence and Explanations*, Part I (table 1), Paris: OECD.

OECD (1997a), 'Economic Performance and the Structure of Collective Bargaining', *Employment Outlook*, July: 63–92.

OECD (1997b), *Implementing the OECD Jobs Strategy: Member Countries' Experience*, Paris: OECD.

OECD (1998), 'Making the Most of the Minimum: Statutory Minimum Wages, Employment and Poverty', *Employment Outlook*, June: 31–79.

OECD (1999), 'Employment Protection and Labour Market Performance', *Employment Outlook*, June: 47–131.

Siebert, Horst (1997) 'Labor Market Rigidities: At the Root of Unemployment in Europe', *Journal of Economic Perspectives*, **11** (3), Summer: 37–54.
Thurow, Lester (1997), *Generating Inequality*, New York: Basic Books.

8.   Can a Rising Tide Raise All Boats? Evidence from the Kennedy-Johnson and Clinton-Era Expansions[1]

L. Randall Wray

The Clinton-era expansion was the longest on record, and while the pace of economic growth was not unprecedented, it was reasonably robust. Perhaps most importantly, the expansion seemed to have successfully moved the economy toward fuller, if not full, employment. Many commentators remarked on the tightness of the 'labor market'[2] over the course of the 'Goldilocks' expansion.[3] Employers from various regions reported difficulty in filling job vacancies, and Federal Reserve chairman Alan Greenspan repeatedly warned that the low inflation rates enjoyed in the 1990s could not continue because labor market 'tightness' would eventually place pressure on wages and thus on costs, and eventually prices (Greenspan, 1998). At the end of the expansion, the Fed raised interest rates in a series of steps as a 'pre-emptive' strike against incipient inflation. However, as the economy slipped into recession at the beginning of the new millennium, and as unemployment began to rise, the Fed relented and lowered interest rates to the lowest levels seen in four decades. The wisdom of the Fed's policy, as well as its contribution to the end of Goldilocks will not be explored here.

Instead, the question we ask here is whether the apparent employment gains enjoyed over the Clinton expansion were shared across the working age population. More specifically, does a rising economic tide lift the boats of those with lower skill levels, or will specific policies be required to provide employment opportunities to help them?

There are several potential measures of the degree to which the Clinton rising tide might have raised the boats of those at the bottom. One obvious candidate would be unemployment rates, which declined across the board over the course of the 1990s. By this measure, then, it appears that job opportunities did indeed improve for all segments of the population. Another indicator of a rising tide would be rising wages and income for low-skilled workers. Here the data are more mixed, although real wages did rise, slightly, in the last few years of the expansion, reversing long-term trends. Similarly, one might analyze the distribution of income – which according to many analyses did narrow slightly, again reversing long-term trends.[4] Alternatively, one might also look directly at the numbers of jobs created for low-skilled workers over the expansion, or at employment rates for the low-skilled. Indeed, some, like Ritter (1998), have specifically pointed to rising employment rates of high school dropouts as evidence that the rising tide indeed lifted all boats.

In this chapter, like Ritter, we will focus on job creation and on employment rates rather than on unemployment rates, income distribution, or wages to determine whether job opportunities have actually increased for the low-skilled. Unemployment rates can provide a misleading picture because, as is well known, many who would be willing to work if a job were made available may not be counted in official unemployment figures. For similar reasons, rising wages of those who have jobs may not tell us much about job opportunities or income of those who are not able to get jobs. Further, income distribution could be improved through social programs to redistribute income, rather than by the effects of an economic expansion. While we do not dismiss the importance of falling unemployment rates and rising wages, nor of income redistribution policies, we believe these do give a skewed picture of the extent to which the Clinton expansion lifted boats at the bottom.

We first provide a general overview of employment conditions during the Clinton expansion. As expected, there is at least superficial evidence for the proposition that a rising tide lifts all boats. We next examine several reasons to doubt this rosy picture: rising incarceration rates over the past 15 years have contributed in a significant manner to falling unemployment rates (and even to rising employment rates) of those with low educational attainment; the employment rate gaps between the college educated and high school dropouts remained huge; and anecdotal evidence indicates that, while employers were experiencing trouble recruiting highly educated workers, job openings still generated long queues of job seekers even at the expansion's peak. More importantly, none of the nearly 16 million net new jobs created between 1992 and 2000 went to the half of the population that has not attended college. In other words, we find that no new jobs trickled down. We next provide a detailed calculation of what we identify as the 'potentially employable' – that is, the population that might be willing to work on some conditions if job offers were forthcoming. We find that there may be as many as 14 million potentially employable individuals, the vast majority of whom are not counted as unemployed, who were left behind by the Clinton rising tide.

The Clinton expansion was often compared to the Kennedy-Johnson expansion of the 1960s. In some ways, that earlier expansion was more robust – economic growth was higher, wages grew faster, unemployment fell to lower levels, and the improvement to income distribution was more marked. We will not pursue these issues here. What we will do, however, is to compare the effects of the two expansions in raising the boats of those at the bottom of the educational ladder in terms of employment rates. At the time of the 1960s expansion, there was a debate over whether economic growth alone would be sufficient to expand employment opportunities to the under-employed. The advocacy of growth as a solution to employment problems is generally associated with the Keynesian position. On the other hand, many economists at the time argued that targeted employment programs would be needed to raise all boats; this is generally associated with the Institutionalist position. Ironically, a number of targeted employment programs were put into place in the 1960s and afterward, a policy victory for the Institutionalists, although academic consensus seems to have coalesced around the view that a rising tide is indeed sufficient. As a result, many of the targeted employment programs were eliminated or at least reduced over the course of the 1970s and 1980s, so that few remained by the time of the Clinton expansion. What we find here, however, is that even the strong expansion of the 1960s failed to raise all boats, although it may have been more successful at doing so than was the 1990s expansion. Whether this was due to the fact that the 1960s expansion was stronger and included growth in sectors that employed workers with low educational attainment, or whether it was due to the active labor market policies in place is beyond the scope of this chapter, although it would make an interesting study.

We conclude that a rising tide, alone – no matter how robust – is unlikely to generate a sufficient number of jobs for all who might wish to work. Thus, we advocate a public service employment program that would be specifically designed to 'hire off the bottom'. This policy is consistent with the Institutionalist view that active labor market policies must be used to supplement 'Keynesian' demand management policies in order to provide job opportunities for those at the bottom. While we do not dismiss the substantial benefits of 'rising tides', the view that a rising tide alone is sufficient does not seem to be supported by the evidence from either of these expansions. If anything, the increasing marginalization of those with low educational status makes it even more imperative to adopt targeted employment policy.

LABOR MARKET CONDITIONS DURING THE CLINTON EXPANSION

Superficially, it would appear that the Clinton tide lifted all boats. Not only were the aggregate employment statistics overwhelmingly positive, but the data also suggest that employment gains were widespread across sex, race, and age categories. For example, Bureau of Labor Statistics data in Table 8.1 show that the unemployment rate for most demographic groups matched or even bettered

Table 8.1 Employment and unemployment data by age, sex, and race

	1950	1955	1960	1965	1970	1975	1980	1985	1990	1995	1998	1999	2000
By age													
Employment rate													
Employment rate 16+	56.1	56.6	56.1	56.2	57.4	56.1	59.2	60.1	62.8	62.9	64.1	64.3	64.5
Teen employment ratio	45.4	43.4	40.5	38.8	42.3	43.2	43.2	44.3	45.3	44.2	45.1	44.7	45.3
Unemployment rate													
Labor force 16+	5.2	4.4	5.5	4.5	5.0	8.5	7.2	7.2	5.6	5.6	4.5	4.2	4.0
Teen unemployment rate	12.2	11.1	14.7	15.0	15.3	20.0	17.8	18.6	15.6	17.3	14.6	13.9	13.1
By sex													
Employment rate													
Males 20+	84.2	84.3	81.9	81.2	79.7	74.8	74.7	73.3	74.3	73.0	74.0	74.0	74.1
Females 20+	31.6	33.8	35.7	37.7	41.2	42.3	48.1	51.0	55.2	56.5	58.0	58.5	58.7
Unemployment rate													
Males 20+	5.3	4.0	4.4	3.4	3.0	6.8	5.6	6.2	4.7	4.8	3.7	3.5	3.3
Females 20+	5.1	4.4	5.1	4.5	4.8	8.0	6.4	6.6	4.9	4.9	4.1	3.8	3.6
By race													
Employment rate													
White teens (16–19)	n/a	44.2	41.5	40.3	44.5	46.5	50.7	48.5	49.7	48.8	48.9	48.8	49.4
White males 20+	n/a	84.7	82.4	81.5	80.1	75.7	75.6	74.3	75.1	73.8	74.7	74.8	74.8
Black teens (16–19)	n/a	n/a	n/a	n/a	n/a	23.1	23.9	24.6	26.7	25.7	30.1	27.9	29.5
Black males 20+	n/a	n/a	n/a	n/a	n/a	66.5	65.8	64.6	67.1	66.1	67.1	67.5	67.6
Unemployment rate													
White 16+	n/a	3.9	5.0	4.1	4.6	7.8	6.3	6.2	4.8	4.9	3.9	3.7	3.5
Hispanic 16+	n/a	n/a	n/a	n/a	n/a	12.2	10.1	10.6	8.2	9.3	7.2	6.4	5.7
Black 16+	n/a	n/a	n/a	n/a	n/a	14.8	14.3	15.1	12.5	10.4	8.9	8.0	7.6

Source: www.bls.gov/cps/cpsatabs.htm.

the low unemployment rates reached during the 1960s. Even teens (16 to 19 years old), traditionally beset by unemployment considerably higher than other population segments, found a more receptive job market. The teen unemployment rate fell to a 40-year low despite the fact that, as we shall soon see, college education is more important today than it was in the past for obtaining and keeping a job.

Table 8.1 also shows that job growth apparently spread to traditionally disadvantaged racial groups. Blacks and Hispanics enjoyed the lowest unemployment rates since the data were first disaggregated by race in the early 1970s. To be sure, both racial groups continued to endure unemployment rates much higher than those of their white counterparts, indicating that there remained considerable room for progress. For example, by the end of the boom in 2000, blacks aged 16 and over had an unemployment rate of 7.6 per cent compared with 3.5 per cent for whites. Employment-to-population ratios (hereafter referred to as employment rates) were more ambiguous but still suggested similar trends. The overall employment rate for people aged 16 and over grew steadily throughout the 1990s, reaching a record high of 64.5 per cent. The expansion also led to improvements in the employment rates for Hispanics, black teens, and black males.

The overall picture then is one of falling unemployment rates and rising employment rates in the mid- to late 1990s. This seems to be consistent with the view that labor markets were tight and that a rising tide increased employment opportunities for all groups. However, closer analysis indicates that this is true only for the half of the population that has attended college.

Labor Market Conditions for Low-Skilled Workers

The 'rising tide' argument might lead one to expect that as an expansion continues and as labor market conditions become tight, employers reach further down the skills continuum so that jobs 'trickle down' to the least skilled. Perhaps an employer would prefer to hire a college graduate, but if the market becomes so tight that college graduates must be bid away from other firms, the employer might settle for an employee who has not earned a college degree and invest in additional training to bring the employee's skills up to the desired level. An employer who would have been happy to hire someone with a couple years of college education might have to settle for a high school graduate. And so on down to the employer who must reach into the pool of high school dropouts.

We might also expect that as labor markets tighten, unemployment rates would fall first for workers of higher skill levels and then for workers with less skill and education. However, labor economists recognize that there are large flows into and out of the labor force, with many individuals becoming employed or leaving the labor force without ever having been counted as unemployed. As

Figure 8.1 shows, the civilian noninstitutionalized population can be divided into two main groups – those who worked (115 million), and those who did not (61 million).

Note that we focus here on the age 25 and over population to eliminate most of those who are too young to work, or who are in school. The figures here include the population over 65, who of course have significantly lower employment rates, but we will also examine the 25–64 age group below (see section on 'A Closer Look at Employment Rates'). The 'did not work' population can be further subdivided into two groups – those who were officially unemployed (3.5 million), and those who were out of the labor force (57.5 million). Finally, note that the unemployed group is counted as part of the labor force (118.5 million), and also is counted as 'did not work'.

While the media often focuses on only the 'unemployed' category, this is a small proportion of the 'did not work' category – most of whom are out of the labor force. This would not matter if those who lost jobs only went into the category called 'unemployed', and if all those who got jobs came from the unemployed category. In fact, flows are much more complex (as represented by the arrows). Those who are employed can become unemployed, or drop out of the labor force, or can leave the population altogether (die). Those who come into the employed category may have previously been unemployed, out of the labor force, or not in the population (they may have been age 24). Further, most labor force statistics are only for the civilian, noninstitutionalized population – excluding the military and penal systems. Hence, for example, the number of unemployed could fall if an unemployed individual joined the army, or became incarcerated.

When job growth is strong, we would expect that many who had been out of the labor force (not actively seeking work) might begin to look for jobs and some of these might then be counted as unemployed. Thus, unemployment rates alone may not tell the whole story, and a better indication of improved job prospects might be the employment rate. We would expect to see rising employment rates, first for the higher skilled and then for the lower skilled. Eventually, if labor markets became sufficiently tight, the labor force participation rates for all skill levels should converge toward some maximum feasible rate, unless there is some reason to expect that the low skilled have a systematically lower desire to work or that employers will not hire the low-skilled no matter how tight labor markets become.[5] On the surface, employment rate convergence appears to have taken place in the 1990s. For example, Joseph Ritter pointed out that 'lower-skill groups have increased their employment rates significantly; since 1994 the ratio for those who did not finish high school rose by about 3 percentage points' (Ritter, 1998, p. 1). Indeed, Ritter reported that all of the growth of the overall employment rate (which grew from 62.8 per cent in 1990 to 64 per cent in 1999) could be attributed to those who have not

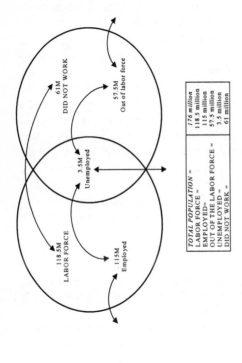

61M
DID NOT WORK

118.5M
LABOR FORCE

3.5M
Unemployed

115M
Employed

57.5M
Out of labor force

TOTAL POPULATION =	176 million
LABOR FORCE =	118.5 million
EMPLOYED=	115 million
OUT OF THE LABOR FORCE =	57.5 million
UNEMPLOYED =	3.5 million
DID NOT WORK =	61 million

Source: Bureau of Labor Statistics (2000).

Figure 8.1 The US labor force in December 2000 (age 25 and over, noninstitutional, civilian)

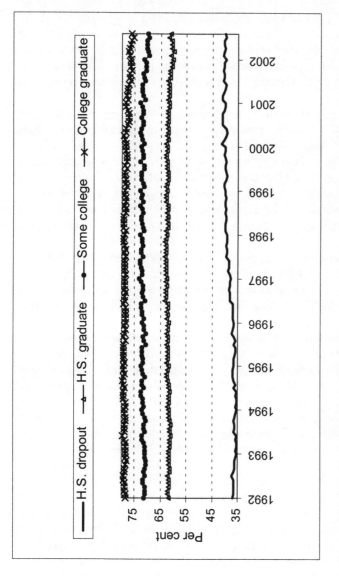

Source: BLS, www.bls.gov/cps/cpsatabs.htm. Data through August 2002. Data for civilian, noninstitutional population.

Figure 8.2 *Employment rates, population of 25 and over, by education, 1992–2002 (seasonally adjusted)*

obtained a college degree, with the greatest gains at the lowest levels of educational attainment.

As Figure 8.2 (which essentially updates the data presented by Ritter) shows, the employment rate for those over age 25 with a college degree or better remained virtually constant through 2000 at just under 79 per cent; the rate for those with some college (those who either did not graduate from college or earned an associate's degree) rose 1.4 percentage points to 72.4 per cent; and the rate for high school graduates rose 0.9 percentage points to 62.7 per cent. In contrast, the employment rate for high school dropouts rose 3 percentage points to 40.[6]

Ritter noted that although 'unemployment rates produce a less dramatic picture' (1998, p. 1), they, too, provided supporting evidence for the view that a rising tide had lifted all boats. For example, between 1992 and 1999 the unemployment rate fell from 3.2 per cent to 1.9 per cent for college graduates, from 5.7 per cent to 2.9 per cent for workers with some college, and from 6.8 per cent to 3.6 per cent for high school graduates. As with employment rates, the largest gain was experienced at the bottom of the educational ladder: the unemployment rate fell 4.7 percentage points to 6.8 per cent for high school dropouts.

Today, 16 per cent of the population 25 and over have not finished high school, 34 per cent are high school graduates but did not attend college, 25 per cent have some college education or an associate's degree, and another 25 per cent have a college degree. Thus, the US population is evenly divided between those who have at least some college and those who have none. Educational attainment is generally regarded as a good proxy for skill level, so the data for employment and unemployment rates seem to support the belief that the current expansion increased job opportunities, with the greatest gains accruing to those with the lowest skill level, or, at least, to those with the least education – and especially for high school dropouts. One could conclude that if the expansion had continued, job opportunities would have continued to 'trickle down' so that eventually both the unemployment rate and the employment rate of high school dropouts might converge toward those for college graduates.

Déjà Vu?

A strikingly similar story was told during the Kennedy expansion, the last time the US experienced such strong, sustained growth, low unemployment and low inflation. Most economists, especially those of the Keynesian persuasion, attributed falling unemployment rates and strong economic growth to government demand management policy, either via tax cuts such as those in 1964, or spending on the war against Vietnam (Marshall et al., 1984). They believed that more government spending was a big part of the reason for prosperity. In contrast, the prevailing view today credits free markets and less government intervention with creating and sustaining the 1990s expansion.

While these views differ markedly in their support for government intervention, they nevertheless share an important underlying premise, namely the view that a rising tide will reach down and help even the least skilled, whether that rising tide results from supply-side or demand-side factors. One economist to challenge this view during the 1960s expansion was Charles Killingsworth, who argued that a significant portion of the fall in the official unemployment rate (to 3.5 per cent in 1969) could be explained by the Vietnam War's direct impact on the labor force.[7] He noted that a large number of the officially unemployed were the first to sign up for the war. As mentioned, virtually all labor force statistics are for the civilian, noninstitutional population, so a decline in the number of unemployed due to a shift of millions into the armed forces would naturally reduce the official measurement of the unemployment rate as it lowered both the numerator and the denominator.

Killingsworth, however, is perhaps better known for his second argument, which rests on the view that strong economic growth alone could not solve what was essentially a structural problem: rapid technological change and a growing shift toward a service-sector economy meant that many workers were in danger of becoming 'obsolete' or unemployable. He argued the unemployment rate would therefore eventually rise (and the employment rate would fall – for the marginalized) and believed that the Vietnam War managed to delay this process only by creating temporary additional demand for unskilled and semi-skilled labor in the military and, secondarily, in the weapons industry. His analysis therefore focused on falling labor force participation rates of the unskilled (what he called 'hidden unemployment'), which he attributed to a long run shortage of job opportunities for this group – a shortage that could not be resolved by aggregate demand management alone. Killingsworth (1970) later demonstrated that, among males, labor force participation rates are lowest for those with less education, regardless of age. During the 1960s, for example, participation rates of college graduates age 65 and over were more than double those of males age 65 and over with some high school education. Furthermore, participation rates of those in the bottom half of the education ladder have been on a long-term declining trend (again, across the age spectrum) even during the booming 1960s economy, while participation rates have been rising for those with the most education.

We will come back in a moment to an analysis of the 1960s expansion. Much as in the 1960s, however, there are good reasons to question the rosy scenario painted by 1990s' official statistics and many of them have a lot in common with Killingsworth's analysis. First, a number of studies have demonstrated that the unemployment rate would be considerably higher if it were adjusted for the rapid increase in the inmate (prison and jail) population –

currently at about 2 million – witnessed during the last 20 years. For example, Beckett and Western (1997) find that the unemployment rate between 1990 and 1994 would have been 7.7 per cent instead of the official 5.9 per cent had it been adjusted to include the inmate population.[8] Moreover, the inmate population is disproportionately made up of young, able-bodied, but poorly educated males, especially black men. According to the US Department of Justice (Gilliard, 1999), more than 41 per cent of the almost 600,000 people held in jails (excluding prisons) as of 30 June 1998 were black. Beckett and Western find that the unemployment rate for black men, when adjusted for those held in prisons and jails, would have been 18.8 per cent between 1990 and 1994 instead of the official 11.3 per cent. This, of course, recalls Killingsworth's suggestion that the unemployment rate during the 1960s was reduced by the large number of unemployed persons joining the armed forces (again, largely young, able-bodied men).

Indeed, growth of the number of prime-age (18–44 years) males in prison has very nearly matched the loss of positions in the military since the late 1960s: well over 1.5 million more men are in prison or jail today, while the military has about 2 million fewer on active duty. Like those in the armed forces, the inmate population is excluded from the official statistics. Evidence suggests that two-thirds of inmates – or about 1.67 million persons – were not employed prior to arrest (although many or most of those would not have been counted in the official unemployment statistics because they were out of the labor force). Note that there were well under 4 million unemployed adults aged 25 years and older at the end of 1999, so the number of jobless males who become incarcerated (and thus disappear from labor force statistics – about 1.7 million) is relatively significant. Indeed, 10 per cent of all prime-age (18–44 years) males without a high school degree are now in prison – more than the number who were officially counted as unemployed in 1999 (Wray, 2000).

While it can be objected that many of those who end up in prison should not be added to the officially unemployed (because they would be out of the labor force if not incarcerated), incarceration does reduce 'excess population' both by lowering the unemployment rate (reducing the number of unemployed in the numerator as well as the number in the labor force in the denominator) and by raising the employment rate (mostly by reducing the population in the denominator). Second, the gaps between those who attended college and high school dropouts are huge, especially for employment rates. Well over half of noninstitutionalized high school dropouts remained out of the labor force even after nearly a decade of growth, compared with only a quarter of those who attended college. If the Clinton expansion raised the employment rate for high school dropouts by only about 3 percentage points over a period of eight years, by simple extrapolation the expansion would have to continue for another 104 years before the gap could be closed. To be sure, these figures are a bit misleading because of the age-educational status interaction in the American population. As average educational levels have risen over the postwar period, the average age of typical high school dropouts has increased. While employment rates rise consistently with educational status, regardless of age (for those over age 65, employment rates are much higher for college graduates than for high school dropouts), employment rates fall with age. Hence to make a more consistent comparison we will separate (below, 'A Closer Look at Employment Rates') the impact of age from that of educational status, but we will still find a large and growing gap based on educational status.

Third, there is anecdotal evidence to suggest that, even at the peak, employers preferred to wait for a strong candidate instead of hiring the 'first warm body off the street'. For example, a *Wall Street Journal* article cited one Florida hotelier who said that a 'tight' labor market means he has to be 'more selective than ever' about filling existing positions or hiring new workers, which is the opposite of what the 'rising tide' argument would have us believe.[9] Unfilled vacancies, in turn, put pressure on existing employees who must bridge the gap by working additional overtime hours, a result that is well documented in the national data (see our discussion of Bluestone and Rose below). In other words, employers were not necessarily willing to lower their hiring standards enough to provide work to the low skilled and ill-trained, because the expected costs associated with training these potential workers were believed to be too onerous.

The fact that hours worked tend to rise late in the expansion is further evidence of the reluctance on the part of employers to hire those they perceive as being ill-equipped, ill-trained, and ill-schooled, not necessarily of a labor shortage. This is bad news for supporters of welfare-to-work programs because if employers prefer to wait for strong candidates they may never lower standards sufficiently to recruit former welfare recipients. A survey by the Jerome Levy Economics Institute (Levin-Waldman, 1999), for example, found reluctance on the part of small businesses to hire former welfare recipients – even in 'tight' labor markets.

Fourth, one would expect the trend toward higher employment rates for the unskilled to be reversed as soon as the economy slows, with the 'last hired' low-skilled workers being the 'first fired'. Many analysts believe that the likelihood of a deep and prolonged recession is high (Godley and Wray, 1999). This means the gaps could become wider than they were in 1992, before the expansion.

Finally, and more importantly, careful analysis of employment and population data casts doubt even on the conclusion that employment opportunities increased significantly for the less skilled during the robust Clinton expansion. While it is true that unemployment rates fell and that employment rates rose, it is less than clear that these data indicate substantially more favorable labor market conditions for the lower half of the skills ladder. Indeed, the apparent improvement may have had more to do with reduction of the civilian population of those who have not attended college. Reflecting rising educational levels in the population over time (see Figure 8.3), the non-institutionalized high school dropout population aged 25 and older fell by 5.4 million; and the number out of the labor force fell by about 3.6 million over the 1990s expansion. This is a case where percentages and rates can be quite misleading; as we will show, almost all the job gains went to the population with at least some college education.

PATTERNS OF JOB GROWTH IN THE 1990s

Figure 8.3 presents the data in diagrammatic form to clarify the situation. The top part of the figure shows that the US population grew by 16.87 million between 1992 and 2000, employment rose by 15.84 million, unemployment fell by 2.92 million, and the number of individuals out of the labor force rose by 3.95 million. The situation, then, appears to be consistent with the view that labor markets were tight because employment grew almost as fast as population.

However, the bottom part of Figure 8.3 shows that virtually all of the population growth consisted of additions of individuals who had some college or had graduated college – two groups that already had high employment rates. The number of high school dropouts fell by 5.5 million, with the largest decline among those who had been out of the labor force.[10] Indeed, somewhat surprisingly, there was no net gain in the number of high school dropouts employed over the whole expansion – on the contrary, 1.2 million jobs were lost.

This means that all of the rise of the employment rate for that group (reported above and by Ritter) was due to a shrinking population and none to rising employment. High school graduates gained just 683,000 jobs, while 16.3 million new jobs went to those who had at least some college education. Although it is true that the number of unemployed fell by 752,000 for high school dropouts, and by 1.3 million for high school graduates, the overall employment picture is not one of substantial improvement for those with low skills – if we think of improvement as an increase in the number of jobs ('trickling down'). One could argue, based on the increase in their employment rate, that the situation of those who did not attend college (high school dropouts and graduates) improved, if one merely focused on the loss of population in the face of a nearly constant number of jobs.[11] Still, over the entire Clinton expansion, no new jobs were created for the half of the population that had not attended college. Thus, we believe the data rather strongly contradict the story that says a tight labor market was forcing firms to reach down to hire the less skilled, since there was actually a net job loss of nearly half a million jobs among the lower skilled. The rise of

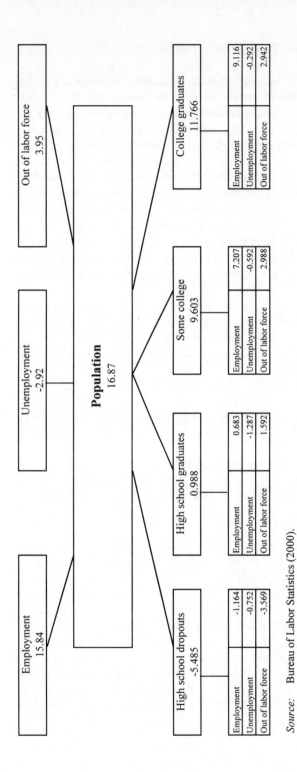

Source: Bureau of Labor Statistics (2000).

Figure 8.3 Changes in population, 25 and over, by employment and educational attainment, January 1992–December 2000 (change in millions)

the employment rate of the bottom half of the population – which was used by Ritter and others as evidence in favor of the belief that a rising tide lifts all boats – was due solely to a decline of population, and not to an increase of employment.

Hence, we find that job creation during the Clinton expansion was just sufficient to provide jobs for college-educated entrants to the labor force. Job creation was not sufficient to draw low-skilled workers from out of the labor force; indeed, in an important sense, there was no improvement of job prospects for low-skilled, out-of-the-labor-force individuals. This can be attributed either to relatively rapid growth of the college-educated population or to the relatively low pace of net job creation. In other words, there was not sufficient job growth to expand employment for both college-educated workers and low-skilled workers. The overall picture is certainly not one of tremendous employment gains for the bottom half of the skills ladder.

This analysis and these results are consistent with a recent analysis of structural shifts in the US labor market from 1971 to 1995 by Pryor and Schaffer (1999). The authors argue that the problem is not merely one of insufficient job growth but rather the 'crowding out' of low skill workers by college-educated workers. Low-skilled positions are increasingly filled by workers 'whose education credentials exceed job requirements', forcing many of the least-educated workers to leave the labor force entirely (Pryor and Schaffer, 1999, pp. 3–4), which again implies that economic expansion alone will not be sufficient to 'lift the boats' of those at the bottom. While we do not want to get into the debate about 'good jobs versus bad jobs' and while it at least superficially appears that better jobs were created during the Clinton expansion than those that were created during the Reagan expansion of the 1980s, we believe that the evidence is strong that college-educated workers have filled the vast majority of the jobs created during the expansion, and that it is quite unlikely that job growth can be sufficiently robust to alter this result.

Our analysis, then, raises questions about the degree of labor market tightness reached over the Clinton expansion. Although it may be true that labor bottlenecks exist, the overall picture is not one of significant pressure on labor markets – job creation just kept pace with the increase of the number of college-educated workers seeking jobs. This analysis is consistent with many other analyses and with the growing recognition that the unemployment rate by itself says little. As noted earlier, Bluestone and Rose (1998) call into question the usefulness of the unemployment rate as a true measure of labor market slack, because it fails to reflect accurately hours worked by people who already have jobs. They show how hours worked climbed steadily since the early 1980s, returning to a level not seen since the late 1960s and leading to a de facto labor supply increase that has kept a lid on wages.

As Bluestone and Rose show, the picture for high school dropouts appears worse still when one looks at data on hours worked. College workers have, on average, the longest workweek, followed by high school graduates, workers with some college, and, finally, high school dropouts. In 1995, for example, the average college worker put in 41.6 hours, 18 per cent more than high school dropouts, who averaged only 35.2 hours, and the gap has been steadily widening. Whereas employees in the college graduate, some college, and high school graduate categories have all increased hours worked since the 1970s, high school dropouts have seen a systematic decline. Thus, not only are high school dropouts stymied by an unreceptive job market, but they are also missing out on one of the few ways that workers have been able to increase real income in recent years, by working additional hours.

We conclude that both the official unemployment rate and employment rates overstate the degree of labor market tightness. While labor economists are generally familiar with problems that can arise when one uses only the unemployment rate (or even the employment rate) as a proxy for labor market tightness, it also remains true that policy makers and most economists do place great weight on low unemployment rates as the primary indicator of labor market tightness. Indeed, Chairman Greenspan consistently cited the low unemployment rates achieved in the 1990s as cause for concern that 'tight' labor markets would sooner or later induce inflation. We believe that a detailed look at the evidence, however, demonstrates that there remained a great deal of slack, especially at the bottom of the skills ladder, even at the peak of the 1990s expansion.

A Closer Look at Employment Rates

As we mentioned above, employment rates fall with age, dropping off markedly after age 65. Furthermore, two-thirds of those age 65 and above have a high school diploma or less, hence, employment rates for those above age 65 are low because of the age/educational status interaction. Still, employment rates even for those age 65 and over are strongly correlated with educational achievement. Approximately 93 per cent of high school dropouts age 65 and above are out of the labor force, versus only 81.5 per cent of college grads in that age group. As average educational levels increase over time, relatively more of the high school dropouts are concentrated in the older age groups. For this reason, employment rates by educational status will be biased downward for the groups with the lowest educational levels. Table 8.2 shows employment rates for the periods 1962–69 and 1993–2000 (two more or less comparable boom periods) for the civilian, noninstitutionalized, population age 25–64.

Table 8.2   *Employment rates, 25–64 years old by educational attainment (percentage of civilian noninstitutional population)*

	H.S. dropout	H.S. graduate	Some college	College graduate
1962	60.93	63.02	66.94	81.40
1963	*NA*	*NA*	*NA*	*NA*
1964	61.60	63.87	67.56	81.55
1965	62.10	64.82	67.07	81.89
1966	62.74	65.93	67.69	80.89
1967	62.60	66.64	68.70	81.49
1968	63.23	67.34	70.53	81.48
1969	63.16	67.96	70.92	81.46
1993	51.86	72.05	77.14	84.61
1994	50.96	72.63	77.63	84.88
1995	53.84	73.31	77.88	86.60
1996	53.65	73.66	78.94	85.97
1997	55.22	74.54	79.07	86.81
1998	57.61	74.68	78.97	86.59
1999	57.84	75.00	79.37	85.14
2000	57.76	75.49	79.71	85.53

Note: Data are not strictly comparable. For the 1960s, the category 'Some college' was 'College 1–3 years' and 'College graduate' was 'College 4 years or more'.

Source: US Census Bureau (for the 1990s), BLS (for the 1960s). Data for 1963 is not available.

In 1962, nearly half of the population aged 25–64 had not graduated from high school; another 30 per cent consisted of high school graduates, while 20 per cent had attended college (with half of those graduating). The employment rate of high school dropouts rose from about 61 per cent in 1962 to just under 64 per cent by 1968 – a rise of slightly less than 3 percentage points. By contrast, the employment rate of college graduates remained nearly constant over the expansion at just under 82 per cent. By 2000, fewer than 13 per cent of the population had not graduated from high school, and almost 55 per cent had at least some college. The employment rate of high school dropouts rose from 52 per cent in 1993 to a peak of 58 per cent by 1998 – a rise of about 6 percentage points – and then remained constant for the rest of the expansion. The employment rate of college graduates remained relatively constant, rising by a maximum of 2 percentage points over the expansion. Hence, what we find is that the employment rate gain by high school dropouts was actually somewhat better during the 1990s expansion than it had been in the 1960s. On the other hand, the employment rate gap between those with the lowest level of educational achievement and those with the highest had increased from just over 20 percentage points in 1962 to about 33 percentage points by 1993. By the end of the Kennedy-Johnson expansion, the gap had been reduced to 18 percentage points, while it remained at 28 percentage points at the end of the Clinton expansion.

Over the longer term, while peak employment rates of college graduates have increased by just under 5 percentage points, those of high school dropouts have declined by 5 percentage points. Thus, even after excluding those over age 64, who have low levels of labor force participation, we find that the employment rate gaps are huge and growing. Economic expansions reduce the gap somewhat as employment rates rise for those with the least education. However, the rise is quite small relative to the gap that remains even at the expansion's peak. Further, as our analysis has made clear, the rise of the employment rate among those with the least education is not due to a greater number of jobs 'trickling down', but rather is due to a declining population of that group.

If we look more closely at the Kennedy-Johnson expansion, we find the same phenomenon. Over the course of that expansion, the population of high school dropouts fell by some 5 million (recall that some of this was due to military recruitment), while the number of jobs available to high school dropouts fell by 2.5 million. Because the population fell faster than the number of jobs lost, the employment rate rose. Over the longer-term, however, job loss for the least skilled has been relatively greater than the decline in this population; hence, employment rates have fallen (the number of jobs fell by some 53 per cent, while the population of high school dropouts fell by 48 per cent between the two expansion peaks). Expansions only temporarily reverse this trend.

Indeed, things are a bit worse than these figures indicate, because we have excluded the institutionalized population. As noted above, in the 1960s the number in the armed forces peaked above 3.5 million, of which many were men with low educational status. For most of these men, service in the military provided an avenue to a decent job in spite of low educational attainment. Today, the military reduces the potential labor force by a much smaller number (about 1.4 million), and no longer takes high school dropouts (virtually all recruits hold a high school diploma, and the average educational level achieved by those in the military is substantially higher than that of the population as a whole). On the other hand, our criminal justice system 'recruits', and removes from the noninstitutionalized population, 2 million inmates. (See Wray, 2000, for sources and calculations related to incarceration figures). About 90 per cent of those are male, nearly half have not graduated from high school, and almost all are 'prime age' (18–44 years). Approximately 600,000 inmates are released annually, with the average releasee committing a dozen crimes annually. In other words, unlike the military in the 1960s, incarceration probably reduces the employability of most prison 'recruits' and helps to develop an 'underclass' of virtually unemployable men who will remain outside the labor force, and will cost society an average of $80,000 per year per inmate released due to crimes committed.

As many as three-quarters of all prime age (18–44) black males without a high school degree are currently under control of the criminal justice system (in prison or jail, or on parole or probation). The comparable figure for white males is just under one-third. Clearly, this is a huge social problem that is not captured in the official labor statistics, which focus only on the noninstitutionalized population, and which usually ignore those who are out of the labor force.

THE POTENTIALLY EMPLOYABLE

As we noted above, unemployment rates for the less educated are significantly higher than for those with at least some college. However, more importantly, the employment rate is strikingly lower for those with the lowest educational attainment; an astounding 60 per cent of the noninstitutionalized 25-and-over high school dropout population was out of the labor force at the end of the 1990s, compared with just under 20 per cent of college graduates in the same age group. For the 25–64 age group, less than 15 per cent of those with a college degree were out of the labor force, compared with about 43 per cent of those with less than a high school degree. (Note, again, that these figures exclude the institutionalized population.) While the gap closed a bit over the 1990s, even after the long and robust expansion more than 56 million noninstitutionalized 25-and-over adults remained out of the labor force in 1999 – a number many times greater than the 3.8 million who were officially unemployed.

Admittedly, many of the 56 million do not wish to participate in the labor force; some are willing to participate only on some conditions, and 28 million are age 65 and over. However, it is useful to try to estimate how many of those currently out of the labor force might be a potential source of labor supply under ideal conditions. This will help us to understand how 'tight' labor markets are, or, alternatively, how much 'waste' of potential human resource there is even after a long, relatively robust, expansion.

Economists have long understood that flows among official categories are large: about half of those individuals who lose jobs become officially classified as out of the labor force rather than as unemployed (Marshall et al., 1984, p. 364). Further, many of those who obtain jobs come from out of the labor force rather than from the ranks of the unemployed, and there are individuals who come from out of the labor force to join the officially unemployed. Some empirical research has even shown that for certain population segments there may be no substantive difference between being unemployed and being out of the labor force (Summers and Clark, 1979; Tano, 1991; Gonul, 1992; Jones and Riddell, 1999). For this reason, one cannot rely solely on data for the officially unemployed to obtain estimates of how many individuals would accept jobs if they became available.

Further, job availability alone does not determine whether an individual will come into the labor force. Individuals may be out of the labor force for a number of reasons: prospective wages may be too low (for example, for those with low skills); family responsibilities may be too great (for example, a person might have to remain home to care for children or sick relatives); cultural norms and expectations may raise barriers (for example, labor force participation by women is frowned upon in some groups); poor health (mental and physical) or personal characteristics (gang membership, criminal record) may diminish individuals' desire to work and their desirability from the perspective of potential employers.

A study by former Bureau of Labor Statistics economist Monica Castillo (1998) provides evidence that individuals classified as nonparticipants are not always unwilling or unable to work. Castillo found that 10 per cent (or 6.2 million) of those classified as out of the labor force in 1994 said they wanted a job. Blacks and young people made up a large portion of these people. Of the 6.2 million who had been out of the labor force in 1994 but said they wanted to work, more than 2.5 million (41 per cent) came into the labor force during the next year. Castillo's study also indicates that prior work experience as well as current participation in the labor force are important factors in determining future employability. For example, only one-third of those who in 1994 were classified as nonparticipants and said they wanted a job were able to find work in 1995, compared with a 53 per cent success rate (in finding a job) for those who in 1994 were classified as unemployed. These data suggest there is a significant pool of potential workers outside the measured labor force with some subset actually flowing into the labor force. However, many of them find it difficult to get a job even when they come into the labor force to search for work.

Low employment rates for those without any college education cannot be attributed only to a lack of available jobs. Many have other characteristics (physical handicaps, racial or gender characteristics that are subject to discrimination, etc.) that make it more difficult for them to obtain a job, or they may have motivational or other psychological issues that prevent them from looking for work. However, we believe it is still worthwhile to obtain what might be thought of as an upper-bound estimate of the number of potentially employable, which would include not only those who are actively seeking work (now counted as unemployed), but also those who are currently out of the labor force but who might be employed if some conditions were met. We will assume that the labor force participation rate for college graduates represents a feasible

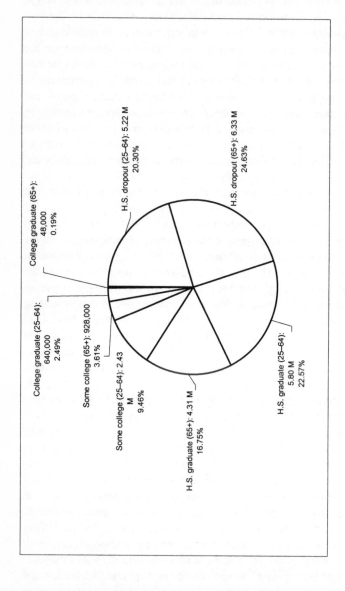

College graduate (65+):
48,000
0.19%

H.S. dropout (25–64): 5.22 M
20.30%

H.S. dropout (65+): 6.33 M
24.63%

College graduate (25–64):
640,000
2.49%

Some college (65+): 928,000
3.61%

Some college (25–64): 2.43
M
9.46%

H.S. graduate (65+): 4.31 M
16.75%

H.S. graduate (25–64):
5.80 M
22.57%

Note: Numbers are in millions. Total potentially employable by age group: 14.09M for 25–64; 11.62M for 65+.

Source: Bureau of Labor Statistics (2000).

Figure 8.4 Potentially employable workers, 25 and over, by age and education, mid-year 1999

maximum on the grounds that given tight labor markets for the highly skilled, it is reasonable to assume that all college graduates who want to work are working or actively seeking work, with only some frictional unemployment and with virtually no one involuntarily out of the labor force. In other words, we assume that college graduates face an 'ideal' labor market with no barriers to finding a job. Using the participation rate of the college graduates as an ideal, we then calculated how many potentially employable individuals existed for each educational category by subtracting the number employed from a target number based on a participation rate of 80.2 per cent of the population for those age 25 and above, or a participation rate of 87.6 per cent for those aged 25 to 64. We find that in 1999, at the expansion's peak, there were 25.7 million potentially employable adults age 25 and above, or 14.1 million potentially employable adults age 25–64. (See Figure 8.4.) Obviously, this number is much in excess of the number of officially unemployed (which was less than 3.8 million for the 25-and-over population midway through 1999).

Some might object that those over age 65 should be excluded from our calculation, which reduces the number of potentially employable from 25.7 million to 14.1 million. There is little doubt that many over age 65 do not want to work, as evidenced by the decline of labor force participation rates even for college graduates as they reach normal retirement age. On the other hand, given that lifetime earnings are significantly affected by educational attainment, we expect that many of the 10.6 million elderly with no college experience that we counted as potentially employable would, if given a chance, supplement their relatively low retirement income (mostly, Social Security) with wages if jobs (especially part-time jobs) were made available. College-educated individuals aged 65 and over are either working or have probably chosen to stay out of the labor force. High school dropouts aged 65 and over probably do not have a choice.

That being said, the figure of 14.1 million potentially employable workers for the 25–64 age group is a reasonable estimate of the number of people who could work under 'ideal' conditions. There is a glaring disparity between the number of potentially employable workers at the low end of the education scale and the number at the high end. Certainly most of the unemployment for college graduates can be accounted for by frictional unemployment. The same cannot be said for high school dropouts or high school graduates who are unemployed or might be involuntarily out of the labor force, what Killingsworth (1970) called 'hidden unemployment'.

Looking at it another way, an additional 14 million jobs would have to be created to bring employment rates for all educational groups between the ages of 25 and 64 up to the rate enjoyed by college graduates – that is, the Clinton expansion created only half the number of jobs required. And, as we have shown above, the jobs created during the expansion went almost exclusively to the highly educated – who already had high employment rates.

Of course, it would be wrong to suppose that the 25.7 million potentially employable people over the age of 25, or the 14.1 million potentially employable in the 25 to 64 age group, produce nothing of value. Many are caring for young children or the sick, many participate as volunteers in a variety of useful activities, many provide household services that make it easier for others to participate more fully in the labor force, and others probably participate in 'underground' activities – some of which may add to our nation's quality of life while others probably reduce it. Also, given our state of knowledge, it is impossible to predict accurately how many of these individuals would voluntarily participate under reasonable conditions (for example, if a job were offered at a minimum wage with a package of benefits that might include health care and child care). Our point is to question the ability of a rising tide to raise all boats, not to claim that it is absolutely essential for every potentially employable person to enter the labor force.

One might object to our analysis on the basis of Occam's razor: perhaps all of those who are currently out of the labor force really are out of the labor force by choice. There are good reasons to believe this is not the case. First, as mentioned above, we know that flows (or 'churning') among the official categories are large – a person currently counted as out of the labor force may well show up in the labor force as employed or unemployed in a later survey. As the study by Castillo demonstrated, many of those currently out of the labor force do want to work and may well enter the labor force over the course of a year. Second, anecdotal evidence indicates that when a major employer announces new positions, long queues of applicants result; employers complain about the quality of applicants, but not about the lack of applicants.[12]

Finally, we believe it is misleading to conduct a 'static' analysis of labor market conditions; what is required is a 'dynamic' analysis. Although it may be true that many of those with low educational attainment really do not want to, or cannot, work, this does not mean that policy should turn a blind eye to the problem. The relatively low employment rate of high school dropouts and even of high school graduates after removal of the 65 and over population indicates there is a serious social problem that apparently cannot be resolved by a robust and long expansion alone. Even if none of these individuals could be drawn into the labor force now, we need to put into place policies that would increase job opportunities for the next crop of young people who for whatever reason do not attend college.

It is highly probable that the longer individuals remain outside the labor force, the less likely it becomes that they will find work, especially if they have low educational attainment. Long bouts of unemployment also entail high personal and societal costs. Various psychological studies have linked prolonged unemployment to a drop in expectations and motivation to seek work (Feather and Davenport, 1981), perception of diminished self-worth (Cohn, 1978), and higher rates of suicide, mental illness, and alcohol abuse (Mallinckrodt and Fretz, 1988). Other studies have shown that unemployment is highly correlated with crime, gang membership, divorce, and loss of human capital. Thus, even if it were true that none of those currently out of the labor force are really 'employable', this should be largely attributed to the negative effects that lack of employment opportunity has on motivation, human development, and general physical and mental well-being. Social costs could be reduced by 'nipping in the bud' whatever barriers to job market entry exist for young high school dropouts before they join the ranks of the 'unemployable'.

Employment opportunities must be created to raise the labor force participation rates of the young who will not attend college. To repeat, half of the US population has not attended college and this ratio is not likely to change rapidly. So, even if far fewer than our calculated 25.7 million (or 14.1 million if we exclude those over age 65) are potentially employable today, well-designed policies could reduce the waste of human potential that undoubtedly exists and will continue to exist when more than 60 per cent of high school dropouts (or over 41 per cent after removing the 65 and over population) and 37 per cent of high school graduates (or 25 per cent after removing the 65 and over population) are not employed, even after a long and robust expansion.

A RISING TIDE IS NOT ENOUGH

Our analysis harkens back to the old debate between Keynesians and Institutionalists on the best way to increase job opportunities for disadvantaged groups. Is an expanding economy with macro policies designed to fine-tune aggregate demand sufficient, as the Keynesians argue, or are well-targeted micro policies required, as the Institutionalists hold?[13] During the 1960s and 1970s the Keynesian position came to dominate. While it is true that interventionist labor market programs were tried even during the Keynesian 1960s, reaching a culmination in the early1970s, they were always small, and were gradually scaled back, if not abandoned altogether, by the end of the 1970s.

Indeed, as our analysis showed, even the robust Kennedy-Johnson expansion only increased the employment ratio of high school dropouts by 5 percentage points – and that was in conjunction with the 'War on Poverty' and during implementation of active labor market policies as well as the Vietnam War build-up. During the Kennedy-Johnson expansion, almost 6.5 million jobs were created, but high school dropouts actually faced a net loss of jobs equal to 2.4 million, with employment rates increasing only due to a decline of 5 million in the noninstitutionalized high school dropout population. Hence, just as in the

1990s, economic expansion did not increase the absolute supply of jobs to the low skilled. In any case, the stagflationary 1970s cast doubt on Keynesian aggregate demand fine-tuning, with most economists concluding that attempts to lower unemployment rates led to unacceptably high inflation. By the 1990s both the Keynesians and the Institutionalists had fallen out of favor.

The prevailing view now is that free markets will generate high growth and low unemployment (or, at least, the 'natural rate' of unemployment). However, many analysts have already remarked on the curious nature of the Reagan-era expansion, during which inequality increased significantly (Peterson, 1994). We have shown here that while job markets superficially appeared to be tight during the Clinton expansion, few job opportunities 'trickled down'. This complements analyses by other authors that show the Clinton expansion did not greatly reduce income inequality (Mishel and Bernstein, 1995; Karoly, 1996; Wolff, 1998).[14] Our conclusion is that neither the Reagan rising tide nor the Clinton rising tide, nor even the Kennedy-Johnson rising tide was sufficient to lift the boats at the bottom in terms of job opportunity. It appears that the Institutionalists were right after all. No matter whether expansions are packaged as demand-led, supply side-led, or free market-led, they must be supplemented with active labor market policy if job opportunities are to be increased sufficiently for those at the bottom.

Policy should provide paths other than college attendance to labor force participation. Even if an expansion could be maintained for decades, this would not increase the employment rates of the bottom half of the population to the rate enjoyed by college graduates. Although it is true that expansions lower unemployment rates of all groups, high unemployment rates are not the major problem for those with low educational attainment. Rather, their problem is one of low employment rates. Expansions appear to promote 'hiring off the top', that is, filling job vacancies with those who have attended college while doing less for those at the bottom. In addition, they promote longer work weeks for the already employed. We expect that inflation would be induced long before firms would 'hire off the bottom' at a pace sufficient to generate significant expansion in real job opportunities for high school dropouts.

The United States has a long tradition of active labor market policies, ranging from informal policies such as unrestricted immigration in the late 19th and early 20th centuries to broad-based policies such as the Comprehensive Employment and Training Act (CETA), which was enacted in 1973. As Marshall et al. (1984) make clear, CETA represented the apex of interventionist labor market policies that took root in the post-World War II era, particularly during the 1960s and 1970s. Prior to this Keynesian period, employment policy was to a large extent an ad hoc method of coping with an immediate problem, such as the influx of soldiers from the first and second World Wars (Smith-Fess Act, 1920; Servicemen's Readjustment Act, 1944) or a temporary measure to cope with the

Great Depression (Wagner-Peyser Act, 1933). Economic policy was dominated by the view that unemployment was at worst a short-term phenomenon.[15] Of course, there were some longer-term strategies, but they were concerned mainly with education (Morill Act, 1862) or apprenticeship programs (National Apprenticeship Act, 1937).

The long history of US labor market policies gives us at least a starting point for understanding what does and does not work. Wage subsidies such as those advocated by Phelps (1997) might induce some private sector employers to hire workers with low educational attainment and provide on-the-job training. However, there is the danger that employers will simply replace existing workers with subsidized workers or that the subsidies will interfere with price signals. Another policy action worth considering is government provision of (or subsidization of) health care and child care benefits, which would make employment more attractive to those who remain out of the labor force due to family commitments or to obtain Medicaid. However, this will not increase employment if the main problem is lack of jobs for the low skilled.

A More Comprehensive Approach

Such policies may be helpful, but we favor a more comprehensive approach. Hyman Minsky argued that an infinitely elastic demand for labor at a fixed wage would guarantee a real job opportunity for anyone who wants to work (Minsky, 1986). Along similar lines, we propose a job opportunity program that would 'hire off the bottom', taking all those who are ready, willing, and able to work but who cannot find employers willing to hire them (Forstater, 1998; Wray, 1998b; Gordon, 1997; Harvey, 1989; 1999; Killingsworth, 1977a; 1977b). The federal government would announce that it would provide the money needed to pay the legislated minimum wage, plus health care and child care benefits, to anyone ready, willing, and able to work. Government agencies at all levels (federal, state, local) and designated not-for-profit organizations could hire as many new employees as desired, with direct labor costs, including health and child care benefits, paid by the federal government. Administration and supervision would thus be decentralized, with participating employers setting reasonable performance standards that would have to be met by program employees. The federal government would require that all these jobs have a significant training component in order to prepare participants for eventual private sector (or public sector) employment. In addition, detailed work records would be kept so that prospective nonprogram employers could recruit from among program participants. The goal would be to create a pool of employable, 'buffer stock' labor from which employers could draw as an alternative to recruiting from colleges.

This program would 'hire off the bottom'; it would provide job opportunities to all who want to work. It would guarantee full employment, or zero unemployment, in the sense that anyone could choose to work in the program at the minimum wage. Clearly, many would choose to remain unemployed or out of the labor force rather than work at the minimum wage; it is doubtful that many unemployed college graduates with substantial work experience would choose to work in the program. However, the program is not designed to solve the unemployment problems of unemployed highly skilled workers, but is focused on those who cannot obtain private sector work, even when aggregate demand is high.[16]

Past US experience with employment policies such as our proposal for a job opportunity program tells us that such a program could prove more effective than other attempts to provide jobs to those at the bottom. Killingsworth (1977b), for example, argued that public sector employment (PSE) programs were far more efficient and effective than any of the larger, macro-policies proposed at the time (such as tax cuts) at getting people to work, stimulating aggregate demand and reducing inequalities.

> One basic purpose of employment policy should be to redress the inequities and inequalities resulting from the 'normal' operations of the labor market. There is persuasive evidence that tax cuts do little or nothing to achieve such redress. Total employment can be increased substantially more with substantially less inflation effect by a PSE program than by tax cuts (Killingsworth, 1977b, pp. 492–3).

Similarly, Gottschalk, in an evaluation of public service employment policies, concludes that 'the U.S. experiments with PSE indicate that minimum-wage jobs would be demanded if offered' (Gottschalk, 1998, p. 93).[17]

One such PSE program was the Youth Incentive Entitlement Pilot Project (YIEPP), which operated from 1978 to 1981 and offered wage subsidies to private sector employers for providing a part-time minimum wage job or full-time summer job to anyone 16 to 19 years old who stayed in school. The program proved successful at, among other things, improving earnings for teens and reducing unemployment differences between blacks and whites. The YIEPP is also instructive in that it showed the limitations of private sector wage subsidies. Only 18 per cent of eligible employers chose to participate in the program despite a 100 per cent wage subsidy for all workers.

Our 'hire off the bottom' policy proposal is much more ambitious than YIEPP. It can achieve a degree of employment that cannot be attained by expansion alone; the problem with traditional 'Keynesian' stimulus programs is that it is feared they might set off inflation long before job opportunities for those with low educational attainment increase. By hiring off the bottom and by fixing the wage in the job opportunity program at the minimum wage, inflation pressures are minimized. Indeed, we believe the buffer stock of labor will lead to greater price stability than can be achieved under the current system, which relies on unemployment to reduce inflation pressures (a point made by Killingsworth, 1977, and Minsky, 1986). For several reasons, discussed in Wray (1997; 1998a), workers employed in the program would constitute a better pool of potential employees than the current unemployed, or out-of-the-labor-force, population. An obvious reason is that someone working in the program is demonstrating that she or he is 'ready, willing, and able' to work to a degree that most of the unemployed cannot. This would present employers with an alternative to bidding up the wages of college-educated workers. In other words, the job opportunity program allows full employment (albeit, a different sort of 'full employment' than can be achieved by 'priming the pump' – which seems to leave behind the least skilled) and price stability to coexist, in contrast to the conventional view of a trade-off between unemployment and inflation.

This analysis has questioned the degree to which labor 'markets'[18] were really tight over the Clinton expansion (and over the Kennedy-Johnson expansion), at least for the half of the population that has not attended college. We have challenged the notion that a rising tide alone can significantly increase job opportunities for this group. While it is true that unemployment rates fall and employment rates rise across the skills spectrum, expansions are woefully inadequate in terms of the sheer numbers of jobs created for the low skilled. We argue, as the old Institutionalists did, that it is time to implement a variety of active labor market policies, with a job opportunity program as the centerpiece. These policies can create conditions for full employment and price stability simultaneously. The moral of the tale is clear: a rising tide alone will not work, but better boats might.

NOTES

1. Professor of Economics, University of Missouri, Kansas City. This chapter draws heavily on Wray and Pigeon (2000). The author would like to thank Marc-André Pigeon for much of the original research and data analysis, and Eric Tymoigne for additional research and for updating some of the data.
2. Note that we reject the notion that there is a 'labor market' in the usual sense of the term, with well-defined supply and demand curves that take real wages as the parameter. See Galbraith (1997) for a position that is close to ours.
3. According to the Bureau of Labor Statistics (BLS), the official unemployment rate fell to 4.3 per cent at the end of the 1990s, the lowest level in three decades. President Clinton was rightly proud of the number of jobs created during this expansion. The long-term downward trend of real wages that began in the early 1970s had stopped. Real wages increased 6 per cent over the expansion, the longest period of sustained increases since the late 1960s and early 1970s, according to the BLS.
4. In this chapter we examine the extent to which the expansion has generated employment opportunities. We do not explicitly address questions related to income inequality. There does

seem to be some evidence that the expansion at least marginally reduced wage inequality. See Galbraith and Cantù (1999) for example.

5.   The maximum feasible rate would depend on a variety of factors including customary norms regarding retirement age, normal age at which one enters the labor force, and female participation in the labor force. In this chapter we will not pursue the possibility that lower-skilled individuals have a lower desire to work. Rather, we adopt the presumption that the lower labor force participation rate of those with low educational attainment is primarily due to differences of opportunities rather than to different preferences. We also reject simple 'market clearing' models that would conclude that low-skilled individuals are outside the labor market voluntarily because their reservation wages exceed market wages, or involuntarily because minimum wages prevent market clearing. We believe, instead, that many of those outside the labor market would work – even at the minimum wage – if jobs were offered. We realize these are contentious issues. Even some liberals believe that the potential labor supply consists only of the unemployed plus a small proportion of those out of the labor force, consisting mostly of 'discouraged' workers (those who self-report in BLS surveys that they primary reason they are not looking for work is because they believe there are no jobs available). In contrast, we take a much broader view of the 'potentially employable', including those who experience barriers to working (family responsibilities, disabilities, health problems), those who believe employers will not hire them (due, for example, to discrimination), and those who have developed attitudes or behaviors antithetical to working (drug or alcohol addiction, gang activity). As we will show, the level of educational attainment is a very good predictor of employment status, which indicates to us that the forces at work are complex. To some extent, those same social advantages that lead one to attain a college degree seem to also lead to high employment rates. We do not believe employment or educational success is merely due to 'preferences'.

6.   We focus on the 25-and-over population (unless otherwise indicated). This allows us to remove most individuals who would still be in high school or who might have completed high school and have not yet attended college, but who might plan to attend college. Thus, if the 25-and-over population of high school dropouts declines, for example, this is primarily due to deaths rather than to an increase in the number graduating high school or attending college.

7.   Killingsworth's argument is presented in Killingsworth (1969; 1977b) and is summarized in Marshall et al. (1984).

8.   A simple calculation reveals that the official (16 and over) unemployment rate in 1998 (the latest year for which we have prison and jail population data) would have been 5.7 per cent instead of 4.5 per cent if the 1.8 million persons in jails and prisons that year had been counted as unemployed. Of course this overstates what the official unemployment rate would have been if those individuals had not been incarcerated, as many (or most) would have been counted as outside the labor market.

9.   'Some Employers Lift Hiring Standards Amid Labor Shortage, Weak Applicants', *Wall Street Journal*, 17 February 1999, p. A2.

10. Presumably, most of the population decline can be attributed to deaths, although some can be attributed to transitions by individuals to higher educational status.

11. A simple example might help. Suppose there was a population of 20 dogs, only 12 of whom had bones to chew. The animal control truck comes by and captures three of them, two of whom did not have bones and one who did. Our 'noninstitutionalized' population now consists of 17 dogs, of whom 11 have bones. Relatively, things have improved because the number of dogs fell by more than the number of bones. The 'excess demand' for bones has in some sense declined. Some might argue that things have improved because if a 'dog eat dog' war broke out, those without bones would now stand a slightly better chance of stealing away with one. But I would be hard pressed to call that an improvement for the dogs. On the other hand, if a thirteenth bone were dropped into our original population of 20 dogs, I would call that an improvement. In my view, a 'rising tide' ought to provide more bones, not simply remove dogs from the population, before it is said to have lifted all boats. Admittedly, not all will agree with this position.

12. Bell South Telecommunications said that it took more than six months to fill 500 newly created jobs in Florida. Even more surprisingly, it went through 10,000 applicants before getting the people it wanted ('Jobs Going Begging, Companies in Florida Adapting', *New York Times*, 22 September 1998, p. C4).
13. See Killingsworth (1970; 1977a; 1977b), Marshall et al. (1984) and Gordon (1997).
14. However, Galbraith and Cantù (1999) disagree with this view.
15. For example, the workers employed in government public-service employment programs were counted as unemployed during the 1930s (Marshall et al., 1984, p. 624). This clearly reflects the then dominant view that the crisis was only temporary and only temporary relief efforts were needed until 'equilibrium' was restored.
16. We do not have space here to discuss the program in detail; the specifics are analyzed in Wray (1998a). Killingsworth (1977) noted that the original draft of the Humphrey-Hawkins Act contained a job guarantee; however, it was dropped in the final version, largely due to fears over costs and possible inflationary impacts. He argued that these fears were unfounded and demonstrated that a job guarantee program would be far more cost effective than alternative means of job creation such as 'Keynesian' tax cuts.
17. Other countries have also experimented with PSE-type programs, most notably Sweden. We do not offer details on such programs but refer interested readers to Ginsburg (1983).
18. As noted above (endnote 2), we reject the concept of a labor 'market' defined by labor supply and demand curves in the usual sense.

REFERENCES

Beckett, Katherine and Bruce Western (1997), 'The Penal System as Labor Market Institution: Jobs and Jails, 1980–1995', *Overcrowded Times*, December: 8–13.

Bluestone, Barry and Stephen Rose (1998), 'The Unmeasured Labor Force, The Growth in Work Hours', *Public Policy Brief Note 39*, Annandale-on-Hudson, NY: Jerome Levy Economics Institute.

Bureau of Labor Statistics (2000), Internet: Bureau of Labor Statistics, http://stats.bls.gov

Castillo, Monica D. (1998), 'Persons Outside the Labor Force Who Want a Job', *Monthly Labor Review*, July: 34–42.

Cohn, R.M. (1978), 'The Effect of Employment Status Change on Self Attitudes', *Social Psychology*, **41**: 81–93.

Feather, N.T. and P.R. Davenport (1981), 'Unemployment and Depressive Affect: A Motivational and Attributional Analysis', *Journal of Personality and Social Psychology*, **41**: 422–36.

Forstater, Mathew (1998), 'Flexible Full Employment: Structural Implications of Discretionary Public Sector Employment', *Journal of Economic Issues*, **32**, 2 June: 557–63.

Galbraith, James K. (1997), 'Dangerous Metaphor: The Fiction of the Labor Market, Unemployment, Inflation, and the Job Structure', *Public Policy Brief Note 36*, Annandale-on-Hudson, NY: Jerome Levy Economics Institute.

Galbraith, James K. and Vidal Garza Cantù (1999), 'Inequality in American Manufacturing Wages, 1920–1998: A Revised Estimate', *Journal of Economic Issues*, **33** (3), September: 735–43.

Gilliard, Darrell (1999) 'Prison and Jail Inmates at Midyear 1998', *Bureau of Justice Statistics Bulletin*, March.

Ginsburg, Helen (1983), *Full Employment and Public Policy: The United States and Sweden*, Lexington, MA: Lexington Books.

Godley, Wynne and L. Randall Wray (1999), 'Can Goldilocks Survive?', *Public Policy Note 4*, Annandale-on-Hudson, NY: Jerome Levy Economics Institute.

Gonul, Fusun (1992), 'New Evidence on Whether Unemployment and Out of the Labor Force Are Distinct States', *Journal of Human Resources*, **27** (2), Spring: 329–61.

Gordon, Wendell (1997), 'Job Assurance – The Job Guarantee Revisited', *Journal Economic Issues*, **31**, September: 826–34.

Gottschalk, Peter (1998) 'The Impact of Changes in Public Employment on Low-Wage Labor Markets', in Richard B. Freeman and Peter Gottschalk (eds), *Generating Jobs: How to Increase Demand for Less-Skilled Workers*, New York: Russell Sage Foundation.

Greenspan, Alan (1998), 'The Economic Outlook and Challenges Facing Monetary Policy', speech before the Economic Strategy Institute in Washington, DC, 8 January 1998. Internet: Federal Reserve Board, http://www.bog.frb.fedus/boarddocs/speeches/default.cfm.

Harvey, Philip (1989), *Securing the Right to Employment*, Princeton, NJ: Princeton University Press.

Harvey, Philip (1999), 'Liberal Strategies for Combating Joblessness in the Twentieth Century', *Journal of Economic Issues*, **33** (2), June: 497–504.

Jones, Stephen R.G. and W. Craig Riddell (1999), 'The Measurement of Unemployment: An Empirical Approach', *Econometrica*, **67**: 147–62.

Karoly, Lynn A. (1996), 'Anatomy of the U.S. Income Distribution: Two Decades of Change', *Oxford Review of Economic Policy*, **12** (1), Spring: 76–95.

Killingsworth, Charles C. (1969) 'Full Employment and the New Economics', *Scottish Journal of Political Economy*, **16**, 1 February: 1–19.

Killingsworth, Charles C. (1970), 'Fact and Fallacy in Labour Market Analysis: A Reply to Mr. Lando', *Scottish Journal of Political Economy*, **17**, 1 February: 95–107.

Killingsworth, Charles C. (1977a), 'The Role of Public Service Employment', in *Proceedings of the 1977 Spring Meeting of the Industrial Relations Research Association*, Madison, WI: Industrial Relations Research Association, pp. 489–95.

Killingsworth, Charles C. (1977b), 'Tax Cuts and Employment Policy', in Robert Taggart (ed.), *Job Creation: What Works?* Salt Lake City, UT: Olympus.

Levin-Waldman, Oren M. (1999), 'Small Business and Welfare Reform: Levy Institute Survey of Hiring and Employment Practices', *Public Policy Brief No. 51*, Annandale-on-Hudson, NY: Jerome Levy Economics Institute.

Mallinckrodt, Brent and Bruce R. Fretz (1988) 'Social Support and the Impact of Job Loss on Older Professionals', *Journal of Counseling Psychology*, **35**: 281–6.

Marshall, Ray, Vernon M. Briggs and Allan G. King (1984), *Labor Economics,* Homewood, IL: Irwin.

Minsky, Hyman P. (1986), *Stabilizing an Unstable Economy*, New Haven, CT: Yale University Press.

Mishel, Lawrence, and Jared Bernstein (1995), 'America's Continuing Wage Problems: Deteriorating Real Wages for Most and Growing Inequality', in Lawrence Mishel and John Schmitt (eds), *Beware the U.S. Model: Jobs and Wages in a Deregulated Economy*, Washington, DC: Economic Policy Institute.

Peterson, Wallace C. (1994), *Silent Depression: The Fate of the American Dream*, New York: Norton.

Phelps, Edmund S. (1997), *Rewarding Work*, Cambridge, MA: Harvard University Press.

Pryor, Frederic L. and David L. Schaffer (1999), *Who's Not Working and Why: Employment, Cognitive Skills, Wages and the Changing US Labor Market*, Cambridge: Cambridge University Press.

Ritter, Joseph A. (1998), 'School and Work', *National Economic Trends*, The Federal Reserve Bank of St. Louis (June).

Summers, Lawrence H. and Kim B. Clark (1979), 'Labor Market Dynamics and Unemployment: A Reconsideration', Brookings Papers on Economic Activity, 1: 13–60.

Tano, Doki K. (1991), 'Are Unemployment and Out of the Labor Force Behaviorally Distinct Force Labor Force States?', *Economic Letters*, **36**: 113–17.

Wolff, Edward N. (1998), 'Recent Trends in the Size Distribution of Household Wealth', *Journal of Economic Perspectives*, **12** (3), Summer: 131–50.

Wray, L. Randall (1997), 'Government as Employer of Last Resort: Full Employment without Inflation', *Working Paper No. 213*, Annandale-on-Hudson, NY: Jerome Levy Economics Institute.

Wray, L. Randall (1998a), *Understanding Modern Money: The Key to Full Employment and Price Stability*, Cheltenham: Edward Elgar.

Wray, L. Randall (1998b) 'Zero Unemployment and Stable Prices', *Journal of Economic Issues*, **32**, 2 June: 539–45.

Wray, L. Randall (2000) 'A Critical Economic Evaluation of American Penal Keynesianism at the Turn of the Millennium', *Challenge*, September–October: 31–59.

Wray, L. Randall and Marc-André Pigeon (2000), 'Can a Rising Tide Raise All Boats? Evidence from the Clinton-Era Expansion', *Journal of Economic Issues*, **34** (4), December: 811–45.

9. Housing and Homelessness in a Globalizing Economy

Dorene Isenberg

OVERVIEW

Is it true that the homeless, like the poor, will always be with us? While it is impossible to answer this very large question in one chapter, it is possible to determine what has happened to produce the very large change in the size, composition, and location of the US homeless population over the last 30 years.

A walk through the streets of a large US city in 1972 would have found only a very small group of people spending the night there. This group, composed predominantly of single white males over 40 years old, would probably be found in an isolated part of the city called Skid Row. These men, called variously hobos, bums, tramps, or derelicts, were associated with having made a choice to live a different kind of life. Rather than commit to a job and build a family, they were seen as having chosen social, economic, and familial independence which manifested itself in social marginality and fierce self-reliance. The life of the hobo emerged from the realities of the Great Depression, but it remained the dominant perception of the composition of the homeless population into the 1970s (Cohen and Sokolovsky, 1989; Rossi, 1989).

Over the next 30 years, the visibility of the homeless population increased as their numbers grew and their composition changed. During this 30-year span, at least three different descriptions of the homeless population emerged.[1] The first description surfaced in the early 1970s. It categorized the homeless as primarily a group of people who had been released from mental institutions, de-institutionalized (Rossi, 1989, pp. 144–7).[2] At the end of the 1960s the mental institutions had altered their policies towards institutionalization. Many of the people who were released from these institutions had nowhere else to go, so they ended up on the streets. Even though these people had medical problems, the reasons behind their homelessness were not identified as personal or medical. The effect of de-institutionalization, while strong in the early 1970s, did not continue to feed into the homeless population after that.

In the early 1980s, another view emerged. The homeless were the involuntarily unemployed. Blau (1992, p. 10) notes that the recessions at the end of the 1970s and the ones in the early 1980s fueled the growth of the homeless population. He notes that, unlike the surge from de-institutionalization, unemployment continued, even into the period of economic recovery, to push people into homelessness. The final description, which emerged in the late 1990s, emphasized the preponderance of substance abusers or other types of 'deficient, pathological individuals in need of rehabilitation' (Bogard, 2001, pp. 425–6). This was a shift to a medicalized view of the homeless.

These changing pictures of the homeless, while reflecting at least a partial reality of who was actually on the street, were even more of a reflection of changing political and social ideologies. The ideological justification for the de-institutionalization of many mentally ill patients from the wards of public mental institutions in the late 1960s focused on the de-humanizing nature of the mental institutions and their seeming inability to heal inmates. When these people were 'freed', however, there was no assurance that they would be provided with other humane institutions to care for them, and so many were left to live on the streets (Wright, 1989, p. 107).

Shifting to the economic reasoning for homelessness, it is important to know that during the 10 years from 1974 to 1984 three recessions came and went in the United States, and a long period of inflation induced greater uncertainty. Two of the recessions were the deepest and one the longest and deepest that the United States had experienced since its 1930s Great Depression. Unemployment skyrocketed to 10.8 per cent in 1982. Inflation was also reaching new highs in this period. The prices of luxuries and necessities experienced a continual rise, with housing prices ratcheting up even more as speculative real estate bubbles inflated their prices. The combination of job loss, rising prices, and falling real and nominal wages left more and more people struggling to pay rent or mortgages. Many more people were put at risk of losing their homes and an increasingly large number of people were pushed out of their homes.

These changes in the source of the problem of homelessness meant that those living on the streets of the small and large cities in the United States encompassed a wider range of men and women, ages, races, levels of education and job experience, and family types than had been seen since the Great Depression. Housing price inflation, changes in US housing policies, and unemployment had driven men, women, and increasingly families out of their homes and onto the streets (Dymski and Isenberg, 1998; Wright, 1989).

By the end of the 1990s, the description of the homeless was changing yet again. Now the homeless population held a higher proportion of children and families, and it was no longer confined to cities. Increasing numbers of homeless people were living on suburban streets and in rural areas (Interagency Council on the Homeless (ICH), 1999). Along with detailing the changing composition of the homeless population, this report also pointed to medical, mental, emotional, and early childhood problems that the homeless population experienced. William Baldwin, an actor who was raising money for the homeless, responded to the findings in the ICH report by saying, 'This report shows homeless people are victims of a downward spiral of personal problems that finally force them onto the streets . . .' (US Dept. of Housing and Urban Development, 1999). The pendulum was again swinging the other way. It was not the economic situation, inadequate attention to housing policy, and housing market problems that promoted homelessness; it was the way the homeless handled their personal problems that accounted for their homeless state.

This movement back and forth between the personal and the economic reasons for homelessness may seem like the social equivalent of the chicken and the egg story. If this were the case, then we would feel like Sisyphus, doomed to repetition and never gaining any ground as we look at the problems of homelessness. But the rest of this chapter will sketch out an argument that veers away from looking at the composition of the homeless population as an indicator of the reasons for homelessness. The analysis focuses less on the personal characteristics of homeless people and more on the structural framework by which housing, the other part of the question of homelessness, is made available and affordable in the United States. Before we jump into that analysis, we need to get a clearer, more extensive view of the US homeless population.

A SKETCH OF THE HOMELESS

How Many People are Homeless?

While a seemingly easy question, the estimates of how many people are homeless vary quite widely, and part of the reason for this variation results from differing definitions of homelessness. First, is a homeless person someone who is living in a shelter or standing on a street for a week or longer? Or is it someone who does not have a place to sleep for at least one night? Or is the problem of homelessness larger than either of these views would indicate? Maybe, the homeless should be counted as the number of requests for emergency shelter regardless of whether they are met or not; or possibly the homeless are those who are 'housed' as doubled up households, living with friends and families because there's nowhere else to go; or maybe, to capture the complexity of homelessness, people living in unstable, provisional arrangements without permanent housing possibilities should also be counted as homeless (National Coalition for the Homeless, 1999).

According to Martha Burt, the lead researcher on the National Survey of the Homeless Assistance Providers and Clients (NSHAPC), the most comprehensive survey to date on the homeless in shelters, between 2.3 to 3.5 million people living in the United States could experience homelessness at least once during a year.[3] Further disaggregation of the homeless population indicates that on any one day 'at least 800,000 people are homeless in the United States, including about 200,000 children in homeless families' (Burt, 2001, p. 1). She continues to describe the size of the homeless population by noting that 'Annual homeless figures exceed 1 percent of the total U.S. population and may represent as much as 10 percent of all poor people in this country' (ibid.). An Urban Institute study by Burt and Laudan Aron also determined that the population had grown by about 200,000 people since the 1987 Urban Institute study (Urban Institute, 2000, p. 1).

Who is Homeless?

The definitional problems again loom when trying to describe the composition of the homeless population. Definitions as well as geographic locations are important when answering this question. Disaggregating these geographically specific populations is important because as Table 9.1 shows, they differ in some important characteristics. Table 9.1 is drawn from the NSHAPC data. As the data in Table 9.1 show, the largest numbers of sheltered homeless people, 71 per cent of the total homeless sample, are found in central cities, which means that approximately 30 per cent of the homeless are found outside central cities in the rural and suburban areas. Since homelessness is usually associated with central cities, acknowledging the 30 per cent who live outside the city is important because this group has experienced the largest recent increase in size.

Looking at some of the other characteristics, we see that in the central cities homeless males account for more than double the percentage of women. The top three rankings in the racial divide shows black non-Hispanics to account for the largest percentage among the homeless, with white non-Hispanic ranking second, and Hispanic ranking third. This ranking reflects the racial composition of the total population in many of the United States' central cities. In terms of age, over 75 per cent of the homeless are between 25 and 54 years old. Finally, the central city homeless are unevenly divided into current lengths of homelessness. 30 per cent have been homeless

Table 9.1   Characteristics of the homeless clients in the NSHAPC sample,
1996

Characteristics	Central cities	Suburban/ urban fringe	Rural
PROPORTION OF HOMELESS	71%	21%	9%
SEX			
Male	71	55	77
Female	29	45	23
RACE/ETHNICITY			
White non-Hispanic	37	54	42
Black non-Hispanic	46	33	9
Hispanic	11	11	7
Native American	5	1	41
Other	1	1	0*
AGE			
Under 25 years	13	12	7
25–54 years	79	77	88
55 years and older	8	11	5
FAMILY – only with children	14	16	17
ECONOMIC			
Mean monthly income	$341	$422	$449
Median monthly income	$250	$395	$475
LENGTH OF			
3 months or less	27%	22%	55%
More than 12 months	48	49	27

Note: * Value is less than 0.5 but greater than 0.

Source: Data taken from Interagency Council on the Homeless (1999), Table 2.9.

Table 9.2 Comparison of homeless clients in central city shelters and soup kitchens, 1987 and 1996

Characteristics	1987	1996
SEX – percentage male	81%	79%
RACE/ETHNICITY		
White non-Hispanic	46	39
Black non-Hispanic	41	46
Hispanic	10	11
Other	3	4
EDUCATION		
Less than 12th grade	48	34
Completed 12th grade	32	39
More than 12th grade	20	27
RELATIONSHIP/ HOUSEHOLD STATUS		
Never married	55	49
Homeless family	10	10
LENGTH OF CURRENT HOMELESS SPELL		
3 months or less	21	30
2 years or more	31	31
RECEIPT OF PUBLIC BENEFITS		
AFDC*	33	58
SSI	4	13
Food stamps	18	37
MEAN MONTHLY INCOME – per person	$189[a]	$267

Notes: [a] Adjustment to 1996 dollars made using CPI-U.
* Only available to families with children

Source: Data excerpted from Interagency Council on the Homeless (1999), Table 2.10.

for less than three months while slightly less than 50 per cent have been homeless for more than one year.

The characteristics of the central city homeless differ from the population in the suburbs along racial and gender lines, and they differ from the rural population in race, age, and length of homelessness. Among the suburban homeless there is a much larger representation of women, making the gender ratios almost equal, and there is a reversal in the rankings of whites and blacks. Whites become the largest racial group with over half the homeless population white non-Hispanic, and one-third black non-Hispanic, while the Hispanic proportion remains constant. Among the rural homeless population, the ranking of the top three racial groups indicates that the white non-Hispanic group, at 42 per cent of the population, barely edges out the native American group at 41 per cent to lead the ranking, and that homeless people who are black non-Hispanic, while third in the ranking, account for only 9 per cent of the population. The racial rankings in the suburbs are driven by the racial characteristics of the total suburban population, but those in the rural areas are not a reflection of the overall population. Additionally, the rural population's age distribution is more concentrated in the 25–54 years-of-age group and their length of homelessness is opposite of that in central cities. Current bouts of rural homelessness are by a 2 to 1 margin short term rather than 12 months or longer.

The characteristics that these geographical sub-divisions share are poverty, a similar percentage of families with children, and similar proportions of people with substance use and mental health problems (not in Table 9.1). All of the homeless population is poor. Actually, they appear to be among the poorest people in the United States. Both the average and the median monthly incomes of the homeless population are at best around 50 per cent of the poverty threshold incomes for 1996.[4] In all of these geographical populations, families with at least one child account for about 15 per cent of each group. People who have had problems with alcohol, drugs, and mental health within the last month account for about 66 per cent of each group.[5]

Along with this current description of homelessness, it is important to know if there have been any major changes in the population over time. In Table 9.2 a rudimentary comparison is made between the populations in central cities in 1987 and 1996. The major differences are in education levels, receipt of public benefits, family status, and race. In 1987 48 per cent of the homeless population had less than a high school degree, but by 1996 that figure had shrunk to 34 per cent. The shift reflects to a large degree the increase in the portion of the total US population getting high school and college degrees between 1987 and 1996. The homeless population of post-high school graduate education rose by 7 per cent between 1987 and 1996, yet in the United States the overall figure rose by 11 per cent, moving from

37 per cent to 48 per cent (US Census Bureau, 2002c). These figures indicate the over-representation of lower levels of education among the homeless compared to the US population in general.

Interestingly, the homeless population has a higher proportion of recipients of public benefits in 1996 than in 1987. In all categories the increase is highly significant and indicates that even with this increasing reliance on public benefits, homelessness still occurs. The safety net as it currently exists does not keep people from falling through. An omission in this list of public benefits is housing benefits. In the nine years between these comparison points, a major change in the structure and availability of public subsidized housing and housing support has meant that fewer households have received this public benefit. The NSHPC study neglects to include housing policy in its study, which is a problematic omission.

The other changes, in racial distribution and family status, indicate shifts which in one case is place specific and in the other, a reflection of the broadened nature of homelessness. When more geographical locations are brought into the picture, the economic deterioration of many of the central cities in the United States and the de facto racialization of the these cities during this time period become apparent. The increase in black non-Hispanic homelessness in the central cities compared to the relative decline in white non-Hispanic homelessness is less about homelessness than it is about race. It begs the broader question of the impoverisation and racialization of the central cities. The process of de-industrialization starting in the early 1960s moved the largest proportion of the good production jobs out of the city and in many cases out of the country. Piggy-backed on de-industrialization is the de-urbanization of the United States. In this process, which started in the 1950s, white and middle-income earning families moved out of the city and into the suburbs. These changes have left many of the central cities destitute.

Contextualizing these statistics in terms of the changing population and concentration and types of jobs in the central cities versus these same parameters in the suburbs helps to explain why the proportion of black non-Hispanic homeless rises when only central cities are counted. As Table 9.1 shows, white non-Hispanic homelessness accounts for the largest proportion of the homeless in geographical areas that have predominantly white populations. The decrease in the never married proportion of the population implies an increase in the married or once married group. This change reflects the spread of homelessness to people who many thought were insulated from this type of life disruption and, again, is indicative of the changing nature of the US population.

These descriptions of the homeless population in the United States may help us see who is in this population, but it does little to help us understand why people are homeless. Understanding the 'why?' of homelessness requires that we look not only at individuals, but also at the economic and social institutions that shape their access to affordable housing. This is the task undertaken in the next section.

It is important to recognize that US housing policy has changed significantly over the last 30 years. To understand what has motivated the change in policy, we need to understand the context in which the housing policy was made. In the first part of the next section we will explain the historical process of globalization. Then in the second part we will look at the development of US housing policy in a pre-globalization period, which will be followed by a look at the changes made in housing policy in the period of globalization.

GLOBALIZATION, MARKET LIBERALIZATION, AND THE STATE: FROM GOLDEN AGE TO GLOBAL AGE

Globalization and Neo-Liberalism

Nations and regions around the world have become more integrated through their trade in goods, labor flows, capital flows, financial flows, and the dissemination of information technology. While this set of world connections may look remarkably new, in the early part of the 20th century, the international market was also considered open and highly integrated. 'By 1913 exports (one of the hallmarks of increasing economic integration) accounted for a larger share of global production than they did in 1999' (Ellwood, 2001, p. 14; see also Streeten, this volume). And in other historical periods, like during the German Hansa, trade among foreign regions, cities, and states was highly developed. What makes our current regime of globalization unique is the particular set of rules under which governments and markets are now operating. These rules call for governments to remove themselves from engaging in interventionary economic policy and for markets to take over decision-making and be the sole determinants of outcomes in all areas that are broadly considered economic.

This vision of the power relationship between government and the market stands in contrast to the one that dominated in the period after the Great Depression. Many economists have argued that the reasons for the Great Depression in the United States, its depth and duration, have to do with under-regulated market activity, especially in the financial sector (Galbraith, 1997; Minsky, 1982). To reshape markets to be less fragile and more stable, and to produce outcomes that were beneficial to the nation's macroeconomic well-being, the US government instituted functional and prudential regulatory controls. It also implemented minimum wage legislation, industrial regulations, and unemployment insurance to further protect residents from negative market outcomes. These organizational and regulatory activities, collectively called the New Deal, continued to be regarded as an important and legitimate part of government's activities through the 1970s.

The macroeconomic disruption created by high inflation and unemployment in the early 1970s fostered a change in this view of government's proper economic role. A 'free market' ideology was emerging which argued that markets were most efficient when they were self-regulated. As this new view, called neo-liberalism, grew in strength, more voices were heard arguing that government should be removed from its regulatory role. Markets should be allowed to operate without regulation and, thus, more efficiently. The idea of efficiency, rather than the broader vision of economic well-being which also includes equity, became the dominating force in the argument for neo-liberal programs.

Underpinning neo-liberalism is the idea that markets, when left to function on their own, operate with the highest efficiency – the greatest quantity of a good produced at the least cost – which translates into the lowest price and the greatest quantity for the consumer. Efficiency is maximized when markets operate by the rules of perfect competition. The assumptions that underlie this efficient-market theory (EMT), and which must be met if its efficient outcomes are to be achieved, are those that govern the operation of perfect competition: firms must not have market power, which means that they must be small enough not to have an impact on market outcomes; consumers, also, must not have market power; firms must be free to enter and exit the market; and information must flow freely and without cost. While the structure of most markets, especially those operating at a national or international level do not adhere to these basic rules, several theorists have produced models that allow for violation of an assumption and will still produce an efficient market result. One example of such a model is contested market theory.[6]

This neo-liberal efficient-market approach has found champions within nation-states as well as with many of the global organizations that set rules for the nation-states. Its proponents include several developed countries, like the United States and Britain; important international organizations like the World Bank and International Monetary Fund; and in some cases, developing countries. At the global level, these are the voices calling for the eradication of governmental regulation of markets and to marketize relations that were historically outside the reach of markets. These are the important actors, operating according to what is sometimes called the 'Washington Consensus', who have made neo-liberalization synonymous with globalization (Ellwood, 2001; Rodrik, 2001).

As the beginning of our description of neo-liberalism implied, this process of market opening and widening leaves little room for other economic actors. The excision of government from its economic roles means that many programs and policies that have been implemented to rectify market distortions, and in so doing produce enhanced well-being to residents, will be eradicated. What the final impact of these changes for residents across the social and geographical spectrum will be is the next question.

The results of this marketization process have been, at best, mixed. At the global level, trade between countries has skyrocketed. During the 1990s it grew at an average annual rate of 6.6 per cent compared to an average annual growth rate of 3.2 per cent in Gross Domestic Product (GDP) (Ellwood, 2001, p. 16). Several developing countries' GDPs have been growing at a rate that exceeds the global average, but that does not mean that they are actually developing (Stiglitz, 2002; Rodrik, 2001). The experience of the 'Asian tigers', South Korea, Indonesia, Malaysia, and Thailand, appeared as a hopeful model in the mid-1990s, but by the end of the 1990s the financial disruption known as the 'Asian crisis' showed the other side of open and integrated markets: contagion.

No one-to-one positive relationship between open markets, growth, and development has been yet been determined. Of equal importance to the question of development is the question of the deterministic relationship between open markets, the expanding skewness in the distribution of national income, and an increase in poverty (ibid.). For our analysis of the roots of homelessness we will show in the discussion that follows how neo-liberal globalization has changed government policies that address poverty alleviation, reduce skewness of the distribution of income, affect the size and structure of the supply of housing, and have thereby affected people's ability to obtain affordable housing.

In concert with the deregulation of the flow of traded goods has been the deregulation of financial markets. These markets, historically composed of important national financial institutions, are being opened to the world. Efforts are underway to integrate them in much the same way that the markets that trade in goods were integrated.

The opening and increased integration of US financial markets has been in process for over 20 years and has produced mixed results in its housing market (Dymski and Isenberg, 1999; 2002). Since the for-purchase housing market is one that relies on credit markets for the final purchase of its produced good, this market is very sensitive to changes in interest rates, the structure of financial markets, and their stability. Several researchers have noted that for people in the market for a 30-year conventional mortgage on a house that is situated in an economically healthy middle-class neighborhood, there have been efficiency gains (Wachter, 1990; Diamond and Lea, 1992).

On the other hand, the homes that are in central cities, working-class, poor, or changing neighborhoods have been less well served. The same neglect is also true for renters who are not at least middle-income earners (Dymski and Isenberg, 1998; Isenberg and Byun, 2002).

The results of markets' decision-making having been substituted for the conscious decision-making processes of governments provide a partial answer to our question about why we have seen such a rise in the homeless population in the United States. As the following sections will detail, the successful housing policies that the US implemented to reduce homelessness after the Great Depression and to increase housing affordability in the 1960s were altered when, at the end of the 1970s, we began to de-regulate markets, promote a greater competition among financial institutions, and remove government involvement in the process of house-building. To understand how this process of financial liberalization affected housing supply and demand, and promoted homelessness, it's first necessary to know how the policies in this 'Golden Age' produced affordable housing.

The Golden Age

The economic and governmental relationships that characterized the 'Golden Age' of the 1950s and 1960s were established as a result of the Great Depression. Institutions and policies were put in place to reduce the risks associated with the private housing market. These risks had materialized in the Great Depression as bank runs and failures, mortgage foreclosures, and a standstill in mortgage lending, had brought a halt to home building. The end result of the financial sector's disarray was loss of family homes for many and a drastic rise in homelessness. To assure that these same financial disruptions would never again occur or lead to mass evictions, the New Deal restructuring of the financial sector aimed to (1) stabilize the financial system; (2) provide an accommodative financial system with the proper incentives to spur the house-building industry to build homes; and (3) provide mortgages that were affordable to the average working family (Dymski and Isenberg, 1997). Since the house-building industry was in disarray and the home finance system was no longer functioning, the home-building industry needed incentives to produce its 'good', the largest single expenditure that a family makes, and assurances that once the home was built it could be easily bought.

Legislation was promoted and enacted that regulated and restructured the entire US financial sector. Integral to this regulation and restructuring were the renovations in home finance. The savings and loan associations (S&Ls), an important part of the set of depository institutions, were reorganized to be the major providers of housing finance.[7] These institutions held the savings accounts of working- and middle-class Americans, and these savings were recycled as mortgages to working- and middle-class homebuyers. This dedication of the deposits in the S&Ls to fund home mortgages acted to segment a portion of all the funds raised by the depository institutions for use by this one sector, the housing sector. It produced a dedicated capital conduit for home finance and segmented the flows in the financial market. Given the insurance provided by the FSLIC and the FHA, the S&Ls came to be viewed as a safe place to deposit savings. Unlike the commercial banks' savings accounts, there was no deposit rate ceiling on an S&L savings account.[8] To maintain their comparative attractiveness, S&L deposit rates were usually higher than the commercial banks', but still low enough to make a house purchase affordable for blue-collar as well as middle-class families. The interaction of deposit insurance, market segmentation, and deposit rate ceilings created a set of house-buying financial arrangements that promoted home buying across a broad income spectrum in the United States especially after World War II.

In addition to producing a dedicated pool of savings for home finance, the restructuring of the financial sector also allowed homebuilders to obtain relatively cheap loans. The legislation that restructured the commercial banks dedicated their savings and checking accounts to be used as commercial and industrial (C&I) short-term loans. The C&I loan in housing construction is the construction and development (C&D) loan. Since these loans were funded by the no-deposit rate checking and low-deposit rate savings accounts of the commercial banks, the interest rates on C&D loans were relatively low. The dedicated fund for short-term loans meant that, as long as the commercial banks attracted accounts and interest rates stayed low, funds to underwrite home building would be available.

The final piece in the restructuring of the U.S. housing finance industry was the mortgage interest tax deduction, which provided an incentive to purchase a home rather than rent.[9] When a home was purchased using a mortgage, legislation made it possible for a portion of the interest paid by the home-purchaser to be deducted from his/her gross income. This reduction in net taxable income meant that the taxes owed on the homebuyer's income were reduced. This tax deduction was, in effect, a subsidy to homebuyers.

While home ownership rose from a century low of 43.6 per cent in 1940 to a century high of 64.4 per cent in 1980, the housing needs of the poor and low income families were not being very well-served by these financial structures (US Census Bureau, 2002a). Understanding that home ownership is not usually affordable for low-income earners or the poor, Congress passed a series of Housing Acts beginning in 1937. The initial Housing Act, aimed at improving sanitation and effecting slum clearance, cleaned up neighborhoods, but did not actually appropriate funds to build public housing.[10] It took until the 1960s to get a commitment to the construction of public housing. At this point the National Association of Home Builders (NAHB) and the Mortgage Bankers Association (MBA) broke with the rest of the housing lobby, which had previously been able to veto all attempts to build public housing. The break with the rest of the lobby came because the business of NAHB and MBA depended upon new house building, and public housing was new housing (Hays, 1985, p. 88).

With the help of the NAHB and MBA lobbyists, the Congressional committees were able to find enough support to pass the Housing Act of 1961, which was followed by additional legislation in 1964, 1965, 1968, and 1969. All but the 1969 act implemented public house-building programs by providing subsidies to the builders. Each program had a house-building goal, and, while these goals were never achieved, the stock of public housing grew and helped to make housing more affordable for the poor as well as other low-income earners and their families.

It was not until 1968 that Congress appropriated the funding necessary to achieve the house-building goals it had set and enacted in earlier legislation. In 1968 change was in the air; it was palpable. The 1968 Housing Act set a goal of building 6 million new housing units for low- and moderate-income families over the next 10 years. This goal would require a major push by the housing industry. Previously, they had only been able to push the level of their subsidized housing starts to 72,000 in 1966 and 91,000 in 1967. Amazingly, subsidized housing starts rose to 197,000 in 1969 and 431,000 in 1970 (Orlebeke, 2000, p. 496). The industry's production achievements in 1969 and after showed that their goals were not out of line with their capacity when proper funding was made available.

The production of subsidized housing continued into the 1970s, but not at the same pace as has been planned in 1968. During the Nixon presidency a moratorium on new building programs was put into force. This building hiatus came to an end during the Carter presidency, when both the executive and legislative branches worked cooperatively to enact and fund programs for subsidized housing production (ibid., p. 504). More new subsidized housing continued to be built throughout the 1970s.

Subsidized housing production, while making a slow start after the Great Depression, had found industry and governmental supporters by the 1960s. The largest quantity of public housing ever built in a 10-year period in the United States was built in the 1960s. Between 1960 and 1987 more than 1.5 million housing units were added to the public housing stock and most of them were added in the 1960s and 1970s (Murray, 1999). This increase in subsidized housing changed the housing profile for low-income and poor Americans. The demand for affordable housing for poor people was always greater than supply, but homeless they were not.

One indicator of how this housing policy boom affected the population can be seen by looking at its effect on the problem of crowding. The effect from increased home ownership and the increased provision of affordable housing for low-income earners and the poor was positive; crowding was reduced.[11] In 1940, 20 per cent of the US population lived in crowded conditions. In each of the succeeding decades, the level of crowding declined precipitously. In 1950 the level was 15.7 per cent; in 1960 it was 11.5 per cent; and in 1980 it reached the century low of 4.5 per cent; it was almost non-existent. The results achieved by the housing policy were all desirable. Home ownership rates rose, more poor people were housed, and crowding was reduced.

But these housing programs were not the only reasons for such positive results. The government had been exploring and implementing other policies that extended the social welfare safety net and reduced poverty. The implementation and funding of Medicare and Medicaid, the expansion of Aid to Families with Dependent Children (AFDC) program, expansion of Social Security benefits, and the more extensive provision of food stamps are some of the programs that aided poor and low-income earners. These programs boosted up the bottom portion of the income distribution and made housing more affordable. Supplementing private income through food stamps and healthcare provision meant that smaller portions of total income had to be spent on these necessities, which left more disposable income to meet housing needs.[12]

It was during the Reagan presidency after 1980 that the commitment to providing subsidized private housing was rescinded. Instead of focusing on the supply side of housing, which was seen by President Reagan and his supporters as an unnecessary governmental intervention into the market, housing policy was shifted to the demand side. This change marks the move to the neo-liberal policy regime. While such a shift may seem innocuous, it was not. This shift in policy is responsible for curtailing the growth in low-cost subsidized rental housing units and producing increased prices for private rental and owner-occupied housing. When these changes are coupled with the deep recessionary period that marked the early 1980s, resulting in unemployment rates of over 10 per cent, the gentrification in the cities, speculative real estate bubbles, and the adoption of neo-liberalism as the ideological system that guided globalization, it becomes clearer why this policy change was so detrimental to housing the poor and low-income earners.

The Globalized Finance System

President Reagan became the US champion for changing the economic role played by government, especially the federal government. During his presidency he was able to effect fundamental changes in how government interacted with the market. While the neo-liberal prescription called for government's removal from the market, Reagan found that government could not be removed from the market, but it could play a different role than it had been playing in the market's operation.

In housing policy, this change in government's role manifested itself in two important ways. First, the financial sector was deregulated, which produced a restructuring of the housing finance system. Second, instead of providing a supply-side subsidy for housing the poor and low-income earners, the government moved its subsidy to the demand side. Supplementing these changes in the role of government were private sector actions that also had supply-side effects. Gentrification, which started in the 1970s, took thousands of affordable apartments and single-room occupancy units (SROs) out of the rental stock, and transformed many of them for the luxury for-purchase market. The first move to turn apartments into condominiums also occurred in this period, producing a negative effect on the rental stock.

In addition to these changes, many low-income rental units in central cities were producing insufficient rental income for landlords to maintain them, so they were abandoned to avoid paying taxes on them. Nearly 1 million SROs were either abandoned or transformed. These units had been the 'housing of last resort' for the destitute, but after a point, even they were no longer available (Wright, 1989, pp. 43–4; Shinn and Gillespie, 1994). This combination of changes produced the affordable housing problem which has affected even middle-class income earners and is at least partially responsible for the move to the streets that so many poor and low-income earners in America have had to make.

THE HOUSING FINANCE SYSTEM AND AFFORDABILITY

Macroeconomic pressures that aided the adoption of neo-liberal policies also put the US banking and housing finance systems under pressure. High nominal interest rates in the late 1970s and early 1980s led to negative cash flow and insolvency for many depository institutions, especially the mortgage-holding savings and loans. As the savings and loan industry imploded, new methods and sources of housing finance were found.

Floating-rate mortgages became common. Expanded government underwriting of mortgage sales led to the rapid growth of mortgage securitization, which in turn opened up new sources of credit supply to replace lost thrift lending capacity. Increased mortgage securitization, in turn, required increased government (and private) underwriting of mortgage sales, and the use of standardized mortgage eligibility criteria in lieu of the earlier system of 'relationship' lending. The home finance system had effectively been deregulated and reorganized into a market-based system. The old system of segmented markets, in which housing finance was deemed a social priority to achieve the goal of providing affordable housing, was replaced by the market priority of efficiency.[13]

Evidence of this transformation is seen in the mortgage originating and holding activities of lenders. In 1970, the mortgage-making depository institutions accounted for 93 per cent of all mortgages originated. By 1997, this figure had been cut almost in half. They accounted for only 48 per cent. Savings and loans alone were responsible for 50 per cent of the mortgage market activity in 1970, but by 1997 that figure had dropped to just under 10 per cent. The void created by the loss of the depository institutions was filled by market-based financial actors. The mortgage pools went from 5 per cent of mortgage activity in 1970 to 42 per cent in 1997. Adding the activity of the mortgage companies and private mortgage-backed conduits to the mortgage pools, they move from being responsible for 3.5 per cent of activity in 1970 to over 50 per cent in 1998 (US Department of Housing and Urban Development, 1998).

At this point, it's important to ask 'why is this change a problem if mortgages are still being originated?' and 'why is this shift in mortgage originators and holders such a big deal?' The nature of the mortgages that the market-based institutions made was very different from that of the depository institutions. The depository institutions had been organized so that they could engage in 'relationship lending'.[14] This type of lending did not rely strictly on a set of standardized criteria that each applicant had to meet. The institution's position in the community, its embeddedness, gave it access to a community member's nonquantifiable qualities and characteristics. Lending decisions were made using both standard and non-standard criteria. This 'art' of lending meant that nontraditional looking credit applications might actually be recognized as good credit risks.[15]

In contrast, the mortgages made by the market-based institutions are 'plain vanilla'. They must adhere to a strict set of criteria about debt load, income, and neighborhood. These mortgages have to be sold into the secondary market where they will probably be 'unbundled' – separated into their component parts – and then rebundled as mortgage-backed securities (MBS) to be sold into the MBS market. Standardization is very important to the actors in the secondary and the components markets. The individual components are not identifiable in an MBS. They have been melded together into a new non-transparent asset, so uniformity in the constituent parts is a necessity. This uniformity reduces the uncertainty that arises from unknown risks and increases the asset's salability.

By reducing risks, the standardization process makes lending cheaper for those who are 'plain vanilla'. By requiring that these secondary market criteria be met, the originator denies access to potential homebuyers who are not 'plain vanilla'. For these people, the chance of buying a home is diminished because the price of risk is high. Lending to a nonstandard borrower can only be accomplished if the loan's interest rate rises to compensate for the additional risk the borrower is perceived to embody. In some cases a risk-adjusted interest rate can compensate for the higher perceived risk, but in other cases the loan will simply be denied. Data on loan denials show that there is a strong relationship between being denied a loan and being a low-income earner, a person of color, an urban dweller and/or a single head of family with children (Dymski and Veitch, 1992; Dymski and Isenberg, 1997; 2002).[16]

The US Census Bureau's housing affordability data provide another glimpse of how feasible home purchase is for different social groups. The 1995 data indicate that people who are currently renters, not owners, have very little chance of buying a modestly priced house in the area in which they currently live (Savage, 1999). In 1995, only 10.2 per cent of renters could afford to buy a house in their neighborhood. This figure gets even worse when renters are disaggregated by family structure and by race. Whereas 15.1 per cent of married couples could afford to purchase a house in their neighborhood, only 5.4 per cent of male-headed households and only 2.9 per cent of female-headed households could purchase a modestly priced house in their neighborhood. These numbers emphasize the importance of a two-income household for making a home purchase affordable.

When Savage (1999, p. 2) disaggregated the sample by racial and family characteristics, some expected results emerged. In his disaggregation of families into those with and without children, the obvious became apparent: housing purchase is even harder for families with children, His analysis of affordability by racial categories also points to additional differences in affordability (ibid., p. 3). Whites lead in the ability to purchase a house. On average 14 per cent of white renter families and 13 per cent of white individuals could afford a modest house in their area. For both black renters and renters of hispanic origin, the already low figures take an even bigger drop. On average, 3 per cent of black and Hispanic origin families, 4 per cent of black individuals, and 1 per cent of individuals of Hispanic origin could afford a modest house. While these figures are quite shocking, the picture gets even worse when home-purchase affordability is seen over time. Savage (1999, p. 2) charts the change in affordability for household type and ownership over time. His analysis begins in 1984, in the middle of the Reagan presidency. For all categories of household and ownership, affordability declined between 1984 and 1995. The only bright spot was 1988, when renter families made a positive jump in their ability to purchase a house. But even that was completely eroded as the housing prices shot up, banks failed, mortgages became more expensive, unemployment rates jumped, and poverty rates rose.

The reduction in for-purchase housing affordability has spillover effects into the rental housing market. The operation of a housing market in which for-purchase housing is affordable to working-class and other middle-income earners means that more close-to-affordable rental housing is made available for poor and low-income earners. The changes in for-purchase housing policies that have been induced since the Reagan presidency have created a situation in which even middle-income people and others who are not able to meet the 'standard criteria' are finding housing less affordable (ibid.). Home ownership rates rose from 1940 to 1980, but by 1990 had dropped slightly, from 64.4 per cent to 64.2 per cent. This stagnation implies that rental housing that would be vacated by new owners is not coming on to the market. The supply-side effect that home purchases produce in the rental market is being impeded. This blockage, along with the other supply-side effects that have been discussed, indicates that housing turnover has slowed down and that the supply of affordable rental and for-purchase housing has been reduced. Given no change in demand, these two supply effects make for higher rents and house prices.

Housing Policy

The neo-liberal precept that markets make more efficient decisions than governmental agencies fostered the change from using supply-side subsidies to demand-side subsidies in housing policy. Even though the government had stopped building government-owned public housing in the 1950s, the 1960s subsidy programs for low-income housing were not popular with the Nixon White House or several important senators. Early in the second Nixon administration, a partial moratorium was imposed on these housing production programs. In the years that followed, Republican administrations reduced the activity of these production programs while Democratic administrations stepped them up. Vouchers for rental subsidies began to be promoted as the better approach to the housing problem, but they did not gather enough support to supplant the production subsidy programs until the Reagan presidency (Orlebeke, 2000).

In 1982, the President's Commission on Housing produced a report proposing a housing payments program as the most efficient way to remedy the housing problems for low-income and poor people. Immediately, the Reagan administration called for a repeal of the still existing production programs and the introduction of a rent voucher program under the terms of Section 8 (ibid., p. 505). The support for switching to vouchers was always couched in terms of a consumer in a market. The proponents' story of how a voucher worked usually emphasized the renter's freedom of choice in the market. Given a voucher instead of an apartment, the consumer could enter into the rental market and choose his or her own apartment. There was no dictate from a governmental entity that indicated where the renter had to live. These visions of consumer choice and freedom within the rental market motivated many voucher advocates.

What the advocates failed to see was how poor families' choices were heavily constrained by the use of vouchers, and the deleterious impact of vouchers on the low-income housing market. First, not everyone who is eligible for a voucher could get one. The number of vouchers issued depends upon funding for the Department of Housing and Urban Development (HUD) program. At the end of 2000, then-Secretary of HUD, Andrew Cuomo, estimated that 5.4 million American families were in need of housing assistance. But at the same time, only about 1.3 million were on average funded annually (Boland, 2000). While the number of vouchers could increase if HUD received more funding for this program, it seems politically unfeasible that all who are eligible for vouchers will actually receive them. Excess demand is huge.

Second, even when families are provided with vouchers, their ability to actually use them to obtain affordable housing is in question. Often, the supply of housing that is made available to voucher users is inadequate. Many landlords do not want to rent to poor people, so they refuse to put their property into the much needed supply. In addition, many landlords refuse to accept vouchers because they do not want to deal with the additional paperwork that vouchers require. Even if the landlord agrees to accept a voucher, then the housing unit, including the level of the rent, has to fit into the voucher guidelines. Finally, the voucher is set for a particular dollar value that is based on the 'standard rent' in the geographical area. The renter is required to pay 30 per cent of family income, and the subsidy provided by the voucher should pay the residual if the actual rent is equal to or less than the 'standard rent'. In reality, many renters, faced with the constraints in their actual market, pay more than 30 per cent of their income because the rental unit's price is higher than the standard rent. The HUD rules allow for families to pay up to 40 per cent of their income, but if it exceeds this level the unit may be categorized as ineligible (Sard, 2001).

With a dwindling supply of housing and a rising demand fueled by renters with vouchers, renters without vouchers, and renters who cannot buy because they are non-standard, the rental price of housing would be expected to rise. Shinn and Gillespie (1994) found that this was the case between 1974 and 1987.

In the 13-year period from 1974 to 1987 median housing costs for all renters went up 16 per cent in constant dollars. Median rents for poverty-level households rose at over twice that rate – 36 per cent. And rents for poor households living in unsubsidized units soared by 41 per cent (Shinn and Gillespie, 1994, p. 510). Instead of making housing more affordable or available, the changes in housing policies have produced the opposite effect.

Exacerbating the impact of these housing policy effects on the housing market are the changes in the government's approach to social welfare programs. Just like the housing policies, the approach to poverty alleviation has been to rely more heavily on the market. In 1996, when President Clinton ended 'welfare as we knew it', the economy was in the midst of a strong expansion that many policy-makers thought should provide jobs for anyone who was willing to work. Cutbacks in expenditures on especially the social welfare programs like AFDC, food stamps, and Medicaid were supposed to induce the recipients of funds from these programs to leave them and rely upon the market for their income.

The result of these cutbacks has been an increase in the poverty rate for families. During the recessions in the early part of the 1980s, the poverty rate for families rose to over 12 per cent. It stayed around 10 per cent for the rest of the decade, but then rose into the 11 and 12 per cent ranges through the middle of the 1990s (US Census Bureau, 2001). Since the late 1980s and the 1990s have been considered periods of good economic growth, the increase in poverty that has accompanied this growth leads one to question for whom the growth has been good. The reality for the poor and low-income earners is that the market has made housing less affordable while government's social spending has been reduced, thereby exacerbating the market's negative effect. There is even less money to spend – income or transfer payment – on housing.

CONCLUSION

In the 'Golden Age' the government was seen as having a legitimate economic role to play because the market had shown how vulnerable it was to disruption in the Great Depression. The flowering of governmental programs to aid middle- income homebuyers, poor renters, and poor families, produced the desired successes, which meant more housing and less crowding. The question of homelessness in the 'Golden Age' never arose. The housing programs may not have produced the level of quality housing that everyone desired, but in terms of quantity there was never a sense that people were on the street because they could not afford shelter.

In stark contrast to this picture stands the 'Global Age'. This is the time period when the homeless were forced out into the streets. They came out in numbers that overwhelmed anyone who had not been around for the Great Depression. Unlike the hobos of the earlier period, these homeless people did not want to 'ride the rails'. They were on the street because they could not afford to keep a roof over their heads. The rollbacks in housing policy and social welfare expenditures that defined the 'Global Age' were also, in large part, responsible for these people being out on the streets. The reduction in the affordable housing supply, coupled with the rise in rental prices, makes it obvious that people needed more, not less, money to keep shelter over their heads. Yet, instead of more money, there was more poverty. The interaction of the government and the market have produced an environment in which governmental entitlements have been reduced, leaving hundreds of thousands of people with only the market to rely on. The market, however, is not set up to care for people, merely to be efficient. The efficient solution, it appears, is homelessness for the very poorest.

This chapter has analyzed some of the major structural shifts that have produced US homelessness, but the story does not end here. There are community, nongovernmental, and governmental organizations still working to make housing affordable and available. Even though the neo-liberal regime has called for market decision-making, it's still the case that the United States continues to provide subsidies for homeowners via the mortgage interest tax deduction and for owners of residential apartment buildings via tax deductions for depreciation. The government is still an active player in the housing market; it is only the nature of its policies that has changed.

Recently, some life has been pumped back into the only program that has been slowly producing low-income housing during the 1990s, the Low Income Housing Tax Credit (LIHTC). While the program relies on a labyrinthine funding process, maintains the tradition of subsidized housing with a short public commitment, and produces a supply of low-income housing that is insufficient to meet demand, it produced over a million low-income apartments between 1987 and 1998. It has also acted to coordinate the activities of non-profit community development corporations such as the Local Initiatives Support Corporation and the Enterprise Foundation (Orlebeke, 2000, pp. 511–15). As these activities indicate, the government continues to intervene in the operation of the housing market, both on the financial and production sides. We need to recognize its presence and redirect budgetary priorities so that the needs of low-income and homeless people are served as well as those of people who are lucky enough to be able to buy a house.

Community and nonprofit organizations, such as Habitat for Humanity, have also become very active in low-income housing production in this period of governmental abeyance. Habitat has become one of the major home-building agencies in the United States. In 1998, it was ranked as the twenty-fourth largest homebuilder and in 1999, its ranking rose to fifteenth. In low-income house building, it is the number one builder in the United States (Habitat for Humanity).

Finally, we need to see that housing costs are relative to incomes. In the United States the poverty rate has been rising, there has been a rise in the skewness of the income distribution, and the bottom of the wage ladder has seen a real decline in purchasing power. The purchasing power of the minimum wage in 1970 was $3.73.[17] As the 1970s inflation ratcheted up prices, the minimum wage was increased in an attempt to keep pace. It did so until 1980. Tying price changes to the level of the minimum wage stopped with the Reagan presidency, so its purchasing power declined. In 1989, it reached its nadir of $2.70. Attempts to push it back up to its earlier value have not been successful. With the last increase in the minimum wage to $5.15 in 1997, its purchasing power only rose to $3.20. This reduction means that people are unable to purchase the same level of goods and services that they could in 1970. The rental housing price index has experienced an increase similar to the overall Consumer Price Index, which means that minimum wage earners are less able to afford housing.

Combating this decline in the real minimum wage would also go a long way towards alleviating some of the housing distress and homelessness that the working poor experience. Some community groups have banded together to show how detrimental this real wage decline has been for individuals as well as the greater community. Through their efforts living wage laws have been passed which mandate a minimum wage that is set in accordance with the cost for actually living in their community. Currently, 102 communities across the United States have adopted living wages ranging from $8.00 to $13.00 an hour (ACORN, 2002).

As the analysis in this article has shown, the problem of homelessness has several components and the problem has changed over time. Neo-liberal policies have reduced the supply of low-income housing and worked towards eradication of the welfare safety net. These changes, while putting more families at risk of losing their homes and being responsible for pushing some people onto the street, are not permanent or irredeemable, as the LIHTC, Habitat for Humanity, and the Living Wage Campaign indicate. Our opening question asked if the homeless will always be with us. The answer appears to be 'no, they don't have to be.'

NOTES

1. What these attempts to categorize the homeless population do is not just give them a name, but provide a reason for the state of homelessness. The interweaving of categorization and source of the problem means that naming the homeless has political overtones that carry very important ramifications. Once they are named, then the source of the problem is defined. Depending upon the reason for the homelessness, economic recession or substance abuser, for example, a plan to remedy the situation emerges based on the cause. If it is a recession, then governmental policy could be helpful, but if it is substance abuse, then it is a problem of personal will. At this point, it is the individual's problem, not society's. This, therefore, is the reason that the definition of who is homeless and the composition of that group are so ardently debated. It is not a problem of counting the number of angels that dance on the head of a pin, but one of whether there's any remedial action or not.
2. Rossi notes that an earlier study of the Skid Row homeless and single-room-occupancy (SRO) hotel occupants estimated that around 20 per cent of this population experienced some form of mental illness. In later studies of various homeless populations between 23 and 26 per cent of the population had mental hospital experience (Rossi, 1989, p. 147). David Snow and Leon Anderson (1994) take issue with the manner in which numerous studies on the homeless have diagnosed people as mentally ill.
3. The Interagency Council on the Homeless (ICH) asked to have this survey completed. It is a working group of the White House Domestic Policy Council and was chaired by Andrew Cuomo, Secretary of Housing and Urban Development. Co-chairs of the council were Donna Shalala, Secretary of Health and Human Services and Togo West, Jr., Secretary of Veteran Affairs. The Census Bureau collected the data; the Urban Institute analyzed it; and a collection of 12 federal agencies funded it (ICH, 1999, p. xiii).
4. The Census Bureau poverty threshold figures for 1996 indicate that a one-person family with a monthly income less than $680 is poor. For a two-person family with two adults a monthly income of less than $875 indicates poverty and for one adult and one child a monthly income less than $901 indicates poverty (US Census Bureau, 2002).
5. This figure stands in stark contrast to the earlier studies that estimate 26 per cent as the highest percentage of mentally ill in the population. See note 2.
6. There are several arguments against contested market theory, and the idea that efficiency is achievable, let alone the real goal of the neo-liberal regime, is also contestable (Crotty, 2002).
7. To provide assurance that the savings deposited into the savings and loan associations would be safe, a series of legislative acts were passed. In 1932, legislation that established the Federal Home Loan Bank Board (FHLBB), which made sure that the S&Ls had a proper level of liquidity available to them, was passed. The FHLBB did for the S&Ls what the Federal Reserve did for the commercial banks. In 1934, the National Housing Act was passed, establishing the Federal Savings and Loan Insurance Corporation (FSLIC). FSLIC insured the savings deposits held by the S&Ls. This insurance was to reduce the risk of savings loss that many depositors experienced in the Great Depression when their S&L failed and to increase the sense of security that the savings institution provided because the deposit was insured against failure. Additionally, the 1934 legislation established the Federal Housing Administration, which insured mortgage lenders against default by borrowers. Lenders, both direct and indirect, were assured through this scheme that the value of their capital would not be lost. Instrumental to the passage of these new laws was the backing of the Housing Lobby, which was composed of US Chamber of Commerce, National Association of Real Estate boards, US Saving and Loan League, National

Association of Retail Lumber Dealers, and National Association of Home Builders (Keith, 1973, p. 29).

8. Commercial banks' liabilities were primarily checking accounts which were mandated to be noninterest bearing. Even though the financial sector was segmented, commercial banks could offer savings accounts to their depositors, but to offer an advantage to the saver in a savings and loan association, the commercial bank savings account had a ceiling on its deposit rate that was determined by Regulation Q. Not until 1966 when inflationary pressures caused market interest rates to jump above the level mandated by Regulation Q were the S&Ls subject to this interest rate ceiling. When Regulation Q was extended to the S&Ls, the savings deposit rate at the S&L was set 0.25 per cent higher than the rate at the commercial bank.

9. This deduction has become known as a middle-class entitlement because of how it subsidizes home ownership. Instead of being a subsidy that would aid a homebuyer by reducing the down payment or the purchase price of a home, this subsidy becomes available only after the house has been purchased. 'In 1989, the mortgage interest and property taxes foregone totaled almost $39 billion . . . Not only was the 1989 figure more than six times the $6 billion spent in direct outlays, but most of it was distributed among upper income taxpayers' (Blau, 1992, p. 63). The entitlement aspect of the subsidy results from it being a forgone tax revenue and not an actual government expenditure. Since no federal money is ever actually spent on this subsidy, it attracts less attention in the budget making process.

10. The term 'public housing' will be used interchangeably with the term 'subsidized housing' which is a more accurate description of US government-sponsored housing. Very little actual public housing was ever built in the United States. The housing legislation passed in the 1960s authorized the building of subsidized private housing units. In exchange for tax breaks the builders agreed to keep the housing in the public domain for 40 years. The United States is now (2002) facing the withdrawal of these units from its stock of affordable housing.

11. A crowded dwelling is defined as one in which there are fewer rooms than there are people, for every person in the household there is a room. Severe crowding is defined as having 1.5 persons per room in the dwelling (US Census Bureau, 2002b).

12. The poverty alleviation programs' success showed up in a reduced poverty rate for the United States. In 1964, the poverty rate for families stood at 15.0 per cent, by 1968 it had dropped to 10.0 per cent, and throughout the 1970s it went above 9.4 per cent only once.

13. Efficiency, in economic terms, is a need-blind concept that defines the highest and best use for each resource according to what people are willing and able to pay.

14. Asymmetric information theorists argue that financial institutions have an advantage over financial markets when information in not uniform. The rationale for bank branching is to gather nonstandard information that allows the bank to make better decisions in lending.

15. Just as lending could be extended beyond the standard borrower, it also could be reduced for particular populations. Since lending standards were variable, it could be difficult to identify discriminatory activities even under strict scrutiny.

16. Government sponsored enterprises (GSEs), such as Fannie Mae and the Federal Home Loan Mortgage Company, dominate the secondary markets. Comparing their mortgage purchases to the depository institutions' holdings of mortgages in their asset portfolios shows in 1995 that depository institutions held a larger portion of their assets in mortgages from low-income areas, underserved areas, low-income earners, and African-Americans (Manchester et al., 1998, table 9).

17. In 1970 the nominal minimum wage was $1.45 and the Consumer Price Index (CPI) for an urban dweller was 38.8. To determine the purchasing power of the minimum wage, which is the same concept as the real minimum wage, simply convert the CPI from its percentage form and divide it into the nominal minimum wage.

REFERENCES

ACORN, Living Wage Resource Center (2002), www.livingwagecampaign.org/ shortwins.php, 12 May.

Bogard, Cynthia (2001), 'Claimsmakers and Contexts in Early Constructions of Homelessness: A Comparison of New York City and Washington, DC', *Symbolic Interaction*, **24** (4): 425–54.

Boland, Tom (2000), 'HUD Releases 80000 More Housing Vouchers', www. csf.colorado.edu/mail/homeless/2000/msg00666.html, 24 December.

Blau, Joel (1992), *The Visible Poor: Homelessness in the United States*, New York: Oxford University Press.

Burt, Martha (2001), 'What Will It Take To End Homelessness?', Washington, DC: Urban Institute, www.urban.org/Template.cfm?Section=Research&NavMenuID= 141&template=/TaggedContent/ViewPublication.cfm&PublicationID=7281.

Cohen, Carl and Jay Sokolovsky (1989), *Old Men of the Bowery: Strategies for Survival Among the Homeless*, New York: Guilford Press.

Crotty, James (2002), 'Trading State-Led Prosperity for Market-Led Stagnation: From the Golden Age to Global Neoliberalism', in Gary Dymski and Dorene Isenberg (eds), *Seeking Shelter on the Pacific Rim: Financial Globalization, Social Change, and the Housing Market*, Armonk, NY: M.E. Sharpe.

Diamond, Douglas B., and Michael J. Lea (1992), 'Housing Finance in Developed Countries: An International Comparison of Efficiency', *Journal of Housing Research* (special issue), **3** (1): 1–271.

Dymski, Gary and Dorene Isenberg (1997), 'Social Efficiency and the "Market Revolution" in US Housing Finance', in Shinya Imura, Takashi Nakahama, and Hiroshi Shibuya (eds), *Evolving Roles of Government in Japan and the United States*, Tokyo: Nihon Keizai Hyoron Sha (in Japanese).

Dymski, Gary and Dorene Isenberg (1998), 'Housing Finance in the Age of Globalization: From Social Housing to Life-Cycle Risk', in Dean Baker, Gerald Epstein and Robert Pollin (eds), *Globalization and Progressive Economic Policy: Real Constraints and Real Options*, Cambridge: Cambridge University Press.

Dymski, Gary and Dorene Isenberg (1999), 'Financial Globalization and Housing Policy: From "Golden Age" Housing to "Global Age" Insecurity', in Paul Davidson and Jan Kregel (eds), *Full Employment and Price Stability in a Global Economy*, Aldershot: Edward Elgar.

Dymski, Gary and Dorene Isenberg (eds) (2002), *Seeking Shelter on the Pacific Rim: Financial Globalization, Social Change, and the Housing Market*, Armonk, NY: M.E. Sharpe.

Dymski, Gary and John Veitch (1992), 'It's Not a Wonderful Life: Housing Affordability in Los Angeles', mimeo, University of California, Riverside.

Ellwood, Wayne (2001), *The No-Nonsense Guide to Globalization*, Oxford: New Internationalist Publications.

Galbraith, John K. (1997), *The Great Crash: 1929*, Boston, MA: Houghton Mifflin.

Habitat for Humanity, www.habitat.org/newsroom/rankings.html.

Hays, R. Allen (1985), *The Federal Government and Urban Housing*, Albany, NY: Statue University of New York Press.

Interagency Council on the Homeless (ICH) (1999), *Homelessness: Programs and the People They Serve*, summary, Washington, DC: ICH.

208   *New Thinking in Macroeconomics*

Isenberg, Dorene and Christie Byun (2002), 'Women, Housing, and Housing Policy in the United States', in Gary Dymski and Dorene Isenberg (eds), *Seeking Shelter on the Pacific Rim: Financial Globalization, Social Change, and the Housing Market*, Armonk, NY: M.E. Sharpe.

Keith, Nathaniel (1973), *Politics and the Housing Crisis Since 1930*, New York: Universe Books.

Manchester, Paul, S. Neal, and H. Bunce (1998*), Characteristics of Mortgages Purchased by Fannie Mae and Freddie Mac, 1993–95*, Housing Finance Working Paper Series, No. HF-003, Office of Policy Development and Research, HUD.

Minsky, Hyman (1982), *Can 'It' Happen Again?*, Armonk, NY: M.E. Sharpe.

Murray, Michael P. (1999), 'Subsidized and Unsubsidized Housing Stocks 1935–1987: Crowding Out and Cointegration', *Journal of Real Estate Finance and Economics*, **18** (1), January: 107–24.

National Coalition for the Homeless (1999), 'How Many People Experience Homelessness?', Washington, DC: National Coalition for the Homeless, www.nationalhomeless.org/numbers.html.

Orlebeke, Charles (2000), 'The Evolution of Low-Income Housing Policy, 1949 to 1999', *Housing Policy Debate*, **11** (2): 489–520.

Rodrik, Dani (2001), 'Trading in Illusions', *Foreign Policy*, March–April, www.foreignpolicy.com/issue_marapr_2001/rodrick.html.

Rossi, Peter (1989), *Down and Out in America: The Origins of Homelessness*, Chicago, IL: Chicago University Press.

Sard, Barbara (2001), 'Housing Vouchers Should Be a Major Component of Future Housing Policy for the Lowest Income Families', *Cityscape: A Journal of Policy Development and Research*, **5** (2): 89–110.

Savage, Howard (1999), 'Who Could Afford to Buy a House in 1995?', *Current Housing Reports*, H121/99-1, Washington, DC: US Department of Commerce, Economics and Statistics Administration, 148.129.75.3/prod/99pubs/h121-991.pdf.

Shinn, Marybeth and Colleen Gillespie (1994), 'The Roles of Housing and Poverty in the Origins of Homelessness', *American Behavioral Scientist*, **37** (4), February: 505–22.

Stiglitz, Joseph (2002), *Globalization and its Discontents*, New York: W.W. Norton.

Urban Institute (2000), 'Millions Still Face Homelessness in a Booming Economy', Washington, DC: Urban Institute.

US Census Bureau (2001), 'Number of Families Below the Poverty Level and Poverty Rate: 1959–2001', table 13, www.census.gov/hhes/poverty/histpov/histpov13.html.

US Census Bureau (2002a), 'Historical Census of Housing. Tables: Home ownership', www.census.gov/hhes/www/housing/census/historic/owner.html.

US Census Bureau (2002b), 'Historical Census of Housing. Tables: Crowding', www.census.gov/hhes/www/housing/census/historic/crowding.html.

US Census Bureau (2002c), table A-1: 'Years of School Completed by People 25 Years Old and Over, by Age and Sex: Selected Years 1940 to 2000', www.census.gov/population/socdemo/education/tableA-1.txt.

US Department of Housing and Urban Development (1998), 'Housing Market Conditions', Washington, DC, www.huduser.org/periodicals/ushmc/winter98/.

US Department of Housing and Urban Development (1999), 'Cuomo Releases Historic Report that Paints Most Comprehensive Picture Ever of Homelessness in America', *HUD News*, 8 December, www.hud.gov/library/bookshelf18/pressrel/pr99-258.html.

Wachter, Susan (1990), 'The Limits of the Housing Finance System', *Journal of Housing Research*, **1** (1): 163–85.

Wright, James (1989), *Address Unknown: The Homeless in America*, New York: Aldine de Gruyter.

PART IV

Macroeconomic Growth and the Environment

10. Debt and Deforestation

Peter Dorman

A leaf by the eye blocks the view of a great mountain. (Mo-zu)

INTRODUCTION

By any standard, deforestation is one of the crucial ecological issues of our time. Appreciation for the essential services provided by forests, a product of our expanding grasp of ecological science, is greater than ever, but it has yet to have much influence on forest policies. Table 10.1 shows the pattern from 1990 to 2000 for a broad sample of developing countries with substantial natural forest cover. Thirty-three of these 36 countries experienced net forest loss, with the aggregate rate of deforestation exceeding 4 per cent. This figure obscures the large differences in national rates; simply by excluding the three nondepleting cases, the aggregate rate rises to over 6 per cent. At this rate, there would be a cumulative loss of more than a third of this forest cover during the lifetime of someone born at the start of the new millenium. Some countries, such as Côte d'Ivoire, Nicaragua, Nigeria and Zambia, would see virtual elimination of their forests, and declines in such critical countries as Indonesia, Malaysia, Mexico and the Philippines would exceed half of the remaining stands.

It is impossible to overstate how catastrophic this trend is. Natural forests make an indispensable contribution to life on earth. To list only the most obvious functions, forests:

- store carbon which would otherwise migrate to the atmosphere and contribute to global warming;
- provide irreplaceable habitat for most of the world's flora and fauna;
- provide stability for montane and riparian soils, without which the rate of soil erosion would increase dramatically;
- provide opportunities for recreation, appreciation and solace valued by people of all conditions and cultures.

Against this backdrop, a debate has been underway over the causes of global deforestation. Clearly, increased demand from industrialized and rapidly industrializing countries (particularly in East Asia) is a significant factor. In part, what we are witnessing is a replay of earlier deforestations in Europe and North America, which fueled (literally and figuratively) the spread of industrial capitalism in the 18th and 19th centuries. A big difference this time, however, is that most of the countries that are cutting down their forests are *not* developing, or at least not developing very rapidly. Indonesia, to take a prominent example, should not be confused with the United States or Sweden, whose deforestations were accompanied by a rapid ascent into the global economic elite. (This should not be interpreted as an endorsement of the earlier waves of forest loss, of course.)

As a result, the search for causes has been broadened; some of this literature will be reviewed shortly. Potential culprits include an upsurge in local corruption, the strategic use of deforestation to uproot and disperse 'inconvenient' native peoples, poverty and land hunger in rural areas, and the liberalization imposed on countries in the process of structural adjustment. Without passing judgment on any of these factors – each of which is probably important in some cases – this chapter will focus on just one: the continuing global debt overhang. The purpose is not to argue that debt is more important than the other causes, or even to demonstrate its place in a reasonably complete account of the big picture. Rather, the chapter's aim is much more limited: to demonstrate that an indispensable part of any explanation is the role that external indebtedness plays in altering the economic calculations by individuals and governments, with the result that long-run and less commodifiable forest values are ignored in favor of short-run exigencies. The empirical methods used will be simple, corresponding to the limited aims of the project.

The hard part is understanding what this process implies for our understanding of the functioning of a credit-based economy. What is it about 'natural capital' that causes it to be sacrificed for the 'unnatural' kind? Why should the financial process bias the direction of development away from the preservation of ecological values? What lessons can we learn from this analysis for fashioning a new economic order that can meet the challenges posed by sustainability? Bluntly, this is to ask of macroeconomics the sort of questions that ecology has long posed to microeconomics. My answers will be provisional and broad-brushed, but I hope they call attention to assumptions in conventional macroeconomic thinking that might otherwise go unnoticed.

EMPIRICAL EVIDENCE

During the decade of the 1980s, the global drama of the Third World debt crisis competed for attention with battles over deforestation in countries like Brazil, Malaysia and Indonesia. Critics of the international financial order began linking the two, first in journalism and then in increasingly sophisticated analytical studies. Some of these were at the level of individual forest tracts, some were national in scope, and others used cross-sectional methods at the international level. In this chapter we will focus our attention on the third group.

A useful starting point is the comprehensive survey undertaken by the Center for International Forestry Research (Kaimowitz and Angelsen, 1998). They reviewed a large number of regression-based studies using national-level data, comparing methodology and results. They found that researchers typically employed similar sorts of variables to explain deforestation: initial forest size, measures of land use competition from agriculture, climate, income or land tenure inequality, the level of development (as proxied by income per capita), regional location and the extent of international indebtedness. The dependent variable was generally a measure of either roundwood production or forest cover loss, as tabulated by the UN Food and Agricultural Organization (FAO) at periodic intervals. Of the studies they considered, 15 employed a debt variable in some form; of these seven found a positive correlation, four found mixed results, and four found no effect (ibid., pp. 84–5).

Of course, all studies do not carry equal weight. Kaimowitz and Angelsen were reluctant to give more credence to any particular set of results, and the subsample I examined did not produce clear winners or losers (Gullison and Losos, 1993; Capistrano and Kiker, 1995; Kahn and McDonald, 1995; Rudel and Roper, 1997). Authors often relied on older, less reliable forest data and did not fully report the winnowing process in model selection. (Earlier FAO data on forest cover were based on fewer direct observations; much of the data were imputed. More recent series contain less error.) The most thoughtful treatment was provided by Kant and Redantz (1997); unlike other approaches, they permit different causal mechanisms to work in different regions of the world.

Kant and Redantz employ a two-step approach. The first considers four direct causes of deforestation: roundwood consumption, forest products exports, expansion of cropland, and expansion of pasture. In the first step total deforestation is decomposed into each of these. The second step consists of four computations in which each of these direct causes is regressed on a set of underlying causes. External debt is one such underlying factor, but it is employed as an explanatory variable only for forest exports in Latin America and Asia and pasture expansion in Latin America. Maximum likelihood estimation is used to adjust for heteroskedasticity and multi-collinearity, which they demonstrate to be substantial. In each equation it appears in, external debt is highly significant. Based on its coefficients and the coefficients on exports and pasture, each $1M US in external debt is associated with 8.4 hectares of deforestation (1981–90) in Asia and 27.2 hectares of deforestation in Latin America.

In this chapter no attempt will be made to reproduce the Kant and Redantz results, since its purpose is more limited. The objective is not to produce the most fine-grained explanation for global deforestation possible, but simply to utilize more recent FAO data to demonstrate the role of external debt. For this purpose, it will turn out that simple OLS methods applied to an undifferentiated set of developing countries yields more than sufficient information.[1] The countries in question are listed in Table 10.1; they were chosen because they are developing in at least a financial sense (their currencies do not play a role as reserves, so they are more subject to foreign exchange pressures), they have significant levels of forest cover, and the necessary data are available for them. Most are tropical, but not all. No particular significance in this study is attached to the nature of the forest habitats at risk. This is because it is not apparent why the causes of temperate forest depletion should be different from those of tropical depletion, all else being equal. Of course, while it is true that biodiversity assets tend to be greater in the tropics, forest loss is of concern everywhere.

The variables employed are presented in Table 10.2. A few points should be made about the purposes they serve. The rate of deforestation is measured positively: forest loss during the decade of the 1990s is reflected in a positive rate of deforestation. The debt measure, debt service as a percentage of GNP, is selected because it provides one of the two best measures of the pressures placed on an economy by external indebtedness. The other, debt service as a percentage of exports, was rejected because exports are themselves related to deforestation, introducing a spurious effect. The base year, 1990, was selected partly because it was assumed that this variable would have a lagged effect, and also because the series is not available for all countries throughout the decade.

Gross Domestic Product per capita can be measured in two ways, as an absolute level and as its natural logarithm. Normally the logged form of most income measures performs better in studies of this sort, but we shall see that this is not true in this case. Both forms are listed in Table 10.2. The Gini coefficient is a common measure of economic inequality; smaller values signify more equal distributions. It was measured for different years in different countries during the decade 1990–2000.

Table 10.1   Forest and financial data for selected countries

Country	Area, 1990	Area, 2000	Change, 1990–2000	Debt service to GNP (%)
Bolivia	54,679	53,068	-2.9	8.3
Brazil	554,745	543,905	-4.0	1.8
Cambodia	9,896	9,335	-5.7	2.7
Cameroon	26,076	23,858	-8.5	4.9
Central African Republic	23,207	22,907	-1.3	2.0
Chile	15,739	15,536	-1.3	9.7
China	145,417	163,480	12.4	2.0
Colombia	51,506	49,601	-3.7	10.2
Cote d'Ivoire	9,766	7,117	-27.1	13.7
Ecuador	11,929	10,557	-11.5	11.1
Ethiopia	5,517	4,593	-8.1	3.5
Guinea	7,276	6,929	-4.8	6.3
India	63,732	64,113	0.6	2.6
Indonesia	118,110	104,986	-11.1	9.1
Korea, Rep.	6,303	6,248	-0.8	3.3
Lao PDR	13,088	12,561	-4.0	1.1
Madagascar	12,901	11,727	-9.1	7.6
Malaysia	21,653	19,292	-11.0	10.3
Mali	14,179	13,186	-7.0	2.8
Mexico	61,511	55,205	-10.3	4.5
Mongolia	11,245	10,645	-5.3	6.0
Mozambique	31,238	30,601	-2.0	3.4
Nicaragua	4,450	3,278	-26.3	1.6
Nigeria	17,501	13,517	-22.8	13.0
Papua New Guinea	31,730	30,601	-3.6	17.9
Paraguay	24,602	23,372	-5.0	6.0
Peru	67,903	65,215	-4.0	1.9
Philippines	6,676	5,789	-13.3	8.1
Senegal	6,655	6,205	-6.8	5.9
South Africa	8,997	8,917	-0.9	3.9
Tanzania	39,724	38,811	-2.3	4.4
Thailand	15,886	14,762	-7.1	6.3
Uganda	5,103	4,190	-17.9	3.4
Venezuela, RB	51,681	49,506	-4.2	10.6
Vietnam	9,303	9,819	5.5	4.8
Zambia	39,755	31,246	-21.4	6.7

Notes: Columns 2 and 3 in Table 10.1 represent the extent in natural forest cover, measured in thousands of hectares. Column 4 is the cumulative change represented by columns 2 and 3. Column 5 is the ratio of debt service to GNP. Both columns 4 and 5 are presented as percentages.

Source: World Resources Institute (2003); World Bank (2003).

Table 10.2   Variables employed in the regression

Variable	Explanation	Source
Deforestation	Percentage loss in natural forest cover, 1990–2000	FAO
Debt	Total external debt service as a percentage of GNP, 1990	World Bank
GNP	Average GNP per capita 1990–2000 in 1995 $US	World Bank
Ln GNP	Natural log of the variable GNP	World Bank
Area	1990 forest area in thousands of hectares	FAO
Land/cap	Average arable land per person in hectares, 1989–1999	World Bank
Pop-growth	Average annual rural population growth rate, 1990–2000	World Bank
Density	Average rural population density in people per km², 1990–2000	World Bank
Gini	Gini index, 1990–2000 (various years)	World Bank
Real r	Average real interest rate, 1990–2000	World Bank
SE Asia	Dummy for South East Asia region	
Africa	Dummy for Africa region	

Source: World Bank (2003); World Resources Institute (2003) for FAO data.

The real interest rate is used because it plays an important role in the economic theory of forest management; high interest rates are thought to encourage higher rates of cutting, although, as we shall see, this is not true cross-nationally. Finally, dummy variables were created for location either in South East Asia or Africa, under the assumption that each of these areas is under particular forms of stress. South East Asia is closer to the timber and fiber markets of the rapidly expanding East Asian economies; African economies have largely stagnated during this period and generally possess less developed infrastructure for extraction.

External indebtedness possesses a strong direct correlation with deforestation; its coefficient is .31, which is significant at the .03 level (one-tailed). The question, then, is whether the significance of this association survives the introduction of other explanatory variables in multivariate estimation, and the answer is that it not only survives, it grows. In the process of evaluating different regression models, 15 specifications were estimated, eliminating variables that appeared to have little explanatory power and keeping those that did. In all of them the coefficient on debt is positive, and it is significant in all but one. More persuasively, the better the regression fit, the better the debt variable performed. The adjusted R2 ranged from .18 to .42, while the t-statistic on debt ranged from 1.57 to 4.02; the correlation between these two measures was a remarkable .86. To summarize, the better a regression model explains cross-national deforestation data, the more confidence we have that external indebtedness is a factor. The five most powerful estimations are grouped in Table 10.3.

Table 10.3 Summary regression data, dependent variable = rate of deforestation, 1990–2000 (t-statistics in parentheses)

Regression	1	2	3	4	5
Debt	.013	.013	.013	.013	.013
	(3.95)	(4.02)	(3.84)	(3.58)	(4.00)
GNP		$1.193\ e^{-5}$	$1.236\ e^{-5}$		$1.221\ e^{-5}$
		(1.39)	(1.41)		(1.42)
Ln GNP				.009	
				(0.58)	
Area	$2.96\ e^{-10}$	$3.414\ e^{-10}$	$3.694\ e^{-10}$	$3.062\ e^{-10}$	$3.607\ e^{-10}$
	(1.68)	(1.93)	(2.01)	(1.71)	(2.02)
Land/cap	.178	.169	.171	.179	.169
	(1.78)	(1.71)	(1.69)	(1.77)	(1.70)
Pop-growth	.024	.043	.038	.030	.039
	(2.01)	(2.40)	(2.04)	(1.86)	(2.11)
Density	$-2.58\ e^{-5}$	$-2.766\ e^{-5}$	$-2.431\ e^{-5}$	$-2.572\ e^{-5}$	$-2.585\ e^{-5}$
	(-2.46)	(-2.66)	(-2.04)	(-2.42)	(-2.43)
Gini	-.001	-.001	-.001	-.001	-.001
	(-0.45)	(-0.61)	(-0.72)	(-0.62)	(-0.66)
Real r	-.002	-.002	-.002	-.002	-.002
	(-2.02)	(-1.97)	(-1.98)	(-2.02)	(-2.06)
SE Asia			-.011		
			(-0.72)		
Africa			.017		.021
			(0.63)		(0.87)
Adj. R^2	.40	.42	.39	.39	.41

Note: N = 36, regressions include constant term.

Considering the wide range of influences on forest cover depletion worldwide, to be able to explain two-fifths of the variation (net of degrees of freedom usage) is somewhat surprising. Rather than offsetting one another, the three variables measuring land pressure (land/cap, pop-growth and density) all perform strongly together – although not necessarily with the expected sign. Land/cap has a positive coefficient, despite the presumption that the clearing of forests would be undertaken in response to a shortage of arable land. One possibility that could be considered in future research is that land-intensive, export-oriented activities, such as ranching, are more likely, at least in a broad sample such as this, to threaten forests than smallholder and subsistence production. Similarly, density enters negatively into the model. It may be that, controlling for other measures of pressure, density proxies a geographical factor favorable to timber extraction. Only population growth plays the anticipated role in these models. Another surprise is that economic inequality, which is thought to contribute to deforestation, perhaps through land pressure, in this model dampens it, although the coefficient is never significant.

Interest rates also consistently play a counter-theoretical role in these specifications. It may be that high interest rates choke off investments that might otherwise be made in timber extraction or land clearing. The initial size of forest cover is very positively related to deforestation, suggesting economies of scale at the operation or, more likely, industry level. The regional dummies do not perform well in models incorporating a sufficient number of economic and demographic variables. It may be that they would do better interacting with these other variables (à la Kant and Redantz), but this possibility was not explored. To summarize, the performance of the non-debt variables presents many puzzles for future research for those interested in a more comprehensive understanding of the deforestation process.

Note that the debt coefficient has high statistical significance in these well-fitting models; its quantitative significance is equally impressive. The mean external debt service to GNP ratio is 6.13 per cent, with a standard deviation of 3.91. Applying the coefficient obtained in regression 2, we find that a one standard-deviation change in this ratio leads to an increased deforestation rate of 5.24 per cent. This is approximately 72 per cent of its aggregate rate during the decade for this sample! Of course, these specific numbers should not be taken as gospel, since the influences on forest loss cannot be decomposed so mechanically in the real world. The true point is that, by any measure, international evidence on the determinants of deforestation strongly point to the role of countries' external debt burdens. It is virtually certain they are relevant and consequential.

Interpretation of the Linkages

How might we understand this linkage between finance and forests? External debt can be thought of as playing both direct and indirect roles. Directly, it alters the incentives face by private and public decision-makers. These include:

- Forest product exports. The need to acquire foreign exchange leads governments to encourage exports of raw logs and processed timber. This has been particularly pronounced in South East Asia, although its influence can be seen elsewhere; e.g. Côte d'Ivoire (World Resources Institute, 2003).
- Investment in industries using forest inputs. As part of a general program to attract inflows of investment, governments may guarantee harvest rights at concessionary prices. The most dramatic case is perhaps the pulp and paper industry promoted by Indonesia in the 1990s (Barr, 2001)
- Investment in industries requiring forest clearing. There is a general consensus that this process accounts for a portion of Latin American deforestation during the 1980s and perhaps more recently. Ranching in particular competes directly with forest cover (Kant and Redantz, 1997)

In addition, the burden of debt can play an indirect role:

- Expansion of subsistence agriculture via deforestation. Financing debt service frequently requires a general program of austerity, and this can have particularly severe effects on poor farmers and landless rural workers. Rather than submit to hunger, these groups may take it on themselves to clear forest land for food production. Brazil provides a well-known case (Andersen, 2002)
- Corruption and diminution of state capacity. Prolonged exposure to the rigors of structural adjustment and periodic financial crises has the tendency to alter the political economy of a country. Policies such as privatization and subsidies to attract inflows of new investment can easily degenerate into open corruption, as was seen in Mexico and Indonesia (Deininger and Minten, 1999; Barr, 2001). Less dramatically but equally as important, the primacy of maintaining debt service tends to elevate finance and trade ministries and their constituents, at the expense of social and environmental interests (Deyo, 2000). Since forest protection usually depends on the willingness and ability of governments to act as an impediment to

private exploitation, it is reasonable to expect that fundamental changes in political economy will lead to forest loss.

In a more detailed study of the causes of deforestation, we would want to know the relative importance of each of these channels, and in which countries they play the greatest role. In the context of this chapter, we can simply take note of what they have in common: they all stem from the pressure of external debt, and in particular a climate dominated by the pursuit of scarce foreign exchange.

One could tell a similar story by focusing on countries that have not deforested. China, India and Vietnam all have modest external debt, due to their pursuit of relatively autarkic development strategies during the principal decades of debt accumulation, and all three of them had positive rates of afforestation in the 1990s. China in particular has been criticized for placing its development goals ahead of natural resource conservation, but deforestation has not occurred (Smil, 1993). Any judgment can only be provisional at this point, but it is at least a question for future research whether the absence of significant debt pressure can account for the relatively benign forest policies of these three countries.

NATURAL CAPITAL: A DANGEROUS METAPHOR

Economics, like all fields of human knowledge, is founded on metaphor. 'The market' is a metaphor, and so are the other building blocks of the theory, such as 'exchange', 'equilibrium' and so on. This is not a criticism, just an observation; there is no escaping the need to think metaphorically. Metaphors foreground particular commonalities between ideas or objects at the expense of their differences. We can say that time is a river, and in some ways it is. The flow of time, its directionality, and the way a few leaves can float side by side for miles on the current – all of this draws our attention to the aspects of rivers that also evoke thoughts of time. But in other respects time and rivers are quite different. Rivers can be dammed and in some cases their flow can be reversed. They have floods and dry spells. There are no analogies here to the way we experience time. Whether the commonalities on which metaphors are based matter more than the differences depends on the purposes we bring to them.

'Natural capital' (like 'human capital') is highly metaphoric. It seizes on certain aspects of natural resource stocks to draw a parallel with assets that serve the function of capital in market societies. Four commonalities suggest themselves:

- Store of value. Natural resource stocks can be held as assets, transmitting value across time. This is true whether they are privately or publicly owned.
- Stock-flow relationship. Resource stocks are productive of flows of value. From this vantage point, their present value can be calculated as the discounted sum of future flows of goods and services.
- Repository of investment. Resource stocks can be augmented through investment. This takes the familiar form of an allocation of resources in the current period to increase expected flows in the future. From this perspective, investments in natural resources can be assigned rates of return in the same manner that any other investment can.
- Potential for disinvestments. Resource stocks can be depleted through harvesting beyond replacement capacity. Thus, just as future value flows can be obtained by investment allocations in the present, they can be diminished by current consumption. From an accounting standpoint, this justifies the use of a depreciation charge on withdrawals from the stock of natural resources, perhaps the main purpose behind the measurement of natural capital.

In all of these respects, a forest is like any other capital fund, and ecological economists are correct to point out that accounting frameworks that fail to incorporate them are incomplete (Repetto and McGrath, 1989; National Research Council, 1994; Costanza and D'Arge, 1997).

The liquidation of forest stocks and their conversion into more conventional capital assets under conditions of current account pressure, however, suggests that the metaphor is imperfect. Why should forests be cut down, while little thought is given to disassembling factories and selling their equipment as scrap? Indeed, the exception illuminates the rule in this instance: in much of the former Soviet Union, factories *were* disassembled and sold for scrap, in many cases without any impetus from external debt. In some cases this could be explained by pointing to the obsolescence of the enterprises – the negative value added to the equipment by their use in production. In others, however, the dismantling was perverse; real wealth was being depleted in order to satisfy the consumption demands of a small number of inside scavengers. What makes this exception noteworthy is that it is a man-bites-dog story; it is unique to a few transitional economies and unheard-of elsewhere. Under 'normal' capitalist conditions, there is no incentive for private owners to destroy the basis of their wealth.

Such is not the case with forests. Owners will often choose to liquidate, even though the present value of forest stocks, taking into account all their future services, exceeds the value of harvest levels that deplete them. This is particularly the case in the presence of debt. One aspect of this phenomenon is well known: increasing debt burdens are associated with higher default risk and therefore supply- and demand-side pressures on interest rates. On the supply side, lenders respond to the perception of increased default risk by attaching a corresponding premium to interest rates. On the demand side, debtors fearing default act in ways that suggest high discount rates – they have shorter time horizons and crave liquidity. In such conditions, fewer investments of any sort will survive the rate of return test, and disinvestment becomes more attractive.

There is a well-known analysis that demonstrates this relationship in the case of biologically reproducible natural resources (Fisher, 1981). Nevertheless, we have seen in the regression evidence that interest rates do not seem to play this role at the present time, and, in any event, current account pressure can be relieved by inflows of foreign investment funds, and this establishes a countervailing tendency for reallocation in debtor economies away from consumption and toward investment in productive assets.[2] In practical terms, why are forests not sold to foreign investors for sustainable management, rather than being liquidated?

Why Forests are not Conventional Assets

I would like to suggest two reasons why forests are not assets in the way conventional assets are assets – two aspects of forests as resource stocks that resist their representation as capital. Briefly, ownership rights in standing forests are intrinsically attenuated; such forests, to the extent they are sustainably managed, are 'tied' entities, inseparable from a set of external relationships over which owners can exercise little control. Also, many of their services are incapable of being commodified; their values are notional in the sense that they arise only in the analysis of economists, not in actual markets in which the contributions of forests are transacted and priced.

A. *Constrained ownership*. In a nutshell, the distinguishing characteristic of monetary economies is that liquidity matters. Flows of money payments are transacted, and payment schedules must be met on pain of default, which is a discontinuous and asymmetric event. (The state of being in default is qualitatively different from that of nondefault, and entry into default differs in cost and kind from exit from it.) Liquidity increases the likelihood that payment obligations can be met under conditions of uncertainty. Thus, increasing leverage, all things being equal, increases the premium on liquidity. Leverage finances investment; liquidity preference discourages it. Rather than being in a timeless, harmonious balance, these two forces ebb and flow, giving rise to the financial cyclicality for which capitalism has always been known.

Since the 1970s, most of the developing economies have been burdened with high levels of external debt, and, to meet their payment obligations, they have required a continuous net inflow of developed country – particularly US – currencies. This in turn has required the marketing of goods, services and assets that can purchase international liquidity. Given the risks – exchange rate and default – faced by buyers/investors initially holding dollars, developing country assets will be closely scrutinized for their degree of liquidity as well as potential return. It is not coincidental that economic models featuring the ease of exit, and not just entry, have gained prominence during this period. Similarly, the degree of liquidity depends on the extent to which assets can be managed or disposed by their owners, which is itself a function of the completeness of ownership. Incomplete ownership rights are more difficult to market, and restrictions on the use of assets limit the ability of owners to manage the magnitude and timing of future revenue flows.

To illustrate the issue, imagine a generic asset called a factory. The factory has financial aspects that promote its relative liquidity, such as share ownership transacted on stable, well-capitalized markets. But it is in the nature of such an asset that the other dimensions of liquidity are satisfied as well. There may be short-term, arm's-length contracts with suppliers (including workers) and customers, permitting investors to withdraw their stake at will or alter the way in which the factory operates or the markets it engages in. There are adequate markets in the factory's physical assets, so that the scale of operations can be altered with relatively little cost. Nor is there any intrinsic reason why investors should be tied to specific locations. Thus ownership stake, contracts, competitive strategy, scale and location are all subject to adjustment at little cost; the degree of commitment demanded of investors is minimized.

A very different asset might be our generic Forest. The ownership structure may lend itself to entry and exit in much the same way as the Factory, but there the similarity ends. Forests generate stakeholders tied to the resource and its management: those dependent on watershed services, fish and game habitat, etc. These are not parties that can be discarded or replaced at will by forest investors. Sustainable harvest practices, if carried out, are highly constraining; the amount and timing of harvests is dictated to a considerable extent by ecological factors and cannot be readily adjusted to changing market conditions. The forest is also tied to a specific location and is at the mercy of events – ecological, social, and political – that affect its profitability. Taken together, these factors suggest that investors must accept a high level of commitment if they intend to manage forest stocks sustainably rather than liquidate them. In this sense, forest resources are reminiscent of real estate; only the biological dimension adds an extra layer of illiquidity.

The practical significance of this stylized account lies in its implications for a debtor country's foreign exchange position. It is much easier to deplete forest stocks through intensive harvesting, and then sell the wood products for foreign exchange, than it is to acquire the same foreign exchange by selling forest stocks to foreign investors. The highly illiquid nature of forest investments requires a price concession greater than one would typically expect in artifactual capital assets like factories.[3] There is more foreign exchange to be had by cutting the forest down and exporting its timber.[4]

B. *Barriers to commodification.* Forests, as we know, have the marvelous capacity to produce a host of services valued on economic and ecological grounds alike. As it happens, only one of these can normally be captured in full by private owners, the generation of timber biomass. None of the others – habitat provision, soil deposition and stabilization, hydrological management, carbon sequestration, human amenities – is satisfactorily traded on markets such that its full value can be returned to forest owners. There is some prospect that markets may soon be in place for carbon storage, but the others will remain nonmarket benefits for the foreseeable future. It is simply not possible to fabricate markets in most of these services.

Faced with this general situation, most countries have evolved regulations or social conventions governing the ownership and management of forests. Their purpose is to protect the non-commodity values that would be lost if the profitability of timber harvest alone were the basis for resource decision-making. Nevertheless, the value of non-timber forest services, while entirely real, is not fungible; they cannot be converted to the liquid assets required for meeting the payment obligations borne by countries with external debt. This leads to an interesting (and depressing) paradox. The services provided by natural forests may be very highly valued, and economists using respectable techniques can put implicit prices on some of them. These values may greatly exceed the value of the timber that can be sold if the forests are liquidated. Nevertheless, the liquidation is still economically rational. The reason is that the relevant comparison is not between the value of the intact forest and its liquidation value, but between the value of the intact forest and the consequences of default (factored by the contribution of timber exports or other forest-depleting activities to the likelihood of default). Hence countries will be induced to substitute lower-valued activities for higher-valued ones, solely because of their payments obligations.

For these reasons, natural capital in the form of a forest is not exactly capital. It has biological and physical dimensions that tie it to other claimants, reducing the scope for owners to manage it as they would other assets, and its services, although real enough in economic terms, are not fully commodified. These differences come to the foreground under conditions of indebtedness, since both restrict the ability of owners to generate a flow of liquidity by means other than the liquidation of the forest stock itself.

CONCLUSION

Among the many sad consequences of the global debt overhang, the rapid and near-universal deforestation of the developing world is one of the most dismaying. It is bad economics and worse ecology. Future well-being depends on our ability to reverse this course, and to do this we need to understand the forces that have brought us to this point.

This study suggests many questions for future research on the causes of deforestation, such as those discussed at the end of the second section, but it leaves little doubt that external indebtedness plays a central role. By fingering debt as a principal contributor, we are brought face to face with the core of the capitalist accumulation process. In the absence of vast, diversified capital funds (which would now have to operate on an international level), we rely on credit to channel capital from its points of acquisition to its points of investment. Given the unevenness of development of the international system, this is inevitably a process of external debt accumulation as well. Moreover, due to its problematic origins decades ago, much of the debt still on the books had no productive counterpart in the world of real assets. The upshot is an onerous schedule of debt servicing, which affects nearly every developing country and to which there is, as yet, no end in sight.

The proper boundary between the pecuniary and nonpecuniary spheres of life – the latter including preservation of natural resources for purposes that do not generate money income – is difficult to determine, but as economies expand, the maintenance of nonpecuniary values becomes more pressing. The assumption of debt service obligations is not neutral with respect to this fundamental question; if payment schedules must be adhered to, money incomes to finance these payments are required. Thus nonpecuniary values are likely to be sacrificed. In the end, for sustainable economics to have a chance, either natural resources must be assigned sufficient money values, or they must be made off limits to private or public owners who would liquidate them, or means must be found to drastically reduce the level of debt required to finance global development.

NOTES

1. Multicollinearity is not an issue in these data; the maximum condition index is 20.5 in the best regression, with nearly all variable proportion accounted for by prior dimensions.

2. Joan Robinson long ago pointed out that flows on the capital account are not necessarily flows of 'capital', based on her work disentangling the monetary and real conceptions of capital. This caveat should be borne in mind, especially in the case of developed economies such as the US, with a panoply of portfolio assets financing consumption.
3. This holds only to the extent that 'investment' in forests adheres to both meanings of the term. That is, we are assuming that ownership claims to the resource are being purchased and that owners are choosing to maintain (invest in) stocks by limiting current harvest levels that would otherwise be feasible and profitable.
4. This stylized account does not include the non-timber uses of existing forest land that may also generate foreign exchange, such as ranching, but the analysis can be extended to them.

REFERENCES

Andersen, Lykke E. (2002), *The Dynamics of Deforestation and Economic Growth in the Brazilian Amazon*, New York: Cambridge University Press.

Barr, Christopher (2001), *Banking on Sustainability: Structural Adjustment and Forestry Reform in Post-Suharto Indonesia*, Bogor (Indonesia): Center for International Forestry Research.

Capistrano, Ana Doris and Clyde F. Kiker (1995), 'Macro-Scale Economic Influences on Tropical Forest Depletion', *Ecological Economics* **14**: 1–9.

Costanza, Robert and Ralph D'Arge (1997), 'The Value of the World's Ecosystem Services and Natural Capital', *Nature*, **387** (6630): 253–61.

Deininger, Klaus W. and Bart Minten (1999), 'Poverty, Policies, and Deforestation: The Case of Mexico', *Economic Development and Cultural Change*, **47** (2): 313–44.

Deyo, Frederic C. (2000), 'Reform, Globalisation and Crisis: Reconstructing Thai Labour', *Journal of Industrial Relations*, **42** (2): 258–74.

Fisher, Anthony C. (1981), *Resource and Environmental Economics*, Cambridge: Cambridge University Press.

Gullison, Raymond E. and Elizabeth C. Losos (1993), 'The Role of Foreign Debt in Deforestation in Latin America', *Conservation Biology*, **7** (1): 140–47.

Kahn, James R. and Judith A. McDonald (1995), 'Third-World Debt and Tropical Deforestation', *Ecological Economics*, **12** (2): 107–23.

Kaimowitz, David and Arild Angelsen (1998), *Economic Models of Tropical Deforestation: A Review*, Bogor (Indonesia): Center for International Forestry Research.

Kant, Shashi and Anke Redantz (1997), 'An Econometric Model of Tropical Deforestation', *Journal of Forest Economics*, **3**: 51–86.

National Research Council (1994), *Assigning Economic Value to Natural Resources*, Washington, DC: National Academy Press.

Repetto, Robert and William B. McGrath (1989), *Wasting Assets: Natural Resources in the National Income Accounts*, Washington, DC: World Resources Institute.

Rudel, Tom and Jill Roper (1997), 'The Paths to Rainforest Destruction: Cross-National Patterns of Tropical Deforestation', *World Development*, **25**: 53–65.

Smil, Vaclav (1993), *China's Environmental Crisis: An Inquiry into the Limits of National Development*, Armonk, NY: M.E. Sharpe.

World Bank (2003), *World Development Indicators Online*, http://devdata.worldbank.org/dataonline.

World Resources Institute (2003), *Earthtrends*, http://earthtrends.wri.org.

11. Reconciling Growth and Environment

Jonathan M. Harris and Neva R. Goodwin

There are good reasons why the word 'sustainability' has become popular. It emphasizes a subject that had become too nearly forgotten in economic theory, as well as in much economic behavior (including both corporate behavior and public policy): that is, the subject of the future, especially when considered in a long-term, generational perspective. Sustainability is about the possibility that the things we value in the present will continue to exist in the future. In this chapter we will assess the usefulness, even the viability, of contemporary mainstream economic theory against the criterion of whether this theory contributes to the understanding and promotion of sustainability in economic systems.

Macroeconomic theory and policy are strongly based on the assumption that economic growth is good. Keynesian and neoclassical perspectives, as well as their many current variants, all accept growth as the goal, while differing over the best means to achieve that goal. However, throughout the development of economics there have been subcurrents challenging the possibility and/or desirability of continual and unlimited growth.

Two lines of thought have suggested limits or significant modifications to economic growth. One tradition is that of J.S. Mill, whose 'stationary state' represented a desirable goal of adequate consumption combined with continued cultural development. His heirs include Keynes himself (see, e.g., Keynes, 1930), as well as recent advocates of 'sustainable consumption', including the small but persistent voluntary simplicity movement (see Durning, 1992). The other tradition is the Malthusian view of physical constraints on population and economic growth. In recent years Herman Daly (1991a; 1991b; 1996) has revived the concept of the steady state as an alternative to unlimited economic growth, advocating the concept of sustainable macroeconomic scale.

Mainstream economics has not been seriously influenced by the perspective of either Mill or Malthus. Current macroeconomic theory reflects the past two and a half centuries' experience of economic growth. The affluence of modern industrialized countries, as they are currently organized, depends on an economic development package that includes:

1. higher per capita purchasing power, resulting from
2. higher output per worker, achieved by
3. accumulation of capital equipment, as well as
4. technological and institutional innovations, along with
5. increased energy use and material inputs, supported by
6. a consumerist culture that assures that the goods produced will be purchased.

The promise of globalization is to extend this package to the presently less developed countries, leading to continual growth in living standards, consumption, and GDP. But a strong environmental critique maintains that we cannot continue with the fifth piece of the package – increased energy use and material inputs – without ecological catastrophe. In this view, current use of materials and generation of wastes is already straining or exceeding the planet's carrying capacity. It is therefore not physically possible for the global South, with still-growing population, to imitate the consumption patterns of the North, any more than it is possible for the North to continue indefinitely increasing output and consumption.

If this environmental critique is well grounded, then the nature of economic growth in the 21st century will be fundamentally different from the resource-intensive growth of the previous two centuries. Economic systems will have to satisfy demands for higher living standards for a larger global population while adapting to inescapable environmental constraints. This would not necessarily mean an end to economic growth, but will require a significant reorganization and reconceptualization of growth that must include some combination of much greater efficiency in resource use, stronger environmental protection, and a shift in the composition of consumption from material goods to services.

There is evidence that all three of these trends are, in fact, occurring in currently developed economies. This leads some economists to believe that the environmental critique is overstated. One argument claims that markets will adapt to ecological limits, without any necessity to deviate from the present growth-dependent course. Such a process of adjustment would, to be sure, require informed government intervention to correct the failure of markets to reflect environmental costs. Microeconomic incentives would have to be changed through higher prices reflecting scarcer resources or internalized environmental costs. The case for this kind of intervention is well established in standard economic theory.

The case for the more radical position of the environmental critics is based on a different assessment of the scale of the problems. If indeed the impact of economic growth on major ecological systems is potentially catastrophic, then more drastic changes are needed in theory and policy, not only at the micro but also at the macroeconomic level.

In this chapter we will examine the macroeconomic impacts of growth in terms of several major areas of conflict between economic demands and ecosystem capacities:

1. energy use and fossil fuel dependence;
2. greenhouse gas emissions and climate change;
3. transportation systems and automobile use;
4. food systems and agricultural productivity;
5. water, forests, and fisheries;
6. toxic chemicals and wastes.

In all of these areas a strong case can be made that current patterns of growth are unsustainable. In each area the problems of limits, overuse, and degradation of resources imply a reassessment of macroeconomic growth goals, a reorientation of policies at both the macro and micro levels, and a rethinking of basic economic theory to accommodate revised goals and policies.[1]

ENERGY USE AND FOSSIL FUELS

Energy has a unique role in all economic systems, and its importance increases in advanced industrial systems with high energy use. The centrality of energy as the essential input to productive processes has always been emphasized by theorists in the ecological economics school (see, e.g., Georgescu-Roegen, 1971; Odum and Odum, 1976; Daly, 1991b; Peet, 1992). However, energy has no special standing in most macroeconomic theory. Economic growth is seen as dependent on inputs of capital and labor, with energy rarely specified as an independent variable. Thus standard growth models have no limits or constraints related to the availability of energy. This is a serious oversight.

World consumption of fossil fuels (oil, coal, and natural gas) quadrupled during the second half of the 20th century, from about 2 billion tons of oil-equivalent in 1950 to close to 8 billion tons by 2000. The use of fossil fuels represents about 85 per cent of commercial energy use, while hydroelectric and nuclear account for 7 per cent and 6 per cent respectively. Solar, wind, geothermal, and biomass account together account for less than 1 per cent. Projections for future energy use during the first two decades of the 21st century show a 59 per cent global increase, with energy use in the developing world more than doubling over 1999 levels (US Department of Energy, 2001). Unless there are dramatic changes in current energy price structures, the great bulk of this additional energy use will also come from fossil fuels.

The 2002 World Summit on Sustainable Development considered, but failed to adopt, a goal of supplying 15 per cent of the world's energy needs from renewable sources by 2010. Even if a target in this range were achieved, fossil fuel use would still be about 30 per cent higher than present levels by 2020. This projection presents grave problems. Even leaving aside issues of atmospheric carbon emissions and global climate change (to which we will return shortly), issues of ground-level pollution associated with fossil fuels are significant, especially in urban areas of developing nations. For oil, in particular, there are also questions of reserve limits. While overall fossil fuel reserves are adequate to meet projected needs for at least two more decades, a number of analysts project a peaking of world oil production between 2010 and 2030 (MacKenzie, 1996; Campbell and Laherrére, 1998). The heavy concentration of oil reserves in the Middle East implies an unhealthy import dependence for major consuming nations, with attendant economic vulnerability to cartels or disruption of supply. This is especially true for the United States, which now imports well over half its oil supplies.

So long as cheap and abundant fossil fuels provided the basis for economic growth, and environmental considerations played a minor role, economic growth models could afford to neglect energy as a specific input. But the approach that worked for 20th-century growth modelers is inadequate for the 21st century. The critical dependence of global economic growth on energy supplies, the centrality of fossil fuels to the global energy system, and the dominant role of oil among fossil fuels, are determining factors shaping economic growth. While a transition to more renewable energy sources is possible, and indeed essential, such a transition will not come about without major policy changes at the macro level. Macroeconomic theory and models of economic growth must reflect the unique role of energy, as well as the natural limits on all of the major energy sources on which the world now relies.

GREENHOUSE GAS EMISSIONS AND CLIMATE CHANGE

Beyond the issues around fossil fuels that were just mentioned, the greatest environmental danger they pose is that of atmospheric carbon emissions which cause global climate change. The 2001 report of the Intergovernmental Panel on Climate Change provides a comprehensive review of the evidence on human-induced climate change. Atmospheric concentrations of carbon dioxide have risen 31 per cent above pre-industrial levels, reaching a level not exceeded during the past 420,000 years, and probably not during the past 20 million years. Global surface temperatures have risen for the past four decades, with a total increase over the twentieth century of about 0.6 °C. Snow and ice cover have decreased, global average sea level has risen, and 'there is new and stronger evidence that most of the warming observed over the last 50 years is attributable to human activities' (IPCC, 2001a). For the 21st century, the IPCC projects a global surface temperature increase of 1.4 to 5.8 °C (2.5 to 10 °F).

The main driver of continued climate change is the carbon dioxide emissions associated with fossil fuel use. Current global carbon emissions are about 6.2 billion tons per year, and this figure will increase with increased consumption of fossil fuels. Despite efforts under the Kyoto protocol to stabilize emissions, they have grown significantly above 1990 levels. Moreover, the stabilization of global emissions at the Kyoto target levels would not be enough to prevent continued and growing atmospheric accumulations of carbon. In order to stabilize the accumulated level of atmospheric carbon, it will ultimately be necessary to cut carbon emissions by 70–80 per cent from present levels. Even if and when this is achieved, effects such as increased ice melting, rising sea levels, and surface temperature increases will continue for hundreds of years (IPCC, 2001a).

It is thus apparent that human economic activity has already had major, irreversible effects on planetary ecology through induced climate change, with a prospect of extremely severe continued impacts during the 21st century even under the most optimistic scenarios. Details in these scenarios include reduction in crop yields especially in tropical and sub-tropical regions, an increased incidence of extreme weather events, increased inland flooding, massive disruption of water systems, decreased water availability in water-scarce regions, an increase in vector-borne diseases, extensive damage to coastal ecosystems, and inundation of low-lying areas. The entire nation of Bangladesh, with 133 million people (projected to increase to 200 million by 2050) is especially at risk of inundation, as are the Netherlands, island nations, low-lying cities such as New Orleans and Miami, and tens of millions more people in coastal areas worldwide (IPCC, 2001b; Population Reference Bureau, 2002). All these impacts will be further magnified if positive feedback effects accelerate warming, disrupt ocean circulation, or cause collapse of the West Antarctic or Greenland ice sheets.

The massive potential impact of global climate change raises a fundamental question about economic growth. The essential assumption underlying growth models is that human well-being will be increased by economic growth. Overall, despite great social inequalities and extensive environmental damage, this has been true during the 20th century. But the projected climate change scenarios raise the possibility that conditions for the current generation of children, and for future generations, will be significantly worse in important respects. The loss of ocean-front property in the US will be painful for those affected, but pales to insignificance in comparison to the devastating loss of homes of homes and lives in store for millions of people in Bangladesh and other low-lying countries. Malaria and other tropical diseases – long a major force against economic development – will infest a much larger portion of the planet. Existing crises in access to clean fresh water (see below), and related issues of health and military conflict, will accelerate.

If human economic activity results in the replacement of a relatively benign planetary climate with one that is more hostile to human well-being as well as to ecosystem diversity, it is difficult to argue that greater economic production will provide an adequate compensation. This is especially so if ever-greater portions of every nation's wealth must be diverted to activities that do not advance well-being beyond its present state, but simply try to make up for what is being lost or destroyed.

Can we hope that these worst scenarios will not be realized? It may be possible that, with an effective policy transition to the promotion of non-carbon fuels, and the reduction of other greenhouse gases, the effects of climate change might be limited, and the general presumption of increasing well-being resulting from economic growth would be affirmed. But this more optimistic outcome is strongly dependent on the nature of economic growth. And the nature of economic growth will be determined by macroeconomic policies that affect carbon dependence. In contrast to the economic development patterns of the 20th century, when it was possible to view macroeconomic goals in terms of the promotion of stable growth, the challenge of climate change implies that macroeconomic policies must be judged not on whether they promote growth, but on what kind of qualitative change in economic systems they achieve.

TRANSPORTATION SYSTEMS AND AUTOMOBILE USE

The major contributor to global warming is the burning of fossil fuels, and the largest single use for fossil fuels is in transportation. The car culture that has been pioneered by the United States, and is rapidly extending worldwide, is the most significant cause of the relentless increase in global transportation fuel consumption.

As of 2000, four-fifths of the world's 520 million automobiles were in industrial countries. In the United States, there were three vehicles for every four people. In Western Europe and Japan, the ratio was about one for every two people (Brown, 2001a). Even if the industrialized countries can be considered to be approaching saturation in automobile use, there is enormous upward elasticity in the demand for cars throughout the developing world. In Brazil, there is about one car for every 10 people, and in China and India less than one for every 100 people. The Chinese government has recently moved to unleash this potential demand by altering policies that favored bicycle transport to policies that encourage cars while banning bicycles from many urban roadways.

The car culture is not just about cars. It determines the mix of public and private transportation options, affecting how materials are shipped as well as the way the individuals travel. It enters our daily lives in the form of pollution, congestion, traffic accidents and parking. Behind these experiences are the materials and energy that go into making cars, the energy used to run them, and the physical space that cars take away from other uses. On a global scale, in addition to the contribution to global warming, loss of cropland to road networks is also an important issue.

In the US, an estimated 61,000 square miles are devoted to roads and parking lots. For every five cars added to the US fleet, an area the size of a football field is paved – and croplands are often the first choice for roads because they are on flat, well-drained soils (Brown, 2001a). The US is a relatively land-abundant country with no domestic food shortage. The competition for land between cars and food can be much more critical in land-short developing nations with much higher population densities.

If China were one day to achieve the Japanese automobile ownership rate of one car for every two people, it would have a fleet of 640 million cars, compared with only 13 million today . . . Assuming 0.02 hectares of paved land per vehicle in China, as in Europe and Japan, a fleet of 640 million cars would require paving nearly 13 million hectares of land, most of which would likely be cropland. This figure is over one half of China's 23 million hectares of rice land . . . While India has only a third the land area of China, it too has over a billion people, and an automobile fleet of 8 million. Its fast-growing villages and cities are also encroaching onto cropland. A country that is projected to add another half-billion people by 2050 cannot afford to cover large areas of cropland with asphalt for roads and parking lots . . . There is not enough land in China, India, and other densely populated countries like Indonesia, Bangladesh, Pakistan, Iran, Egypt, and Mexico to support automobile-centered transportation systems and to feed their people. The competition between cars and crops for land is becoming a competition between the rich and the poor, between those who can afford to buy automobiles and those who struggle to buy enough food. Governments that subsidize an automobile industry with revenues collected from the entire population are, in effect, taxing the poor to support the cars of the wealthy (Brown, 2001a).

The model of consumption that encourages this path is the middle-class car culture of the developed nations. This model cannot be replicated in the developing world without disastrous impacts on the environment and perhaps also on food production.

This does not mean, of course, that the existing automobile-centered systems of the US, Europe, and Japan are sustainable while those planned for the developing world are not. The significant contribution of the transportation sector in the industrialized nations to global carbon emissions means that these countries are in no position to preach to developing nations about the need for restraint. The envisioned development of 'hyper-cars' getting 80–100 miles to the gallon, and the use of advanced fuel-cell technologies, could significantly reduce emissions problems. But these technologies are, under optimistic projections, 12–15 years away from realization, and during the intervening period many millions of current-technology vehicles will be added to the world's automobile fleet. And, of course, more efficient automotive technology cannot solve the problem of land use conflicts in densely populated countries.

The transition to a more environmentally-friendly transportation system in developed nations will be a huge challenge, requiring substantial social investment as well as modification of the consumption-oriented ethos which is presently driving continued increases in traffic congestion and in emissions. Macroeconomic issues of social investment and infrastructure, as well as social goals and values, are crucial to determining the future of transportation networks and land use.

FOOD SYSTEMS AND AGRICULTURAL PRODUCTIVITY

Between 2000 and 2020 an average of over 70 million people a year will be added to the world's population. To feed these additional people at the current world average consumption rate of 350 kg/cap of grain would require about 25 million additional tons of grain each year, a cumulative increase of 25 per cent over present production levels.[2] The actual increase required, however, is likely to be much larger than this, because, as incomes rise, there is a well-documented tendency for people to shift to more meat-intensive diets, which require significantly more grain use as animal feed. This in turn requires more land, water, and input use. The International Food Policy Research Institute, for example, estimates a cumulative global increase in grain demand of 35 per cent between 1997 and 2020, with a 49 per cent increase in the developing world (Rosegrant et al., 2001).

How much of a strain will this increased food demand impose on world agricultural production systems? Increases in the range of 40 per cent clearly cannot be met by expanding cropland. There has been little expansion in global cropland since the 1980s, and most additional land theoretically available for cropping is in forested tropical areas, generally poorly suited for agriculture and involving significant ecological costs to convert. Moreover, housing as well as transportation systems and other infrastructure for growing populations create pressures on croplands. For all these reasons, there is general agreement that the great bulk of the projected demand increase must be met through increasing yields.

But worldwide yield growth from agriculture is slowing. Rates of growth in yields averaged 3 per cent per year in the 1960s, and about 2 per cent in the 1970s and 1980s. During the decade of the 1990s world yield growth rates were only 1.3 per cent per year (Harris and Kennedy, 1999). This trend reflects diminishing returns from the Green Revolution. Rapid rates of increase in yields were obtained from grain varieties that were bred to accept large quantities of fertilizer and irrigation water, converting much of these inputs to grain for consumption rather than to the leaves and stalk of the plant. The requirement for high input use has resulted in significant environmental problems of fertilizer runoff and water pollution and overdraft. By 2000, the benefits of the Green Revolution technologies had been largely exploited, leaving little room for additional yield growth from these input-intensive techniques.

Current grain yields average a little over 2 metric tons per hectare in developing nations (excluding China), as compared to 3.7 metric tons per hectare in developed nations. To accommodate a 40 per cent increase in grain demand, average global yields would have to rise to about 4 metric tons per hectare, assuming a modest increase in land use (Harris, 1996; Harris and Kennedy, 1999). Doubling grain yields in the developing world in a 20 year period would require rates of growth in yields in excess of 3 per cent per year – well above current trends. For this reason, almost all projections for global food supply and demand envision the developing world importing much larger quantities of grain. The International Food Policy Research Institute reports that

> Cereal production in the developing world will not keep pace with demand, and net cereal imports by developing countries will almost double between 1995 and 2020 to 192 million tons in order to fill the gap between production and demand. Net meat imports by developing countries will increase eightfold during this period to 6.6 million tons. (Pinstrup-Andersen et al., 1999, p. 5)

Does this indicate a Malthusian outcome, with increasing danger of food shortfalls and famine? Not in the classic sense, since global export capacity will probably be adequate to meet the demand. It does, however, raise several troubling possibilities. One relates to the special case of China, which has had rapid success in raising yields to over 4 metric tons per hectare. However China's population is still projected to increase by nearly 200 million (Population Reference Bureau, 2002), cropland loss to urban and industrial uses continues, erosion is a serious problem, water overdraft is severe, and pollution from fertilizer runoff is widespread. Should China fall significantly short of self-sufficiency in grains, its entry into the world market as a major importer could raise prices, creating great hardship for import-dependent but poorer nations, especially in Africa. In addition, the experience of China indicates that environmental problems resulting from the push to raise agricultural yields can be enormous.

Africa is closer to a genuine Malthusian crisis. With the world's most rapid population growth, Africa is projected to double in population before 2050, even taking into account the increased death rate from AIDS (Population Reference Bureau, 2002). Water constraints are extreme, with only 4 per cent of cropland irrigated, and yields in Africa have barely increased in the past several decades, averaging only slightly over 1 ton per hectare. Much cropland and grazing land is being lost due to degradation, while deforestation is bringing ever more marginal land into production (Paarlberg, 1996).

The true neo-Malthusian threat in the 21st century is not that we will run out of food, but that agroecosystems will suffer such high environmental costs that water supplies and soil quality will be seriously degraded, leading to even greater dependence on artificial inputs and accelerating damage to future sustainability, especially in the developing world. Many environmental problems associated with agricultural production are long-term in nature: the effects of soil erosion and water overdraft, for example, may not affect productivity significantly for decades, but will eventually have devastating impacts when the topsoil is lost or the aquifer runs dry. In the short term, however, the negative effects are usually masked by increases in agricultural productivity from additional inputs. This means that farmers have few market incentives to conserve resources for the longer-term future, since the immediate economic incentives promote more intensive production and resource use.

During the period 1950–2000 global agricultural production nearly tripled, running steadily ahead of population growth. We are already experiencing a shift from that experience of rapid growth in per capita food production to a situation of slower growth and tightening environmental constraints. This suggests that the concept of carrying capacity is relevant in analyzing the combined effects of population and economic growth. Carrying capacity is a relatively straightforward concept in population biology, and clearly applies to analyses of, for example, grazing stocks or fisheries. Economists have generally rejected it as inapplicable to human economic growth, essentially because technological progress allows escape from resource constraints – or at least enormous elasticity in extending those constraints. But in the area of global agricultural production it appears that we are already stretching the limits of biophysical production systems.

The introduction of carrying capacity constraints into economic theory would fundamentally change the role of technology in growth models. In most such models, technology appears as an inexhaustible source of increased production, raising the productivity of capital and labor in a secular fashion without limit. But with significant environmental constraints it seems that we must at least ask the question, 'What kind of technology?' Some technologies will worsen environmental problems, directly or through unforeseen consequences (as in the case of impacts on ecosystems and genetic diversity). The market does not necessarily supply incentives for the development of environmentally friendly technologies. Thus, rather than simply seeking to provide stable conditions for economic growth, macroeconomic policy needs to be concerned with the direction of growth. In agriculture, this could imply moving subsidies from technologies that encourage overproduction and high input use to those that promote conservation and ecological technologies – a different approach from the standard economic recommendation for elimination of subsidies and free trade in agricultural commodities.

WATER, FORESTS, AND FISHERIES

[H]umanity has entered the endgame in its traditional, historical relationship with the natural world. (James Gustave Speth, Dean of the Yale School of Forestry and Environmental Studies – Speth, 2002, p. 19)

The meaning of Speth's statement is especially evident in relation to renewable resources such as water, wood and food harvested from the oceans. History provides many examples of local catastrophes for peoples who exceeded the local limits of such resources. Humanity is now, for the first time, encountering on a global scale the limits placed by the natural ecosystems of the planet on the availability of renewable resources.

At present about one-third of the world's population lives in countries suffering from moderate to high water stress, and in less than 25 years this figure is projected to be two-thirds of the world's population (United Nations Environmental Programme, 2002). The global supply of fresh water is fixed, with an annual freshwater runoff of about 47,000 cubic kilometers per year, or 7,000 cubic meters per capita (Gleick, 2000). The portion of global runoff that is stable and available for human use (i.e. excluding floods and remote areas) is significantly less. Since the available total can be increased only marginally through dam or river diversion projects, per capita availability falls steadily as population increases. Uneven regional distribution of water means that global per capita figures do not accurately indicate the frequency of regional water stress (less than 2,000 cubic meters per capita) and water scarcity (less than 1,000 meters per capita). All major areas of irrigated agriculture currently suffer from groundwater overdraft, often with severe impacts including restriction of urban water supplies, land subsidence, and salt-water intrusion into aquifers.

Similar, though less easily quantifiable, limits exist for the sustainable yields available from the world's forests and fisheries. Current patterns of forest loss in developing countries – about 13 million hectares annually, equal to 0.65 per cent of forested area per year, or 6.5 per cent per decade – arise from a combination of wood and firewood demand plus conversion to (often short-lived) agricultural uses. On the positive side, forested area in developed countries is increasing, as is plantation forest area worldwide. In theory, improved forest management practices and increased reliance on plantation forests and recycling of wood products should make it possible to prevent excessive demands on natural forests. But such improved practices are a long way from reality, and demand for wood, which has grown steadily over the past 40 years, is projected to continue to increase from 3.28 billion cubic meters in 1999 to about 4.35 billion cubic meters in 2015 (FAO, 2000a; 2001; Brown, 2001b).

Overexploitation of ocean fisheries is a worldwide problem, with 11 of the 15 major fishing areas and over 60 per cent of major fish species either fully exploited or in decline (McGinn, 1999; FAO, 2000b). Here also better management practices could reduce excessive pressures, but achievement of sustainable harvesting, especially in international waters, is extremely difficult. The global harvest of wild fish appears to have peaked around 90 million tons in the 1990s, and growth in fish consumption is now coming primarily from aquaculture. Aquaculture, however, is encountering serious environmental problems of physical and biological/genetic pollution. Per capita fish harvest, including both wild and cultivated, has barely increased since the late 1980s, and FAO projections envision little future increase in wild harvest, with expansion of aquaculture being essential to any increase in per capita consumption (FAO 2000b; Gardner, 2000).

TOXIC CHEMICALS AND WASTES

As economic systems grow, their 'throughput' of energy and materials tends to increase.[3] This net effect results from two opposing trends. One is the increase in per capita consumption of output. The other is 'dematerialization' – decreasing material use per unit of output (Wernick et al., 1996; Ackerman, 2001). In general, while intensity of materials use tends to decline with technological progress, this has been outweighed by increasing per capita consumption, leading to long term national and global increases in materials use (Gardner and Sampat, 1998). This raises questions of possible resource and environmental constraints. The original *Limits to Growth* report in 1972 (Meadows et al., 1972) focused on issues of exhaustion of mineral resources, but for most resources this prospect is still fairly distant due to technological progress, resource substitution, and discovery of new reserves. More recent discussion, including the 1992 update *Beyond the Limits* (Meadows et al., 1992), has focused on environmental impacts associated with expanded resource recovery and disposal. This is of greatest concern when the products and byproducts of resource throughput are toxic to humans or damaging to ecosystems.

By the late 1990s global output of chemical products for industry and agriculture totaled over $1.3 trillion. Chemical industry production is projected to grow slightly faster than gross world product through 2020 (OECD, 2001; McGinn, 2002). Only about 10 per cent of approximately 72,000 industrial chemicals have been thoroughly screened for toxicity, and only 2 per cent have been tested to determine if they are carcinogens, teratogens, or mutagens (Miller, 1998). Chemicals in widespread use that are known to be both highly toxic and long-lived include halogenated hydrocarbons, dioxins and furans, and heavy metals such as lead, mercury, cobalt, and cadmium (McGinn, 2002). As global production increases, especially in the developing world, the threats posed by the known and unknown dangers of toxic emissions and wastes intensify.

The 2001 Convention on Persistent Organic Pollutants (POP) seeks to ban ten of the most damaging chemicals – but even if the POP convention succeeds, this addresses only a small portion of the global toxics problem. Persistent lead and mercury pollution are widespread throughout the world, despite recent reductions in emissions. Stockpiles of toxic wastes exist in almost all developed and developing nations, often with little regulation or adequate techniques for disposal. Common products such as PVC plastics, whose production, use, and disposal involve a range of toxic emissions, are expanding in use with little attention to problems of immediate toxicity or of long-term disposal. One of the most troubling problems is the migration of toxic chemicals from agriculture, industry and transportation into aquifers – another source of stress on the world's potable fresh water. This virtually irreversible problem is becoming evident both in industrial areas and in increasing nitrate and pesticide pollution of groundwater in agricultural areas (Sampat, 2001).

The use of toxic materials appears inextricably integrated into current production systems. A massive shift to 'industrial ecology' systems, involving extensive recycling and substitution of environmentally benign materials, could significantly reduce the long-term pollution and health problems associated with toxic emissions and wastes, but such a shift is not now on the horizon. In effect, there is a race between the spread of 'greener' technologies and rapid industrial growth using current technologies. In this context, economic growth is both a promise and a threat. The outcome will be determined by institutional and policy factors; there is no guarantee that economic growth in itself will improve, rather than worsen, the situation.

IMPLICATIONS FOR MACROECONOMIC THEORY

The major areas of economic/environmental conflict that we have reviewed offer ample evidence that the nature of economic growth will have to change, and that there are real global limits on energy and resource use. This argument is not new (see, e.g., Daly, 1992; Goodland, 1992) nor is our presentation of the issues either unique or comprehensive (see, e.g., Brown, 2001b). But our review of these major areas indicates that the problems have grown worse over the last decade, and cannot be expected to ameliorate in coming decades without drastic policy action. This has – or should have – significant implications for macroeconomic theory and policy.

The first essential area for reorientation of macroeconomic thinking is with respect to the goal of increasing consumption. Macroeconomic theory is implicitly or explicitly oriented towards achieving this goal, either through raising current consumption or through greater investment, which makes possible higher future consumption (see, e.g., Goodwin et al., 1997). No distinction is made between consumption of essentials and luxuries, nor is much attention paid to the distribution of consumption expenditures. In a standard macroeconomic perspective, a rising tide lifts all boats, and the object of macroeconomic policy is to keep the tide rising. The picture of environmental limits that we have sketched implies a much more critical view of increasing consumption. Growth in consumption is not necessarily undesirable, but needs to be weighed against its negative effects on resources and environmental services.

In this perspective, it is clear that growth of consumption in developing nations must be viewed differently from growth of consumption in the developed world. For the developed countries a good case can be made that current material consumption is sufficient (or perhaps excessive). For these countries, J.S. Mill's 'stationary state', with continued development in cultural and intellectual areas but not in material consumption, may be a relevant model. Here the problem should be to assure the sustainability of current living standards, and to improve equity, but not to promote a continued rising tide. This clearly poses a major challenge for macroeconomic theory, since we currently have no theory that indicates how to achieve a stable, full-employment economy in the absence of continual growth.

For the developing world, increased material consumption is essential, but a distinction needs to be drawn between consumption of basic needs, health services, and education, and a broad range of consumer products such as the automobile. The former need to be promoted, while the latter must be evaluated in terms of environmental feasibility and the availability of more sustainable alternatives. This, of course, raises questions about the unregulated provision of consumer goods through the market – a basic assumption in standard macroeconomic models. The importance of social investment, social provision of goods and services, and the regulation or redirection of market-based production, all need to be recognized in macroeconomic theory.

On the production side, standard macroeconomics assumes an aggregate production function based on supplies of labor and capital, with output determined by total factor productivity. These supply factors determine the basic pattern of economic growth, while demand fluctuations explain deviations from the long-term trend (see, e.g., Solow, 1997). Our survey of resource and environmental issues indicates that this generally accepted approach is fundamentally wrong. In every case where there is serious conflict between economic growth and the environment, the important issue is what kind of production takes place, and whether the direction of growth is compatible with environmental limits. This implies that there is no inevitable long-term growth trend – everything depends on which technological path is chosen. This choice is partly market driven, but is also a product of conscious social and economic policy. Automobile transport, for example, is dependent on infrastructure investment in road systems as well as energy tax policy and strategic choices regarding oil supply.

Thus we cannot say that there is 'a' path of economic development over time. There are many paths; the choice of path and the issue of economic fluctuations around the path are both issues of macroeconomic policy. This, of course, has been true in the past, especially regarding social policy and the provision of goods such as education and health care – among the Western economies, there are clearly different path choices between, say, the US and the Swedish models. In the future, the environmental aspects of these macroeconomic choices will be paramount – regarding fuel use, land use, water systems, industrial ecology, and natural resource use. Economic growth and its measurement will look very different depending on which choices are made.

The fallacious concept of a unique 'natural' growth path for the economy is reflected in the one-dimensional output measure of GNP/GDP. While critiques of GNP/GDP as a measure of well-being are extensive (see Tinbergen and Hueting, 1992; England 1997; Harris, 1997), no single alternative measure has emerged. This is not surprising, since the essence of the critiques concerns the reductionist nature of standard national income measures. There is no simple way to include the many dimensions of human well-being and ecosystem sustainability that are omitted or distorted in standard GDP accounts. Very broad measures such as Daly and Cobb's Index of Sustainable Economic Welfare (ISEW) or the Genuine Progress Indicator (GPI) are conceptually valuable, but difficult to use for analysis because of the many value judgments they necessarily embody (Daly and Cobb, 1994, Cobb et al., 2000). This poses a dilemma for the reform of macroeconomic analysis. Shall we continue to use a measuring rod that we know to be faulty, or abandon it when no other well-defined measurement concept is in sight?

Two major approaches have been taken to resolving this dilemma. One is to adopt a partial system of correcting existing accounts for resource and environmental depreciation (see, e.g., Hamilton and Clemens, 1997). Another is to employ satellite accounts measuring environmental factors in physical terms, an approach now systematized by the UN (United Nations, 2000). Either or both may have significant implications for the formulation of macroeconomic and trade policies especially when natural resource sectors are a significant portion of output, as they are in many developing economies (El Serafy, 1997). In general, it will be necessary to escape the trap of measuring and thinking about all macroeconomic problems in terms of GDP – even though the existing alternative measurement systems are necessarily incomplete. Awareness of the multiple dimensions of human well-being and ecosystem health will broaden macroeconomic goals beyond the narrow objective of increasing measured GDP.

IMPLICATIONS FOR MACROECONOMIC POLICY

Standard macroeconomic policy tools can be reoriented to respond to environmental goals. One widely discussed approach is tax shifting to promote a 'greener' economic growth path. The most widely discussed example is a carbon tax, but other 'green' taxes include taxes on virgin raw materials or on waste flows. The use of such a tax at the microeconomic level is based on a simple Pigouvian analysis of internalizing external costs. When employed on a large scale, the macroeconomic issues involved include whether or not the taxes are designed to be revenue neutral and whether there is a 'double dividend' of environmental and economic benefit from recycling green tax revenues to reduce taxes on capital and labor. There is an extensive literature on this debate (see, e.g., Bovenberg, 1999). There is also some experience with environmental taxes in practice, especially in Europe (Roodman, 2000). One important issue relates to the equity implications of environmental taxes. If implemented on a large scale, the impacts are potentially quite regressive unless offset with progressive systems of tax rebates.

Without a wholesale shift to environmental taxes, especially in the area of carbon-based energy sources, it is unlikely that any major transition away from current resource-using economic paths will occur. Even with significant technological progress in energy efficiency and renewable sources, the market mechanism places a significant roadblock in the way of an energy transition. So long as fossil fuels remain cheap, any successful effort to conserve or reduce demand for carbon-based fuels will tend to lower their price further, causing significant 'leakage' from any carbon reduction policy. In effect, the fact that some consumers use less fossil fuels will simply encourage others to use more, through the market signal of lower price. Only a macro-level, and ideally global, system of carbon taxes or the equivalent can avoid this problem.

Another major area of environmental macroeconomic policy is social investment and the provision of public goods. In a standard Keynesian view, social spending can serve the function of maintaining full employment. From a narrow perspective, the nature of the spending is not important, only its amount and employment multiplier effects. But in a broader view, public expenditure is not merely filling a gap in aggregate demand. It is compensating for the failure of private markets to take adequate account of future social needs. This rationale, especially regarding educational and health, has always been central to the political success of Keynesian policies of public expenditure. It is not just the employment effects, but also the perceived social benefit from government investment in these areas, that makes them politically feasible. Economic theory has generally taken the narrower view, and with the decline of Keynesian theory within the mainstream of economic thought, both kinds of benefits from social investment have been downgraded in favor of goods supplied through the private market. But as Thurow and others have pointed out, this ignores the fundamental need for social investment – a need that has grown more, not less, pressing in modern economies (Thurow, 1997, Ch. 13).

The massive investments required on a global scale to respond to environmental problems introduce a new dimension to the discussion of government provision of public goods. Funds must be raised and spent both at the national and international levels. Proposals for new mechanisms such as the Tobin tax on international financial transactions, as well as new institutions for transfer of environmental investment funds to developing nations, have the potential to reshape the global macroeconomic environment (Haq et al., 1996; Kaul et al., 1999). Joseph Stiglitz, former World Bank chief economist and recent Nobel laureate, has made an eloquent appeal for reform of current international financial institutions, arguing that their narrowly conservative policies have done major damage to the developing world (Stiglitz, 2002; see also Streeten, this volume). Both from the point of view of traditional macroeconomic concerns – employment, price stability, and economic stabilization – and in terms of new environmental imperatives, a new approach is clearly needed.

The 21st century will see continued population and economic growth, including unprecedented growth in the developing world. This growth could lead to a global system that is even more inequitable, unstable, and environmentally unsound. Or it could be mediated and directed towards a more stable global system, with moderated consumption, environmentally oriented technology, and more equitable distribution. It is folly to leave this choice of outcomes to undirected market forces. The needed response must come through intelligent macroeconomic policy, drawing on the best of earlier Keynesian theory while adapting to the new realities of environmental constraints on human economic activity.

NOTES

1. The case that the world has reached, or will soon reach, environmental limits, has been made by Goodland (1992) and Daly (1992), among others. We seek here to review and update this assessment, and to examine its particular significance for macroeconomic theory.
2. These grain figures include direct consumption and indirect consumption (grain used as animal feed). They use the UN Food and Agriculture Organization system including unmilled rice, and

are therefore higher than estimates, such as those of the US Department of Agriculture, which use milled rice. Grain output supplies about 50 per cent of global calorie consumption and uses about 50 per cent of world agricultural land, so it can be used as an (imperfect, but easily quantifiable) proxy for total food production.

3.   The term 'throughput', introduced by Herman Daly, denotes both the input of materials and output of wastes resulting from the use of energy and resources by economic systems.

REFERENCES

Ackerman, Frank (2001), 'Materials, Energy, and Climate Change', in Jonathan M. Harris, Timothy A. Wise, Kevin P. Gallagher, and Neva R. Goodwin (eds), *A Survey of Sustainable Development: Social and Economic Dimensions*, Frontier Issues in Economic Thought, vol. VI, Washington, DC: Island Press.

Bovenberg, Lans A. (1999), 'Green Tax Reforms and the Double Dividend: An Updated Reader's Guide', *International Tax and Public Finance*, 6 (3): 421–43.

Brown, Lester R. (2001a), *Paving the Planet: Cars and Crops Competing for Land*, Earth Policy Institute, http://www.earth-policy.org/Alerts/Alert12.htm, accessed 28 October 2002.

Brown, Lester R. (2001b), *Eco-Economy: Building an Economy for the Earth*, New York: W.W. Norton.

Campbell, Colin and Jean Laherrère (1998), 'Preventing the Next Oil Crunch: The End of Cheap Oil', *Scientific American*, 278 (3): 77–83.

Cobb, Clifford, Mark Glickman and Craig Cheslog (2000), *The Genuine Progress Indicator: 2000 Update*, Oakland, CA: Redefining Progress, www.rprogress.org.

Daly, Herman E. (1991a), 'Elements of Environmental Macroeconomics', in Robert Costanza (ed.), *Ecological Economics: The Science and Management of Sustainability*, New York: Columbia University Press, ch. 3.

Daly, Herman E. (1991b), *Steady State Economics*, 2nd edn, Washington, DC: Island Press.

Daly, Herman E. (1992), 'From Empty-world Economics to Full-world Economics: Recognizing an Historical Turning point in Economic Development', in Robert Goodland, Herman E. Daly, and Salah El Serafy (eds), *Population, Technology, and Lifestyle: The Transition to Sustainability*, Washington, DC: Island Press, ch. 2.

Daly, Herman E. (1996), *Beyond Growth: The Economic of Sustainable Development*, Boston, MA: Beacon Press.

Daly, Herman, and John B. Cobb, Jr (1994), *For the Common Good: Redirecting the Economy Toward Community, the Environment, and a Sustainable Future*, Boston, MA: Beacon Press.

Durning, Alan (1992), *How Much is Enough? The Consumer Society and the Future of the Earth*, Worldwatch Environmental Alert Series, Linda Starke (ed.), New York: W.W. Norton.

El Serafy, Salah (1997), 'Green Accounting and Economic Policy', *Ecological Economics*, 21 (3): 217–29.

England, Richard W. (1997), 'Alternatives to Gross National Product: A Critical Survey', Part X in Frank Ackerman, David Kiron, Neva R. Goodwin, Jonathan M. Harris and Kevin Gallagher (eds), *Human Well-Being and Economic Goals*, Frontier Issues in Economic Thought, vol. III, Washington, DC: Island Press.

Food and Agriculture Organization of the United Nations (FAO) (2000a), *Forest Resources Assessment (FRA) 2000*, http://www.fao.org/forestry/fo/fra/index.jsp, accessed 28 October 2002.

Food and Agriculture Organization of the United Nations (FAO) (2000b), *The State of World Fisheries and Aquaculture,2000*, Rome: FAO Fisheries Department.

Food and Agriculture Organization of the United Nations (FAO) (2001), *Agriculture: Toward 2015/30, Technical Interim Report*, Geneva: FAO Economic and Social Department.

Gardner, Gary (2000), 'Fish Harvest Down', in Lester R. Brown, Michael Renner, and Brian Halwell (eds), *Vital Signs 2000: The Environmental Trends that are Shaping our Future* (Worldwatch Institute), New York: W.W. Norton.

Gardner, Gary and Payal Sampat (1998), *Mind Over Matter: Recasting the Role of Materials in Our Lives*, Worldwatch Paper No. 144, Washington DC: Worldwatch Institute.

Georgescu-Roegen, Nicholas (1971), *The Entropy Law and the Economic Process*, Cambridge, MA: Harvard University Press.

Gleick, Peter H. (2000), *The World's Water 2000–2001*, Washington, DC: Island Press.

Goodland, Robert (1992), 'The Case That the World Has Reached Limits', in Robert Goodland, Herman E. Daly, and Salah El Serafy (eds), *Population, Technology, and Lifestyle: The Transition to Sustainability*, Washington, DC: Island Press, ch. 1.

Goodwin, Neva R., Frank Ackerman and David Kiron (eds) (1997), *The Consumer Society*, Frontier Issues in Economic Thought, vol. II, Washington, DC: Island Press.

Hamilton, Kirk and Michael Clemens (1997), 'Are We Saving Enough for the Future?' in *Expanding the Measure of Wealth: Indicators of Environmentally Sustainable Development*, Washington, DC: World Bank, ch. 2.

Harris, Jonathan M. (1996), 'World Agricultural Futures: Regional Sustainability and Ecological Limits', *Ecological Economics*, **17** (3): 95–115.

Harris, Jonathan M. (1997), 'Critiques of National Income Accounting and GNP', Part IX Overview Essay in Frank Ackerman, David Kiron, Neva R. Goodwin, Jonathan M. Harris and Kevin Gallagher (eds), *Human Well-Being and Economic Goals*, Frontier Issues in Economic Thought, vol. III, Washington, DC: Island Press.

Harris, Jonathan M. and Scott Kennedy (1999), 'Carrying Capacity in Agriculture: Global and Regional Issues', *Ecological Economics*, **29** (3): 443–61.

Haq, Mahbub ul, Inge Kaul and Isabelle Grunberg (eds) (1996), *The Tobin Tax: Coping with Financial Volatility*, New York: Oxford University Press.

Intergovernmental Panel on Climate Change (IPCC) (2001a), *Climate Change 2001: The Scientific Basis*, J.T. Houghton (ed.), New York: Cambridge University Press.

Intergovernmental Panel on Climate Change (IPCC) (2001b), *Climate Change 2001: Impacts, Adaptation, and Vulnerability*, James J. McCarthy (ed.), New York: Cambridge University Press.

Kaul, Inge, Isabelle Grunberg and Marc A. Stern (eds) (1999), *Global Public Goods: International Cooperation in the 21st Century*, New York: Oxford University Press.

Keynes, John Maynard (1930), 'Economic Possibilities for our Grandchildren', in J.M. Keynes (1972), *Essays in Persuasion*, The Collected Writings of John Maynard Keynes, vol. 5, Cambridge: Macmillan.

MacKenzie, James J. (1996), Oil as a Finite Resource: When is Global Production Likely to Peak? Washington, DC: World Resources Institute.

McGinn, Anne Platt (1999), *Safeguarding the Health of Oceans*, Worldwatch Paper No. 145, Washington, DC: Worldwatch Institute.

McGinn, Anne Platt (2002), 'Reducing Our Toxic Burden', in Christopher Flavin, Hilary French and Gary Gardner (eds), *State of the World 2002*, Washington, DC: Worldwatch Institute, ch. 4.

Meadows, Donnella H., Dennis L. Meadows, Jørgen Randers and William H. Behrens (1972), *The Limits to Growth*, New York: Universe Books.

Meadows, Donnella H., Dennis L. Meadows and Jørgen Randers (1992), *Beyond the Limits: Confronting Global Collapse, Envisioning a Sustainable Future*, Post Mills, VT: Chelsea Green.

Miller, G. Tyler, Jr (1998), *Living in the Environment*, 10th edn, Belmont, CA: Wadsworth.

Odum, Howard T. and E.C. Odum (1976), *Energy Basis for Man and Nature*, New York: McGraw-Hill.

Organization for Economic Cooperation and Development (OECD) (2001), *OECD Environmental Outlook for the Chemicals Industry*, Paris: OECD.

Paarlberg, Robert L. (1996), 'Rice Bowls and Dust Bowls: Africa, not China, Faces a Food Crisis', *Foreign Affairs*, **75** (3): 127–32.

Peet, John (1992), *Energy and the Ecological Economics of Sustainability*, Washington, DC: Island Press.

Pinstrup-Andersen, Per, Rajul Pandya-Lorch and Mark W. Rosegrant (1999), *World Food Prospects: Critical Issues for the Early Twenty-First Century*, Washington, DC: International Food Policy Research Institute.

Population Reference Bureau (2002), *2002 World Population Data Sheet*, Washington, DC: Population Reference Bureau.

Roodman, David M. (2000), 'Environmental Tax Shifts Multiplying', in Lester R. Brown, Michael Renner and Brian Halwell (eds), *Vital Signs 2000: The Environmental Trends that are Shaping our Future*, (Worldwatch Institute), New York: W.W. Norton.

Rosegrant, Mark W., Michael S. Paisner, Siet Meijer and Julie Witcover (eds) (2001), *Global Food Projections to 2020: Emerging Trends and Alternative Futures*, Washington, DC: International Food Policy Research Institute.

Sampat, Payal (2001), *Deep Trouble: The Hidden Threat of Groundwater Pollution*, Worldwatch Paper No. 154, Washington, DC: Worldwatch Institute.

Solow, Robert M. (1997), 'Is there a Core of Usable Macroeconomics We Should All Believe In?', *American Economic Review*, **87** (2): 230–32.

Speth, James Gustave (2002), 'A New Green Regime: Attacking the Root Causes of Environmental Deterioration', *Environment*, **44** (7): 16–25.

Stiglitz, Joseph E. (2002), *Globalization and its Discontents*, New York: W.W. Norton.

Thurow, Lester C. (1997), *The Future of Capitalism: How Today's Economic Forces Shape Tomorrow's World*, New York: Penguin Books.

Tinbergen, Jan and Roefie Hueting (1992), 'GNP and Market Prices: Wrong Signals for Sustainable Economic Success that Mask Environmental Destruction', in Robert Goodland, Herman E. Daly, and Salah El Serafy (eds), *Population, Technology, and Lifestyle: The Transition to Sustainability*, Washington, DC: Island Press, ch. 4.

United Nations, Department of Economic and Social Affairs, Statistics Division (2000), *Integrated Environmental and Economic Accounting: An Operational Manual*, New York: United Nations.

United Nations Environmental Programme (2002), *Global Environmental Outlook 3*, http://www.unep.org/GEO/geo3/index.htm, accessed 28 October 2002. Also London: Earthscan, 2002.

US Department of Energy, Energy Information Administration (2001), *International Energy Outlook 2000*, Washington, DC: US Government.
Wernick, Iddo K., Robert Herman, Shekvar Govind and Jesse H. Ausubel (1996), 'Materialization and Dematerialization: Measures and Trends', *Daedalus*, **125** (3): 171–98.

Afterword: A Japanese Social Initiative – The Relevant View[1]

John Kenneth Galbraith

It is now a lifetime since I encountered first-hand the Japanese economy; it was in 1945, a few weeks after the end of the war. I was in charge of a study – a grim experience of which I've often told – of the effect of the air attacks on the Japanese economy, the work of a noted organization of the time in Germany and Japan: the United States Strategic Bombing Survey. In ensuing months and years I remained in touch, shared the wide admiration of the brilliant way Japanese government, industry and people had recovered from the war. Physical reconstruction went rapidly. The standard of living, with some exceptions, was restored. Employment was strong. In a very few years Japan again had a good domestic and international economic system. This was widely accepted – for many it was the economic marvel of the time.

Leading the effort were some of the most talented and effective economists of the time. One of particular note was a close friend of mine, Professor Shigeto Tsuru. He was later brought back to Harvard University for an honorary degree that celebrated his achievements. The phrase was common: The Japanese Miracle. However, admiration of this achievement was, I suggest, to cloud further innovative thought and policy. In Japan and elsewhere, notably in the United States, past policy commanded a change in thought and action. There is need for further thought and action.

What was successful past action can now be effectively out of touch with present need and needed policy. In Japan the Japanese economy is no longer celebrated. There is unemployment, an economy of stagnant growth verging on permanent economic recession. Public works expenditure, central bank policy and low interest rates do not work as they once did. Reference to the Japanese Miracle has disappeared from both Japanese and international discourse. An economy once a world model is seen to have a serious problem. It is time for a better view of economic and social success. So, if less urgently, in other lands including the United States.

Economic change has rendered obsolete the old and established measures of economic achievement. Japan, as in the postwar years, is still an economic model. It is time for action in the modern, socially developed economy.

The basic and unrecognized fact is that the tests of achievement applied to the modern industrial economy, the measures of progress and performance, are obsolete. These are focused firmly on a steadily rising gross domestic product – a sharp increase in the total of goods and services produced. Here is the test of economic and social performance. This and the employment and income so provided are the measure of economic and social performance. The enjoyment of life is set and the quality of life is measured by employment and the production of goods and services. Here the quality of life. An improving life is increased production, full employment, increased possession and consumption. The good life is given by the production of things and, more than incidentally, the employment thus required. There is no serious concern as to what is produced. Over the centuries it was artistic, literary, architectural and then intellectual, including scientific, achievements that were important. Now it is employment and a growing gross domestic production.

Once it was thought that leisure, freedom especially from physical or monotonous toil – membership in the leisure class – was a basic human aspiration. So indeed it was. Now public merit is for how hard the individual works; all praise is given to the good, reliable worker, not, certainly, the leisured enjoyments of the fortunate.

Here, one sees Japan. Having solved the economic problem, the Japanese people, the first in our time, are ripe for other values. Why hard work if unemployment is possible? Better, perhaps, a small income and the pleasant use of time. Freedom from dreary, repetitive toil can be a basic human freedom. Better are other activities or, better for some, idleness itself. Were I in Japan at an earlier age, I would not leave the scholarly pleasure allowed by unemployment compensation for labored effort building a new post office. I do not now assess the quality of life by a simple numerical measure of the gross domestic product. I wish to know the rewards, personal and for the community, for which it is produced and, more urgently, the response to the things and services produced. On many journeys to Japan over a lifetime I have enjoyed my encounters with Japanese intellectuals, artists and entertainers. New railroads and more automobiles are not the prime test of achievement.

Japan is thought to have a serious economic problem: recession reflected in low physical production, low employment, strained public and corporate budgets, and an unduly casual attitude toward work and debt repayment. There is a deeper fact. The most advanced of industrial economies, Japan has now to adjust to its achievements. In the economically advanced country, performance can no longer be tested by the production and possession of physical goods or by the employment of people who prefer an easier life, or who are attracted away from industrial production by the arts, by literary enjoyments, by recreation, by athletics or simply a lower-paid leisure including from unemployment compensation. Of life, there is only one; its goal cannot necessarily be the commitment of those scarce and terminal days to an automobile assembly line or to a computer. As history since World War II has shown, Japan can be economically and peacefully ahead of other countries in its commitment to the realities of the modern world. My hope is that Japan will take the lead to assure the deeper, more varied, more civilized enjoyments of life, as it led the way in the perhaps far easier economic task after the war. No longer is economics the guide and test; instead the diverse enjoyments of life and its service to true well-being.

NOTE

1.   This article appeared in the *Nihon Keizai Shimbun*, 3 January 2003.

Index